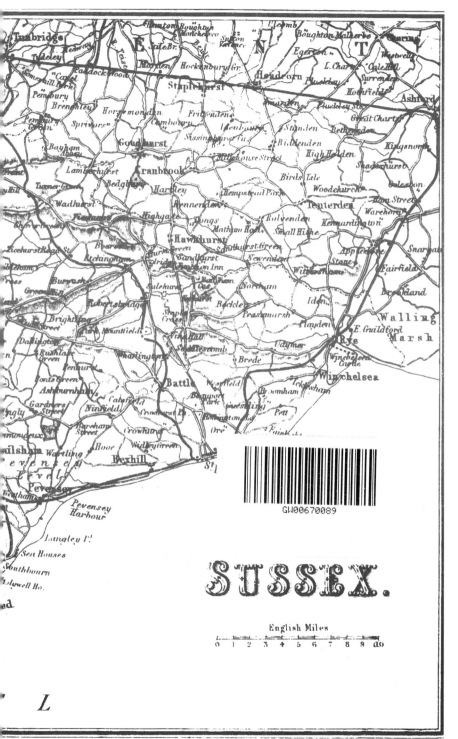

SUSSEX.

English Miles

0 1 2 3 4 5 6 7 8 9 10

Drawn & Engd by J.Bartholomew. Edinr

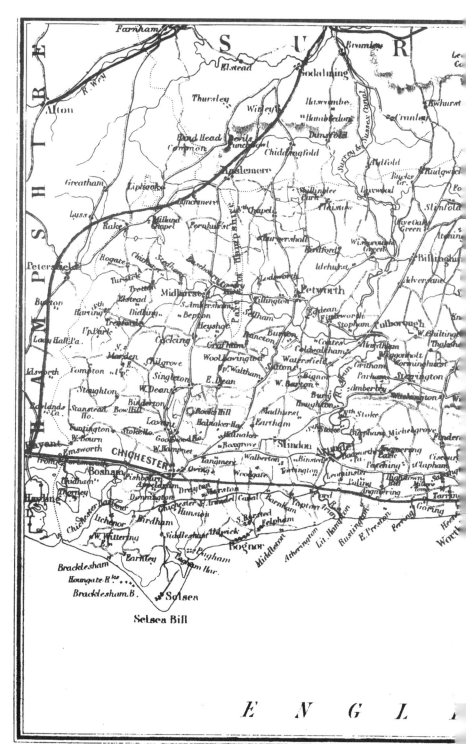

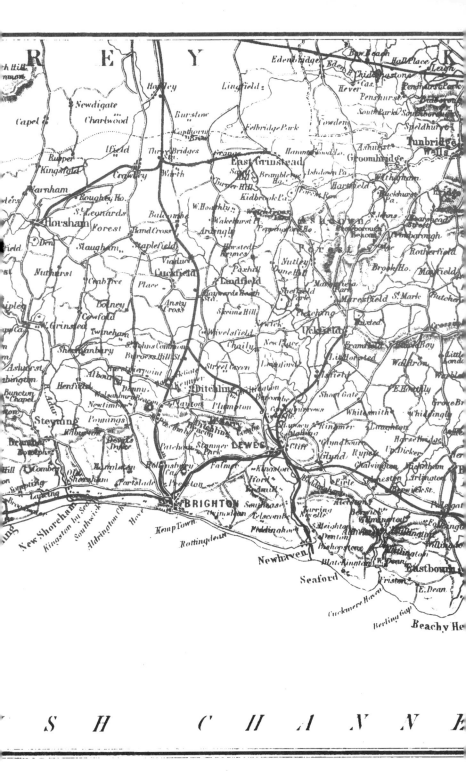

BLACK'S GUIDE

TO THE

SOUTH-EASTERN COUNTIES OF ENGLAND.

SUSSEX.

BRIGHTON.

BLACK'S GUIDE

TO THE

SOUTH-EASTERN COUNTIES OF ENGLAND.

SUSSEX.

With Map and Numerous Illustrations.

EDINBURGH:

ADAM AND CHARLES BLACK.

1861.

Published by:
Country Books
Courtyard Cottage, Little Longstone, Bakewell, Derbyshire DE45 1NN England
Tel/Fax: 01629 640670

ISBN 1 898941 21 1

From the 1850s until the end of the nineteenth century, Adam & Charles Black of Edinburgh published a series of guide books covering the country at a time when the railways and the industrial revolution were in their infancy. Who would have thought in 1861 that the population of Crawley would much exceed 447 people?! Only the aristocracy and the wealthier middle classes could afford to travel and so the books were produced in small numbers — original copies are now both scarce and expensive.

The **1861 Black's Guide to Sussex** forms part of the South-Eastern Counties of England series. There is a folding map of the county and steel engravings of the chain pier at Brighton, Hastings and Chichester cathedral. Major towns are covered as well as the smaller villages. I have included the newspaper cutting from *The Times* dated 24th August 1865 describing the opening of the tomb of Canute's duaghter at Bosham.

This volume includes **Breads's 1859 Guide to Worthing** and the **1859 Guide to the Miller's Tomb**. Steel engravings of the tomb on Highdown Hill, the water tower at Worthing, Broadwater church and Lancing. The Worthing guide contains information on the origin, situation, climate and mortality of the town. There are sections on the extent, buildings and population; sanitary provisions (*a subject of great interest to Victorians!*); government; charitable institutions; social conventions; geology; botany; entomology and ornithology; walks, rides and drives in the neighbourhood There is a list of streets in the town and details of the town well, etc.

COUNTRY BOOKS are in the process of reprinting the entire series of Black's Guides. Please ask for a prospectus on other counties of interest Numbered limited editions in cloth or leather bindings are available only by subscription from the publisher.

Printed in Englnad by:
MFP Design & Print, Longford Trading Estate, Thomas Street, Stretford, Manchester M32 0JT
Tel: 0161 864 4540

PREFACE.

THIS volume has been carefully compiled from the best topographical authorities, and from the results of the writer's own personal observation. In conjunction with its fellow-volumes, it presents a full and comprehensive Guide to the Southern Counties of England, and to the neighbouring islands : exploring a portion of our fatherland, which is eminently attractive from its natural beauties and historical associations. It has been the writer's aim to point out— not only the "shady bower" and the rippling stream, the sheltered cove and the "sunny spot of greenery,"—not only the picturesque and beautiful in nature—but all that is note-worthy in art and science ; "whatsoever," to adopt Lord Bacon's stately phrase, "is memorable in the places where we go : churches and monasteries, with the monuments which are therein extant ; the walls and fortifications of cities and towns, and so the havens and harbours, antiquities and ruins, colleges, shipping and navies, houses and gardens of state and pleasure, armouries, arsenals and magazines of state." It is, therefore, presumed that this volume may be of some service in the library, as well as in the hands of tourist or excursionist.

Errors will doubtless have crept in, despite of the compiler's utmost care, and corrections afforded by competent persons will be gratefully acknowledged and adopted.

The system of Routes and Branch Routes, on which the volume is based, the compiler believes to be novel, and trusts will prove serviceable and intelligible to the traveller.

"Peregrination," says quaint old Burton, "charms our senses with such unspeakable and sweet variety, that some count him unhappy that never travelled—a kind of prisoner, and pity his case that, from his cradle to his old age, he beholds the same—still, still the same, the same." An "unspeakable and sweet variety" is, indeed, presented to him whose "peregrinations" embrace the fair counties of South-Eastern England; and the writer heartily wishes to the tourist, who accepts him for a cicerone, that gratification and delight which he has himself enjoyed in viewing the scenes described in the present volume.

LONDON, July 1861.

CONTENTS.

———◆———

SUSSEX.

SUSSEX.

ROUTE X.—RYE to LEWES.

[Winchelsea, 2 m. ; Hastings, 11 m. ; Bexhill, 2 m ; Pevensey, 6 m. ; Polegate, 4 m. ; Berwick, 4 m. ; Glynde, 5 m. ; Lewes, 3 m.]

" Whate'er of beautiful or new,
Sublime or dreadful, in earth, sea, or sky,
By chance or search, was offer'd to his view,
He scann'd with curious and romantic eye.
Whate'er of lore tradition could supply
From Gothic tale, or song, or fable old,
Roused him, still keen to listen and to pry."

BEATTIE.

The road from Rye to Winchelsea is one of no peculiar interest. It runs along the edge of the salt marshes, nearly in a line with that branch of the river Rother, which, by its junction with the Channel, forms Rye New Harbour.

WINCHELSEA (population, 778)—*Inn :* the New Inn—retains but few traces of its former importance ; yet one may discern the lines of its principal seats—ruins of groined vault and crypt—a fragment of a shattered tower—the ivy-grown remains of an ancient chapel—mute but eloquent witnesses to present decay and bygone prosperity. But of all the impoverished old towns along the coast, Winchelsea, as Mr. Thorne has observed, is the best worth visiting. " It owns itself a wreck, and does not try to get rid of the ruins, and put on an appearance of smartness. The wide space which the town originally covered helps now not a little to increase the reverend air it carries as a ruin. You wander about its outskirts among pleasant bye-ways, and are startled to come upon some fragment of a chapel or an old house, when you thought yourself a long way beyond the limits of the town." Let us, then, " go visit the reliques of this city," and hear what they have to tell us of the brave and palmy days that are gone.

Old Winchelsea occupied a site, about three miles south-east of the present town, upon land which the sea has long since claimed as its own. It was a complete peninsula, connected with the mainland on the west side, and defended by fortifications which were then considered of unusual strength. Like all the old sea-fortresses, it was continually suffering from the depredations of the lawless Norsemen, and its inhabitants, in their turn, became notorious pirates, and ravaged the narrow seas with their swift galleys.

Here King William landed on his return from Normandy in 1063 ; here, in 1170, disembarked two of the knightly murderers of Thomas à Becket ; and such was its general prosperity that it furnished, in 1229, ten out of the fifty-seven vessels which formed the contingent of the Cinque Ports. A few years later, and its downfall began. In 1236, the waters, for the first time, broke beyond their ancient limits, and rolled in upon the doomed city. Again in 1250, on the eve of October 1st, when the cruel Winchelsea pirates had boarded a small bark freighted with pilgrims for the Canterbury shrine, and had foully murdered them, and the sea—as the old tradition runs—flooded the town in vengeance of the sacrilege. In 1264-5 it sided with De Montfort against Henry III.—an act of rebellion which Prince Edward terribly punished, when, on the 4th of August, he took it by assault, and put to the sword almost all its male inhabitants. From this severe blow it never recovered, and another disastrous inundation on the eve of St. Agatha, 1287, completed its ruin.

Edward I. now resolved to remove the town to a less exposed site, and the hill of Higham, now rising above the marshes like a natural watch-tower, was selected by the lord-treasurer, Kirkby, Bishop of Ely, despatched for that purpose. The sea bounded it on the east and north, on the south and west convenient roads struck inland to Robertsbridge and Hastings. The harbour was safe and commodious. So the town was laid out with the utmost regularity, and stout walls enclosed an area of 170 acres, subdivided into thirty-nine squares or quarters. It had three gates, and on the west side a deep fosse or trench. On the south-west rose a castle, adjoining St. Leonard's Church ; in the centre, the stately tower of a church dedicated to St. Thomas à Becket. When completed, King Edward paid it a visit, and reviewed his fleet in its haven. As he rode onward near the Strand Gate, his horse, terrified by the sudden clangour of a windmill, leaped over the wall, and his attendants were in sore affright, believing he was killed. But the earth had been rendered soft by incessant rain, and the king re-entered the town uninjured by his fall.

Here, in 1350, King Edward the Third embarked on board his fleet, and in the offing defeated a Spanish fleet richly laden with Flemish goods on the 29th of August. Nine years later, and during the great Plantagenet's absence in France, 8000 Frenchmen landed, set fire to the town, and slew many of the townsmen who were assembled at mass in the great church. The spot where the unfortunate Winchelsea men were buried is still known as Dead Men's Lane. In 1359, it was assaulted by the French fleet of 120 sail, under the Comte St. Pol; and, in 1377, they again sailed along the coast, ravaged Rye, and would have taken Winchelsea, had not Haymo, abbot of Battle, drawn together his men-at-arms and made so gallant a show that the enemy withdrew discomfited. But in 1380 it was sacked by John de Vienne, and, for the last time, in 1449, was once more set on fire by the French.

From the assaults of its enemies it might, however, have recovered, and that its consequence was not inconsiderable may be inferred from the vast vaults and crypts built by the inhabitants for storehouses ; but the rapid withdrawal of the sea, and destruction of its harbour, were not to be contended against. When, in 1573, it was visited by Queen Elizabeth, and its citizens and magistrates clothed themselves in scarlet, she was so pleased with its apparent prosperity that she christened it "Little London ;" but, even then, not more than 60 families remained in the town, and it has never since held up its head. It is, as Wesley called it in 1790, when he preached his last sermon under a wide-spreading ash tree adjoining the west side of St. Thomas' Church, the "poor skeleton of ancient Winchelsea," and into its dead bones not even the Genius of the Steam Engine has been able to infuse any life.

The notable objects to be here examined are, however, many ; first, there is the old STRAND GATE, an Early Decorated structure, which you pass under as you come from Rye—"a picturesque old pile, having a wide gateway between massive round towers. Looking through it from the inside, the town of Rye is seen seated on its hill, as though a picture, set in a heavy antique frame." LANDGATE, or PIPE WELL, or FERRY GATE, on the road to Udimore, is a mere shapeless mass of gray old stone, near which à few dull houses straggle. It bears a shield with the word *Helde* inscribed upon it, supposed to be the name of the mayor during whose supremacy it was erected. NEW GATE, on the Icklesham road, is a mile from any houses, and has no architectural pretensions, but stands in a lovely nook, embowered among trees, and opening into a lane whose banks, in the spring, are flush with primroses. The foundations of the stout earthwork, and the line of the deep fosse, which defended the town, may still be traced between the two latter gates.

In the centre of the town stands the CHURCH—or all that remains of it—dedicated to St. Thomas a Becket. The nave was probably destroyed by John de Vienne, in 1380 ; the chancel and side aisles are still extant. The style is Early Decorated, and from its purity deserves particular examination. Remark the exquisite fidelity of the sculptured foliage ; the curious corbel heads ; the rich foreign tracery of the side windows ; the piers of Bethersden marble and Caen stone ; the sedilia in the chancel (restored in 1850); the Perpendicular English Windows ; and the light and airy three-bayed choir. In the south aisle is the ALARD CHANTRY, originally the Chapel of St. Nicholas, where particularly observe the noble Alard tombs—one to *Gervase Alard*, Admiral of the Cinque Ports, 1303 and 1306, with a recumbent effigy, cross-legged—the hands clasping a small heart —a lion at the feet, growling, and half rising as if to spring upon you—and over all a noble arched canopy, adorned with heads of Edward I. and Queen Eleanor. The other to *Stephen Alard*, grandson of the above, and Admiral of the Cinque Ports, in 1324 —with some fine foliaged ornamentation, and a canopy resembling that already alluded to. In the north aisle is the CHANTRY of *John Godfrey*, d. 1441, and *Maline* his wife. Remark the three canopied tombs, *temp.* Henry III., with effigies of a mailed templar, a lady, and a young man, robed. In the chancel floor is inserted a brass for a priest, d. 1440.

The triple gable of the chancel, externally, is luxuriantly shrouded in ivy, and connected with the ruined transept walls. Observe over the porch, which is of later date, the arms of Winchelsea. (The town confers an earldom on the Finch family.) The rectory, valued at £278, is in the patronage of Sir A. Ashburton, Baronet.

On the south side of the town lies the FRIARY PARK, or the FRIARS (R. Stileman, Esq.), to which admission is only obtainable on Mondays. The present house was erected in 1819, when the old Franciscan monastery was pulled down. The exquisitely beautiful ruins of the CHAPEL OF THE VIRGIN have happily escaped profanation. It was founded in 1310. The apsidal choir is entered by a noble arch, 26 feet broad. " The Friars" was the residence, in 1780, of two daring burglars, George and Joseph Weston, one of whom was actually appointed church-warden of Winchelsea, and both brothers living here, under assumed names, on the plunder acquired in their daring excur-sions, were held in much repute. After robbing the Bristol mail they were detected, apprehended, and one of them was hung. James, the novelist, in one of his best romances, has made good use of these circumstances.

There are no ruins of the ancient Dominican Priory, founded by Edward II. The Court House and Gaol have Norman door-ways, but are not peculiarly interesting. Of many old buildings there are vestiges, and the vaults are large and curious, but we have tarried as long as may be among the shards and débris of the ill-fated Winchelsea—twice grievously injured by the sea —and must resume our onward way. Up to the time of the Reform Bill it returned two members to parliament. Henry Lord Brougham represented it from 1815 to 1830. It is governed by a mayor and twelve jurats.

[About three miles north-west of the town is UDIMORE (population, 435), for whose name tradition supplies a curious etymology. While its church (a small and ancient building) was being built in a different situation, a spirit-voice, during the lonesome night-hours, came sighing across the wold, "O'er the mere! O'er the mere! O'er the mere!" and spirit-hands removed the stones. So the builders took the ghostly hint, erected the church on its present site, and named the village UDIMORE, a corrupted version of the spirit's cry. The perpetual curacy, valued at £100 per annum, is in the gift of T. C. Langford, Esq.]

Leaving Winchelsea by the New Gate, we follow a shady and agreeable road to ICKLESHAM (population, 728), which passed by marriage from the family of Alard to that of Finch. The CHURCH, dedicated to St. Nicholas, is mainly Norman in style. The north aisle is Early English ; the East Window, Early De-corated, and a good example. Observe the capitals of the pillars in the nave, and the round-headed windows of the south aisle. There is an altar-tomb for *Henry Finch*, d. 1493. The vicar-age, valued at £715, is in the patronage of the Bishop of Oxford.

From White Hart Hill, beyond the church, the view of sea and land is broad, magnificent and constantly chequered with exquisite effects of light and shade.

" Through a fertile swelling country, varied with beautiful woods," we continue our route, and passing BROOMHAM HALL, a good stone house in a fair demesne, which has belonged to the Ashburnham family since the days of Edward IV., quickly enter

GUESTLING (population, 860), where we need only pause to examine its CHURCH, dedicated to St. Lawrence, a Transitional Norman building, with its tower surmounted by a low spire, standing about 300 yards from the road. The Ashburnham chantry is divided from the south aisle by three pointed arches; the nave from the north aisle by two Norman arches with chevron mouldings. In the vestry stands an old richly carved " Flanders chest." The rectory, worth £401, is in the gift of the Rev. J. M. Lukin.

At Maxfield, in this parish—an old timbered farm-house— was born Gregory Martin, the translator of the Rheims edition of the Bible.

At this point we turn aside towards the shore to PETT (population, 364), where a church, dedicated to Sts. Mary and Peter, is noticeable for its deformity. The rectory, valued at £460, is in the gift of R. Thornton, Esq. At Cliff End, below Pett, commences the low marshy ground extending from the sand-stone of the Hastings ridge to the chalk of the Folkestone heights. The Hastings sand stretches from this point over the whole valley of the Weald, bordered north and south by the chalk ranges. The Forest Ridge, alternating between sandstone and clay, includes Fairlight, Hastings, and Bexhill, and gradually unités with the Wealden.

The tourist may now follow the coast line through Fairlight, or, regaining the high road, cross Fairlight Hill, and descend into the valley where Hastings so quietly reposes. Just beyond Pett the cliffs rise into something like grandeur of elevation at HOOK POINT. The next headland is called GOLDBURY POINT. Here we turn aside (a little to the right), and climb the bold, bleak ascent of FAIRLIGHT DOWN, 600 feet above the sea, and commanding the whole sweep of the coast from Beachy Head to the South Foreland. The inland views are of the most varied and interesting character.

FAIRLIGHT (population, 625)—originally Fair-leigh—has a new and pretty CHURCH, dedicated to St. Andrew, which was consecrated in 1846. The vicarage, valued at £502 per annum, is in the gift of C. Young, Esq. Passing FAIRLIGHT PLACE (Countess of Waldegrave) we descend into the leafy and blossomy depths of FAIRLIGHT GLEN, and make our way to the DROPPING WELL, where, in the shadow of a glorious beech-tree, plashes over the rock a bright shimmering streamlet. A path along the hill side leads hence to the famous LOVER'S SEAT, where, to use a local rhyme,—

"Where youth, from sympathy, a visit pay,
　And age to pass the tedious hour away,"—

where you may rest yourself upon a rude oaken bench, and look out afar over a sea which seems lit with a thousand suns. This, we are told, was (at the close of the last century) the favourite trysting-spot of a pair of true lovers—the heiress of the Bogs of Elford and Lieutenant Lamb, who commanded a revenue-cutter stationed off this coast. Their stolen interviews led, in due time, to a clandestine marriage in Hollington Church. The lady, after presenting her husband with a daughter, sickened and died; the widowed husband, while sailing up the Southampton river, was smitten overboard by the boom of his yacht.

We may now continue our stroll to the shingled beach of Covehurst Bay, and keep along to Ecclesbourne (or Eagle's bourne) Glen, a picturesque gap in the cliffs which are here 250 feet above the sea. Ascending the height we pass the coast-guard station, and afterwards, on the right, the grounds of ROCKLANDS, where Canning used occasionally to retire from the strife of St. Stephen's. We soon gain the elevation of the East Cliffs, where are visible enough the lines of a Norman entrenchment.

Either by the road or the fields, the walk into Hastings will be found a pleasant one. Let us, therefore, conduct the tourist without delay into that picturesque seaside town which Elia so agreeably anathematized as "a place of fugitive resort, an heterogeneous assemblage of sea-maws and stockbrokers, Amphitrites of the town, and nurses that coquet with the ocean. If it were what it was in its primitive shape it were something. I could abide to dwell with Meschech ; to assort with fisher swains and smugglers."

HASTINGS (*i.e.*, THE SETTLEMENT OF THE HÆSTINGAS.)

[Population, 21,215. *Inns:* The Albion, Castle, Swan, and Victoria (at St. Leonards). 74 m. from London, by London and South Eastern Railway; 60 m. by road; 11 m. by rail from Winchelsea; 23 m. by rail, from Ramsgate. ☞ The Railway Station is about ¼ m. from the town.]

"We have been," says Charles Lamb, "dull at Worthing one summer, duller at Brighton another, dullest at Eastbourne a third, and are at this moment doing dreary penance at Hastings ! I love town or country, but this detestable Cinque Port is neither. I hate these scrubbed shoots thrusting out their starved foliage from between horrid fissures of dusty innutritious rocks, which the amateur calls ' verdure to the edge of the sea.' I require woods, and they shew me stunted coppices. I cry out for the water-brooks, and pant for fresh streams and inland murmurs. I cannot stand all day on the naked beach, watching the capricious hues of the sea, shifting like the colours of a dying mullet. I am tired of looking out of the windows of this island prison. I would fain retire into the interior of my cage." But the tourist will err wofully if he accepts Charles Lamb's delightful badinage for truthful description. Hastings is not only not a dull, but it is even a romantic and picturesque town, while it has enough of London comforts to satisfy the most fastidious Londoner. It has good hotels, and good lodging-houses, and a German band, and a circulating library, and the shops are exceedingly smart, and the prices (in the season) are aristocratically high ! The newest bonnets and the latest developments of crinoline may here be noted. Its suburb of St. Leonards, connected with it by rows of handsome houses, is quite the abode of the exclusive.

The town of Hastings lies for the most part in a hollow, snugly sheltered by good-sized hills, except where it slopes, southward, to the sea. "The original town is believed to have extended some distance to the south of the present one, its site being now partly covered by the waves. Very few of the houses in the present town appear to be old, but there has for the last 25 years been a continual effort to render every part of the town, except the quarters inhabited by the poor, as modern-looking and smart as possible ; and any traces of antiquity are, therefore, scarcely to be expected."—(*Thorne.*) Its chief support is derived

HASTINGS.

from its fishery, boat-building, and lime burning ; its lime-kilns lying up at the valley, at some small distance from the sea. Messrs. Rock and Son have here a large and celebrated coach-factory. The principal thoroughfares are Pelham Crescent, Pelham Place, Wellington Street, the Marine Parade, and Robertson Street. Under the East Cliff, varying from 170 to 218 feet in height, Dutch fish-auctions are often held. The TOWN HALL is in High Street, and was built in 1823. It boasts of a shield taken from the French at the conquest of Quebec. To the west stretch the lofty and breezy terraces of St. LEONARDS, almost as far as Bulverhythe, or "the townsmen's haven." The Marina, a parade 600 feet in length, was designed in 1828 by Decimus Burton, the architect, and the Esplanade was also erected on his plans. Its new church was built in 1833.

Hastings, as may be supposed, has had its "distinguished visitors." Charles Lamb was here, as we have already shewn, and indulged his usual good-humoured vein of satire. Lord Byron was here in 1814, " swimming and eating turbot, and smuggling neat brandies and silk handkerchiefs, and walking on cliffs, and tumbling down hills." Here Campbell resided for five years, and wrote his beautiful " address to the Sea." Here the Rev. Charles Honeyman (*vide* " The Newcomes") displayed his white handkerchief and his lachrymose eloquence in Lady Whittlesea's chapel. Prout, the artist, lived at 53 George Street. Sir Cloudesley Shovel and Titus Oates—not exactly "Arcades ambo," though we class them together—were born in All Saints' Street. Louis Napoleon, the exile, resided at Pelham Cottage, in 1840, and Louis Philippe, ex-King of the French, at the Victoria Hotel, 1848.

The CLIMATE in the higher parts of the town is vigorous and bracing ; in the lower range it is well adapted, from its mildness, to the most delicate pulmonary invalids. St. Leonards is, however, the healthiest and most genial quarter. According to Dr. Harwood, the average mean temperature, at 9 a.m., is, in November 45° ; December 47°, January and February 44° ; and out of 64 days the S.W. wind prevails 22, S. 11, N. 8, W. 8, S.E. 6, N.E. 4, N.W. 3, and E. 2.

The botanist will find in this vicinity—peppermint, catmint, calamint, wild cabbage, psamma arenaria, samphire, tamarisk, scorpion grass, henbane, wild celery, and pellitory. The kestrel, tern, bee-eater, phalarope, landrail, hobby, snipe, plover, and gull are met with along this coast from Hastings to Rye.—(*A. E. Knox.*)

Hastings, as the termination *ing* indicates, was a settlement of the Saxon Hæstingas, and cannot be connected with Hasteñ, the old Danish jarl. Edward the Conqueror erected it into a seaport, and its contingent to the Cinque Ports' fleet was estimated at 21 ships, each bearing 20 men and a boy. Its component limbs, or members, were—Pevensey, Seaford, Bekesbourne, and the Ville of Grange, Rochester. As late as the reign of Elizabeth it could boast of a wooden pier, but it has now neither pier nor haven, and it is at considerable risk that a collier occasionally beaches here, and when exhausted of its cargo, puts out to sea at the next high tide.

On this shore William the Conqueror landed on the 20th of September 1066, and, while his Knights stared at each other aghast, lost his footing as he leapt ashore. With the promptitude of a great mind he grappled the sands with his fingers, and exclaimed, " It is thus I take seisin of the land which shall shortly be ours." The table—a slab of rock—at which he is said to have taken his dinner, is now placed at the gateway of the old Subscription Gardens. His vessels, meanwhile, were moored in a line from Pevensey to Hastings. From this place he marched along the downs to Telham Hill. On the level, near the Railway Station, he formed his camp where his army passed the night in prayer and singing hymns.

HASTINGS CASTLE stands upon the brink of the cliff. Its principal entrance was necessarily on the land side, where the portcullis groove, and the hooks for the gate-hinges may yet be examined. The castle area occupied about an acre and a quarter. The south side was 400 feet long ; the east side 300 feet long, with a fosse, and a massive wall strengthened by three semicircular towers whose fragments are still interesting. The north-west side was 400 feet in length. To the west, both a square and a circular tower are still standing, and a doorway which formerly opened into the ·chapel of St. Mary, a Transitional Norman structure, 110 feet long, with a nave, chancel, and aisles, now a mass of ruins.

The manor was bestowed by King William on the Count of Lee, who may have erected the castle. It remained in the hands of his descendants until the middle of the fourteenth century when, according to tradition, it was consumed by fire. In December

1093, William Rufus was detained here by contrary winds, and Archbishop Anselm consecrated—in the Castle Chapel—Robert Blovet as bishop of Lincoln. Adela, daughter of King William, presided here as Queen of Love and Beauty at the first tournament celebrated in England, and smiled upon the doughty deeds of Stephen, Count of Blois. From Hastings Castle King John dated the famous proclamation which asserted for England the sovereignty of the seas. It now belongs to the Earl of Chichester, and "admittance may be gained at any time, except on Sundays, to see the ruins, by payment of threepence ; or to subscribers at sixpence per week, the gate is always open."

We turn now to the CHURCHES which, sooth to say, are of no great beauty or special interest. At the foot of East Hill stands the Perpendicular pile of ALL SAINTS' CHURCH, with a nave, chancel, south porch, and west tower, 73 feet high. Observe the sedilia in the south wall ; and the octangular font. It contains a brass to *T. Goodenough.* In the graveyard lies *Edward Mogridge*, d. 1854, better known as "Old Humphrey." The rectory, valued at £300, is in the gift of the Rev. S. Foyster.

ST. CLEMENT'S CHURCH, in High Street, is another Perpendicular building, rebuilt about 1380. It contains a chancel, nave, north and south aisles, and west tower. The two balls fixed to the tower commemorate the attack made upon the town by the Dutch fleet, under De Ruyter, in 1666. The font is Decorated and octagonal. There are brasses to *Thomas Weekes*, d. 1563, and *John Barley*, d. 1592. The east memorial window, to the honour of a late rector, was set up in 1857 ; and in the north aisle a similar window is dedicated to the fame of the gallant Viscount Chewton, slain in the Crimea. The rectory is in the gift of the Rev. S. Foyster. The perpetual curacy, valued at £100, is in the patronage of the Bishop of Chichester.

ST. MARY'S-IN-THE-CASTLE, a Grecian structure, in Pelham Crescent, was built and endowed by the Earl of Chichester in 1828. ST. MARY MAGDALENE'S was consecrated in 1852 ; ST. CLEMENT'S, Halton, in 1838 ; and the MARINERS' chapel in 1854. ST. LEONARD'S (perpetual curacy, valued at £314, in the gift of Rev. C. W. Leslie) was erected in 1833.

The town of Hastings has given its name to a distinguished family, which did good service in the old chivalric times ; and, in 1808, conferred a marquisate upon the celebrated Governor General of India.

A fragment of wall at the PRIORY FARM is the sole relic of a house of Augustinian canons, founded by Sir W. Bricet, *temp.* Richard I.

[HINTS FOR RAMBLES. 1. To Fairlight Down, and thence to Guestling. Cross the country to Westfield. Keep northward, across the Rother, to Brede. Visit Sedlescomb, and return by the main road. About 17 m. 2. Through Hollington to Battle Abbey. Return by way of Catsfield and Crowhurst, 12 m. 3. Through St. Leonards and Bulverhythe to Bexhill. Strike across the country northward to Crowhurst. Gain the high road by way of Crowhurst Park, and return *vià* Ore to Hastings. 4. To Winchelsea by rail. Return, by the road, to Pett, and thence by way of Fairlight Down, the Lover's Seat, the Dropping Well, and Ecclesbourne Cliffs to Hastings.]

We subjoin the distances from Hastings of the following localities :—

To Belleport, 3 m. ; Crowhurst, 2¾ m. ; Dropping Well, 2 m. ; Ecclesbourne Cliffs, 2 m. ; Fairlight Glen, 2¼ m. ; Glen Roar Cascade, 2½ m. ; Hollington, 2 m. ; The Lover's Seat, 1¾ m. ; Old Roar Cascade, 2½ m. ; Ore, 1¾ m. ; Westfield, 5 m.

BRANCH ROUTE FROM HASTINGS TO LAMBERHURST.

Winding up the fair Hastings valley we turn to the right, at (or near) the 62d milestone from London, and ascend the hill to ORE (population, 1745), facing the bold and abrupt elevation of Fairlight Down. Its Perpendicular CHURCH is dedicated to St. Helen, and contains a brass to an unknown worthy, d. 1400. The rectory, valued at £480, is in the hands of certain trustees. ORE PLACE (Lady Elphinstone) retains, it is said, some portions of the ancient house erected by John of Gaunt.

Another route which the tourist will find, perhaps, the most picturesque, is by way of HOLLINGTON (population, 579), which lies about 2 miles north-west of Hastings. Its " lion" is its CHURCH, dedicated to St. Leonard, a quaint little Early English structure, hidden away in a mass of leafiness, at some distance from the village. Its steeple is a low pyramid, sloping on the west side beyond the roof, and supported by a massive but deformed buttress. It contains an old pentagonal font, and some memorials of little interest. The tradition attached to it may be compared with that of Udimore. " When a church was begun in the neighbouring village, the Evil One, jealous of the encroachment on a spot which he had marked as his own, every night undid what the workmen had accomplished in the course of the day. Priests were summoned to lay the fiend, and they had prepared to commence their potent conjurements, when a voice was heard offering to desist from opposition if the building were erected on the spot *he* should indicate. The offer was accepted. The church was raised, and then sprung up all around it a thick wood, concealing it from the general gaze"—(*Thorne*).

The vicarage, valued at £209, is in the patronage of the Eversfield family.

The views from the Hollington hills are very beautiful— " charming reaches of down alternating with masses of rich foliage, with here and there a fine old farm-house, or old-fashioned Sussex cottage, and everywhere the ocean filling up the breaks in the distance."

We cross from Hollington to OLD ROAR (2 miles) by a pleasant path leading across fields and through hop-grounds. It lies in a leafy hollow, near Roar Farm, close by which is a blasted oak of bolder and more picturesque form than Salvator ever designed. It derives its name from " the tremendous noise made by a large body of water tumbling over a perpendicular rock, 40 feet high, which might be heard half a mile off." It won't roar now, not even for the gratification of a cockney enthusiast; but the nook is a romantic and sequestered one, and worth seeing. About a hundred yards higher up is GLEN ROAR, "a smaller edition of Old Roar," and only to be reached by the adventurer who makes light of brambles.

We now pursue the high road to Lamberhurst, and as we keep along the sandstone ridge, may see below us, on our right, 5 miles from Hastings, the pleasant village of WESTFIELD (population, 900), and its Early English church, a small but pleasant edifice, containing many memorials, but none which will induce us to turn aside to visit them. The vicarage, valued at £372, is in the patronage of the Bishop of Chichester.

[About two miles beyond, and across the Rother, lies BREDE (population, 1059), at a short distance south of the Winchelsea road. Here, on the slope of a gentle acclivity, stands the quaint old manor-house of BREDE PLACE, *temp.* fourteenth century, now made use of as a farm, but anciently the residence of the Attefords, from whom it passed, early in the reign of Henry VI., to the Oxenbridges. Of these Sir Goddard, who about 1530 made considerable additions to the mansion, is traditionally reported to have lived upon human flesh, with a particular relish for that of infants. Neither bow and arrow, nor axe, nor sword, nor spear, could slay this redoubtable giant, but some of the country folk about here succeeded at length in making him drunk, and sawing him in half with a wooden saw ! His house, about a century ago, was tenanted by a gang of smugglers, who, by inventing strange sights, and uttering unearthly noises, contrived very effectually to secure it to themselves, undisturbed by any over-curious hind. The hall, and a room beyond it, with their Caen stone-work and enriched windows, should be carefully examined.

The CHURCH is equally worthy of notice. The Brede chantry was enlarged and repaired by Sir Goddard Oxenbridge, who chiefly employed French workmen, and their skill and fancy may be admired in the window-traceries and the foliated decoration of the doorway. Observe the monument, and effigy in Caen stone, of Sir GODDARD OXENBRIDGE, d. 1537.

The patronage of the living, a rectory valued at £1023, is in the hands of T. Frewen, Esq.

A bridge which spans the rivulet, near Brede Place, is called the GROANING BRIDGE, in recollection, perhaps, of the noises artfully produced by the smugglers. On the left of the road, towards Udimore, is Great Sowden's Wood. It contains a large and well-known heronry.]

SEDLESCOMB (population, 714) straggles along the high road, at a distance of about seven miles from Hastings, in a pleasant valley, whose sides are not indifferently clothed with wood. Here the Romans had established an iron work, as appears from the Roman coins discovered in a recently opened cinder-bed, some of which were greatly corroded, and others had evidently been burnt—(*Lower*). The CHURCH, a noticeable old building, is Early English, with some Perpendicular insertions in the chancel. Its rectory, valued at £267, is included in the Lord Chancellor's patronage.

At Cripses' Corner we turn to the left, and regain the principal road, near Vine Hall. At Soins Cross the Battle road effects a junction with the Hastings one, and we soon reach the village of ROBERTSBRIDGE (population, 270), *i.e.*, Rother's-bridge—where there is a station on the Ashford and Hastings branch of the South-Eastern Railway ; an INN, The Old George ; and a cluster of old-fashioned, red-brick houses, intermingled with some bran-new villas. On the river bank, in one of those sweet, sequestered valleys, so dear to the Cistercian monks, moulder the scanty ruins of a Cistercian abbey, founded, in 1176, by Robert de St. Martin. The site of the chapel is still discernible, and there are materials for observation in a cone-roofed "oast-house," and a groined crypt. A volume preserved in the Bodleian Library contains a quaint inscription :—"This book belongs to ST. MARY of ROBERT'S-

BRIDGE ; whoever shall steal or sell it, let him be anathema maranatha." Underneath is the following commentary :—" I, John Bishop of Exeter, know not where the aforesaid house is, nor did I steal this book, but acquired it in a lawful way." Despite of the Bishop's ignorance, the Abbey was one of some importance, and its abbot was sent—in company with the Abbot of Boxley, another Cistercian dignitary—to discover the place of Cœur de Lion's detention in Germany.

☞ The tourist should here turn aside to SALEHURST and BODIAM. SALEHURST (population, 2191) lies at the foot of a really bold ascent, SILVER HILL, whence the view over Kent and Sussex is one to be enjoyed and remembered. When Walpole was here in 1752, his dilettantéism warmed into an almost poetical enthusiasm :—" It commands," he cries, " a whole horizon of the richest blue prospect you ever saw." The landscape is not deteriorated by the occasional passage of a rapid train on the neighbouring rail—a white rolling column of smoke marking its swift transit through grove and over meadow. In this neighbourhood are IRIDGE PLACE (Sir S. Meiklethwaite), COURT LODGE (J. Smee, Esq.), and HIGHAM (Mrs. Luxford). The hop-plantations are of considerable extent. The Early English CHURCH, dedicated to St. John the Baptist, is neat and picturesque. Its situation is eminently agreeable. The font has an oaken cover. The vicarage, valued at £503, is in the gift of J. Hardy, Esq.

Crossing the Rother at Bodiam Bridge, we see the CHURCH on our left, and the Castle of BODIAM (population, 306) to the right, on the river bank. A deep fosse, filled with water, and fed by the Rother, encircles it. A round tower fortifies each angle of the area (165 feet by 150); the great gateway, approached by a causeway, is conspicuous on the north side ; and in the centre of the other sides rise up stout, square towers. The central court is 87 feet by 78 feet. Over the main gateway, observe the armorial bearings of the Bodiams, Dalyngrugges, and Wardeuxs— into whose hands the castle successively passed. The outer portcullis may still be examined, and the tourist will find much to interest him in the remains of the hall, chapel, and kitchen.

From the Dalyngrugges the manor and castle passed, by marriage, into the Lewknor family. Sir Lewis Lewknor, its representative, *temp.* Charles I., was a hot-headed cavalier, whose stronghold was taken and dismantled by Sir William Waller's forces. It was built in 1386, by Sir Edward Dalyngrugge, one of the gallant knights who fought so brilliantly at Creçy and Poictiers. A. E. Fuller, Esq., of Rose Hill, is the present proprietor.

BODIAM CHURCH, dedicated to St. Giles, at the other end of the village, is an Early English building, of some interest. Thomas Cubitt, Esq., is the patron of the vicarage, valued at £280 per annum.

From Bodiam we may cross the hill to the north of Salehurst, and regaining the high road, descend into ETCHINGHAM (population, 852); The village is one mile distant from the station. ETCHINGHAM CHURCH is one of the most interesting in the county. Its general character is Decorated, with a massive square tower, a staircase turret, a roof of unusual height, and windows ornamented with rich flamboyant tracery. The chancel is noticeable for its length—its south door—and Early English font. The founder of the church was one Sir *William de Etchingham*, d. 1387, to whom there is a brass in the chancel (much injured), and an inscription which may be compared with that on "the Black Prince's tomb at Canterbury." An enriched canopy overhangs a brass to a later Sir *William*, d. 1444, his wife, and son, and the south aisle is adorned with an Etchingham helmet. In the nave a monument, with a bust and a neat Latin inscription, commemorates *Henry Corbould*, the father of the brothers Corbould, the artists. The church has been recently and tastefully restored. A noble yew flourishes in the graveyard.

The rectory, valued at £518, is in the hands of trustees. The present rector, Hugh Totty, D.D., is 104 years old (1860), and has held the living since 1792.

We now move northward, leaving altogether the line of the railway, and at Hurst Green cross the Lewes road. Near the 47th milestone a winding road leads off through a pleasantly undulating country (3 miles) to TICEHURST (population, 3148). This populous village is seated on an eminence, and surrounded by fertile hills and valleys, quite 3¼ miles distant from the Ticehurst road Railway Station. The hop-grounds here are extensive ; and a considerable amount of arable land is carefully cultivated. At Stonegate and Flimwell are two small churches of recent date. Much of the venerable wood which anciently gave name to this countryside, and which was haunted by the mischievous Saxon fairy *Tys*, to the great wonder of the woodmen and their households, still clothes the sides of the hills and involves their combes in heavy shadows.

  . The CHURCH, Perpendicular in style, and dedicated to St. Mary, was completely and carefully restored in 1856. The stained glass was then introduced. Both pulpit and font are curiously and elaborately carved. Observe the brass to *John Wybarne*, d. 1490, and his two wives—the figures evidently copied from an older brass, perhaps from that to Sir William de Etchingham, in Etchingham Church.

The Dean and Chapter of Canterbury have the presentation to this vicarage, which is worth £700 per annum.

By way of Dane Hill and Fleniwell, we regain the high road, and cross the boundaries of Kent. A mile beyond Stone Crouch we again return into Sussex, and at 40 miles from London, and 23 miles from Hastings, reach LAMBERHURST (population, 1734), *i.e.*, the Lambs' wood. To the right of the Bayham road, a short distance from the village, are the remains of the once celebrated GLOUCESTER FURNACE, the largest of the Sussex iron-works, where the iron balustrade, weighing 200 tons, and worth £11,202 : 0 : 6, was cast. At the time of its completion the foundry was visited by the Princess (afterwards Queen) Anne and the young Duke of Gloucester, whence the name. A cottage, formerly the counting-house, and the mill-pond, with some traces of the foundry walls, are the only *vestiges* of the once busy iron-works.

As we enter the village we pass, on our right, QUEEN VICTORIA'S OAK, planted by loyal hands on the Queen's marriage-day, February 10, 1840. A few paces farther and we reach the GEORGE INN. At the other end of the village, on the hill, stand the COURT LODGE (W. C. Morland, Esq.); the VICARAGE, a picturesque Elizabethan structure ; and the CHURCH, an interesting building, with a fine Perpendicular window at the west end. The carved oaken pulpit, date 1630, should be examined. The chancel is separated from the Scotney chapel by an Early English arch, of earlier date than the rest of the church. A noble and venerable yew adorns the garth.

The vicarage, valued at £401, is in the patronage of the Dean and Chapter of Rochester.

In the neighbourhood (1 mile) is SCOTNEY CASTLE (E. Hussey, Esq.), a stately Elizabethan pile of recent erection. Of the old castellated and moated mansion of the Scotneys remains a machicolated tower, and a part of the gate house. There are also extant portions of a later house, designed by Inigo Jones.

From Lamberhurst the tourist may proceed to PADDOCK'S WOOD, 7 miles, or TUNBRIDGE WELLS, 8 miles ; or he may cross the country to WADHURST, 6 miles, and return by rail, reversing the route we are now about to describe.

BRANCH ROUTE FROM HASTINGS TO TUNBRIDGE WELLS.

The view of Hastings from St. Leonards is one of exquisite beauty. The town is certainly seen to most advantage from this point. "The lofty and handsome range of Pelham Crescent, the church of St. Mary-at-Cliff, and other modern buildings, occupy a prominent place in the picture, and wear an imposing air as they stand contrasted with the meaner houses at their base, and are backed by the noble cliff which rises far above, and which has been carved away to afford room for them. The houses of the older part of the town running irregularly up the higher grounds, and opposing to each other every variety of size, and shape, and colour, prevent anything like formality, which the preponderance of the newer buildings would otherwise produce ; while the gray fragments of the ancient castle, crowning the summit of the lofty cliff, impart an air of dignity to the humble dwellings beneath. And then, to complete the picture, a large fleet of fishing smacks and boats, with numerous fishing boats moving about them, are seen on the beach ; and the ever-varying sea sweeps round the foreground, to give animation to the whole"—(*Thorne*).

After enjoying this agreeable panorama we shall be in fitting mood for our railway excursion. We leave ST. LEONARD'S STATION at 9.27 ; stop at Battle, 9.42 ; leave Battle, 12.31 ; arrrive at Tunbridge Wells at 1.22 ; return from Tunbridge Wells, at 7.49 ; and reach St. Leonards at 9.2. These, at least, are the best trains available according to the *summer arrangements* of the South Eastern Company.

On our right rises the sandstone ridge terminating in Fair-light Down, and beneath it in the woodland, the church and village of HOLLINGTON (*See* p. 480). At 2½ miles, we pass CROW-HURST PARK (T. Papillon, Esq.), the ancient demesne of the famous Sussex Pelhams. It extends as far as the Battle road. On our right, and near the line, stands CROWHURST (population, 591), a pretty village in a well wooded valley, with clumps of dark green yews springing up at every point of vantage. The church, dedicated to St. George, was re-built (except the tower) by Teulon, in the Decorated style. There are fragments of painted glass in the tower window. In the tracery, and over the door-case, remark the celebrated device of the Pelhams; a *buckle*, adopted in commemoration of the capture of John of France at Poictiers—a "deed of derring-do," in which Sir John Pelham bore a conspicuous part. A wooden buckle was long suspended from the gallery front. A glorious old yew, 27 feet in girth at four feet from the ground, renders the churchyard memorable. The rectory, valued at £177, is in the gift of T. Papillon, Esq.

South of the church, notice the ancient COURT LODGE, 40 feet by 23 feet, and Early Decorated in character. It was a parallelo-gram in plan, but the only remains now extant are the east gable, and a porch at the south-east gable. Probably it had a hall on the south side, and was of greater importance than its present ruins indicate. Its erection is ascribed to a certain Walter de Scotney, of Crowhurst, Chief Steward of Clare, Earl of Glou-cester, who was executed in 1259, on the charge of having poisoned his lord and his lord's brother.

[CATSFIELD (population, 550) lies beyond Crowhurst to the north-west. Its Church is small, and not peculiarly interesting. The rectory, valued at £311, is in the patronage of the Earl of Ashburnham.]

At 6 miles from Hastings we reach the BATTLE STATION, where we quit the train, and proceed on a pilgrimage to the scene of the great fight which, in its mighty influence upon the destinies of England and the world, can never be over-estimated. A view of the abbey gateway—"one of the finest gate-houses belonging to a religious establishment that remain in England" —and of the leaf-encompassed church, may be obtained from the railway. Lord Harry Vane is the proprietor, and the property is only thrown open to the public on *Tuesdays* and *Fridays*. Even then the tourist will find himself hampered by certain disagreeable restrictions, and he will feel the full force of the old vulgar saw—" we must not look a gift-horse too curiously in the mouth !"

Before we enter into any minute examination, however, of BATTLE ABBEY, it will be advisable to put together a few details of the great victory which its founder designed it to commemorate. Fuller particulars than we can here afford will be found in Sharon Turner's History, and Thierry's Conquest of the Normans ; while an erudite and most interesting paper in Mr. M. A. Lower's " Contributions to Literature" should be consulted by the tourist. In our own sketch we shall be greatly indebted to it for topographical information. Our historical notes are principally drawn from the old monastic chroniclers.

THE BATTLE OF HASTINGS.

[A.D. 1066. Duke William landed on the English shore, September 28th, 1066. After resting his men, and fortifying the more important positions in the vicinity of Hastings, where he had congregated his forces, he marched along the hills from Fairlight to Battle, passing through Crowhurst Park to Hetheland (now called Telham Hill, south of Battle, and distinguishable by a modern farmstead), which he reached on the morning of October 14. Meanwhile, Harold's camp occupied the ascent now crowned by Battle Abbey, was protected by deep trenches, and a breast-work—or *chevaux de frise*—of osier hurdles. To the east extended broad morasses and an almost impenetrable wood—to the west stretched the fastnesses and jungles of the vast Andreds-leas. Victory was, therefore, imperative for the Normans. The only alternative was—not simply defeat, but ruin.

The morning dawned all coldly and darkly upon Norman and Saxon. Then the half brother of Duke William, Odo, bishop of Bayeux, celebrated a grand mass, and afterwards mounting a large white steed, drew up the cavalry in line. William divided his army into three divisions or columns ; in front were the light infantry, chiefly armed with arrows ; in the centre, the heavy armed foot ; all the best and bravest of the Norman chivalry, with the great duke at their head, formed the last division. Then he addressed his soldiers in stirring words. ." Remember," said he, " to fight bravely, then shall we conquer and be rich. What I gain ye will gain, what I conquer ye will conquer ; if I win this land ye shall have it." With a loud shout of " God help us !" and singing the old Norman song of " Roland," and of " Roncesvalles," the whole army moved impetuously forward.

The English, chiefly infantry, were drawn up by Harold in the form of a wedge. Firm, motionless, impregnable as were their children at Waterloo and Inkermann, their shields covered their bold hearts, their sturdy arms wielded the ponderous battle-axe. Harold was amongst them, and on foot. His banner was planted near him, and on its folds was blazoned in gold the device of a fighting warrior. When the English saw their monarch in their midst, they burned for the battle, and shouted enthusiastically " The Holy Cross ! the Cross of God !"

At length there comes a rush upon the startled air. The archers have discharged their arrows, and they speed on their deadly way, like the bolts of heaven. Forward press the Norman spearmen, forward up the grassy hills, forward to the very defences of the Saxons ; and then there are shouts, and groans, and loud outcries of rage, despair, exultation, and agony. From behind their ramparts the Saxons ply, with arms strengthened by patriotic fervour, their heavy battle-axes, and many a stout knight falls beneath the ponderous blow. In vain the Normans fill up the places of their slain, in vain they display the most heroic valour. Did the Saxons possess a reserve, or a body of cavalry, William's hopes of the English crown verily would be nought. As it is, his sixty thousand men find themselves unable to break through the noble Saxon phalanx, though they outnumber it by one-third. Great is their dismay, heavy are their hearts ; and hark ! there is a cry, uttered first by a few faint voices, but quickly taken up by many others, and soon swelling over the field—"The Duke is fallen ! Duke William is dead !" A passion of terror seizes the Norman troops, and they fling down their arms, and take to flight. Then out from the *melée*, all maddened with indignation, sweeps Duke William ! He rushes among the fugitives ; he smites them with his spear. Throwing off his helmet, he turns his flashing brow and glowing eyes upon them, and he cries, "Behold ! I live ; and with God's help I will conquer ! What madness makes ye fly? How will ye escape ? Those whom, if ye willed, ye might slay like cattle, are destroying you. Ye fly from victory—from immortal glory ! Ye rush upon your ruin !"

These fiery words reanimate the dispirited troops. And now the astute Norman, seeing that it is in vain his best soldiers charge that impenetrable wall, conceives a wary stratagem. His troops pretend to retreat—to fly in confusion ; the Saxons, elate with the hope of victory, pursue them, and break for the first time, their firm array. Alas ! it is their perdition. The main body of the Duke's army charges them in their flank with a horrible slaughter. Twice is the stratagem repeated, twice are the Saxons deceived. The great banner of the Fighting Warrior is seized by some daring Normans. The rival chiefs fight in the *melée* like the meanest soldiers. William's half brother, Odo of Bayeux, the warrior priest, in a fit of holy enthusiasm, wields his battle-axe with signal valour.

The sun is setting in the western seas, going downward in a sky as red as blood. Alas ! it is the last sunset that shall shine on the eyes of Saxon Harold ! Even while the issue of the dread fight is still uncertain, a random arrow flashes through the air, and smites the gallant monarch in the brain. He falls !—the ominous tidings of his death thrill through the Saxon ranks. Their leader dead ; what is left them but despair ? The Normans rush again to the attack ; and, as the moon rises in silver light over the fatal field, it gleams upon William the Conqueror, and gilds the victorious banners of the Normans ! Thus was the crown of England lost and won !

During the pretended flight of the Normans, and their impetuous pursuit by the Saxons, a terrible incident occurred. "In the plain," says Wace, "was a fosse. The English charged, and drove the Normans before them, till they made them fall back upon this fosse, overthrowing into it horses and men. Many were to be seen falling therein, rolling one over the other, with their faces to the earth, and unable to rise. Many of the English also, whom the Normans drew down along with them, died there. At no time in the day's battle did so many Normans die as perished in that fosse," which thenceforth was called MAL-FOSSE, and has been identified with the rill flowing at the foot of Caldbeck Hill, in the direction of Watlington. "This rivulet still occasionally overflows its banks, and the primitive condition of the adjacent levels was doubtless that of a morass, overgrown with flags, reeds, and similar bog vegetables."]

At the place now called Battle (and formerly Epiton), Mr. Lower believes that " no town, or even village, existed in Saxon times. It was probably a down covered with heath and furze,—a wild rough common, without houses, and almost without trees. The Saxon Chroniclers had no better mode of indicating the locality of the hostile meeting than by saying that it occurred at the HOARY APPLE TREE (at thære háran apuldran),—probably from some venerable tree of that species growing near at hand."

That portion of Battle town which now lies east of the church is called the Lake, and sometimes SANGUELAC, or Seulac, —*i. e.*, "the lake of blood,"—so named it is said, by the Conqueror, "because of the vast sea of gore there spilt." It was called SANT LACHE, however, long before the battle of Hastings. In like manner, the springs of chalybeate water hereabouts, which form the sources of the Asten, derived their redness from the blood of the slaughtered Saxons.

"Asten, once distained with native English blood,
    Whose soil yet, when but wet with any little rain,
    Doth blush, as put in mind of those there sadly slain."
                                   (DRAYTON—*The Polyolbion.*)

CALDBECK HILL was corrupted with "Call-back-Hill," because at that point the Duke "called back" his pursuing troops; "TELHAM" was made "Tellman," as the spot where the conqueror counted his forces; a large tree, on the London road, is named "*Watch Oak;*" and at *Standard Hill*, either William or Harold traditionally set up his standard. But Harold's banner, in truth, was first pitched at Battle, and there it remained until supplanted by the oriflamme of the conqueror; and there subsequently arose that majestic edifice "The Abbey of the Battle"—an expiatory offering for the terrible slaughter which had taken place.

THE ABBEY OF BATTLE.

The Abbey of St. Martin DE BELLI LOCO—" of the place of the battle "—was erected on the very spot where the Norman knights humbled the Saxon "Fighting Man," within ten years of that great event. Very nobly did William carry out the vow he uttered upon Telham Hill, and richly did he endow his new foundation. William Faber, a Norman knight who had heard the vow, and had assumed the cowl and robe in the Benedictine Abbey of Marmontier, had the superintendence of its erection. A circle of three miles diameter spreading around the Abbey was set apart by William as a "lowy" or "leuca," over which it had unlimited jurisdiction, and peculiar rights and privileges were conferred upon its abbot. "Here William intended to place 140 Noman monks, for the full discharge of its pious services ; but he was prevented by death from executing the whole of his design. He had endowed it with lands equal to the support of such a number ; and had bestowed on it the privileges of a sanctuary, and a multitude of others usual in those days. He peopled it with religious from the Benedictine monastery of Marmontier in Normandy, and appointed one of them, Robert Blankard, first abbot. He being drowned in his passage, was succeeded by Gaubertus. William (Rufus?) honoured the church with his presence, probably at its consecration, and offered at the altar his sword and the robe he wore on his coronation"—(*Pennant*).

At the time of its dissolution this wealthy and "mitred" Abbey had fallen into a most unsavoury condition, and the royal commissioner, Layton, wrote of it as "the worst he had ever seen," as inhabited by "the blake sort of dyvellyshe monks." Its annual value was then returned at £880 : 14 : 7, according to Dugdale, or £987 : 0 : 10, according to Speed. The site was conferred upon Sir Anthony Browne, "the same who had the courage to bring to his royal master the fatal message of death," and by his descendant, the fourth Lord Montacute, was sold to Sir Thomas Webster.

Sir Anthony Browne converted the monastic buildings into a stately mansion. Fronting the street still stands, in excellent preservation, the GATE-HOUSE, late decorated in style, and probably erected by Abbot Bethynge, *temp.* Edward III. The house nearest to it, on the west side, was the Pilgrims' HOSPITIUM, and is called the ALMONRY ; the range of buildings to the right, now in ruins, was long made use of as the TOWN-HALL. Passing within the entrance, we first inspect the HALL, 57 feet by 30 feet, very lofty, and timber-roofed ; the DORMITORY, now converted into a corridor and bed-rooms ; and the BEGGARS' HALL, a vaulted apartment underneath. Next we visit the terrace, traditionally reputed to have been the BANQUETING-ROOM, and overlooking the scene of the great battle. Below it are eight vaults, each of them 29 feet by 14 feet, which had been "the magazines for provisions and fuel in the flourishing days of this great foundation"— (*Pennant*).

Viewing afterwards the east front of the splendid pile, we

remark its nine arches enriched with Perpendicular tracery. On the site of the flower-garden stood the conventual CHURCH, whose foundations were excavated in 1817, and the apse of whose crypt and the bases of its columns still remain uncovered. " Siste, viator ; heroa calcas :"—it was here that Harold fell. " When William of Marmontier and his brethren, some time after the battle, engaged in the work of rearing the abbey, not liking the place on account of its lack of water, they proceeded to build on a more eligible site on the west side of the hill, at a place called HERST ; but the Conqueror, hearing of what they had done, waxed wroth, 'and commanded them with all haste to lay the foundation of the temple on the very place where he had achieved the victory over his enemy.' The brethren suggested the inconvenience which would arise from the dryness of the site, when William gave utterance to the memorable promise that, if God would spare his life, he would so amply endow the establishment, that wine should be more abundant there than water in any other great abbey. The chronicler goes on to inform us that, ' in accordance with the King's desire, they wisely erected the high altar upon the precise spot where the ensign of Harold, which they call the Standard, was observed to fall ' "—(*Lower*).

The Early English REFECTORY, with its lancet-windows and buttressed walls, and the vaulted rooms beneath it, must next be visited. One of the latter, the largest, has been called the SCRIPTORIUM, or LIBRARY, and among the books which Leland found here was Prior Clement of Llanthony's highly edifying treatise on " the Spiritual Wings and Feathers of the Cherubim."

The Battle Abbey roll of Norman knights, from which Duke William, it is said, called over his band of followers on the morning of the fight—but which, probably, was a later fiction, or, at least, compilation, of the Battle monks—was preserved in the monastery until the Dissolution, and afterwards removed to Cowdray, where it was destroyed in the great fire. Copies of it, but widely varying among themselves, may be consulted in Leland's Collectanea, in Holinshed, and the Normanni Scriptores.

On leaving this " hallowed ground"—this spot so sacred in the eyes of every intelligent Englishman—the visitor will join, we fancy, in the reprobation which has been pretty generally expressed of the mean and selfish restrictions here designed, as it would seem, to minister to his especial discomfort. Surely a place like this might be left for Englishmen to examine, unshackled by half a score of absurd conditions, and free from the constant supervision of a greedy janitor, whose cry, like the horse-leech's daughters', is—" Give! Give!"

BATTLE CHURCH is Transitional Norman in style, with a few Decorated additions. It contains a little stained glass ; and in the chancel stands the white marble tomb of Sir *Anthony Browne*, with recumbent effigies of that gallant knight and his wife *Abie*. Observe the brasses for a knight in armour, d. 1425 ; Sir *W. Arnold*, d. 1435 ; *Richard Cleve*, d. 1430, and *John Wythines*, Deans of Battle, d. 1615.

The vicarage of Battle, valued at £500, is in the patronage of Lord Harry Vane, who, as lay abbot, has the appointment of a dean ; and he, independent of the bishop, has complete sway over the ancient abbatical jurisdiction. The population of Battle, in 1851, is 3849.

Battle is famous for its gunpowder-mills, which are situated at some distance from the town beyond the woods. In the neighbourhood the lover of wild blossoms will meet with the field geranium, pansy, rue-leaved saxifrage, ivy crowfoot, corn-pheasant's eye, and cornwort.

On our way from Battle to Robertsbridge we pass SEDLES-COMB on the right, WHATLINGTON (population, 458), and MOUNTFIELD (population, 769), on the left. The latter is agreeably situated in a fair and leafy landscape, surrounded by low but pleasantly-verdurous hills.

At 62 miles from London we pass the Robertsbridge station ; 3 miles further and we reach ETCHINGHAM. About 3 miles to the right, on the hills, stands BURWASH (population, 2227), a large and busy village, with an interesting CHURCH, noticeable for containing " a curious specimen of the iron manufacture of the fourteenth century, and the oldest existing article produced by our Sussex foundries. It is a cast-iron slab, with an ornamental cross, and an inscription in relief. In the opinion of several eminent antiquaries, it may be regarded as unique for the style and period. The inscription is much injured by long exposure to the attrition of human feet. The letters are Longobardic, and the legend appears, on a careful examination to be —

'ORATE P. ANNEMA JHONE COLINE' (or COLINS).
' Pray for the soul of Joan Collins.'"

The living (a rectory and vicarage), valued at £699, is in the patronage of the Rev. J. Gould.

Either from Robertsbridge, Etchingham, or Ticehurst station (through Burwash) we may visit BRIGHTLING (population, 812), a spot assuredly not to be neglected by the tourist who has a brain and a heart to appreciate "the all-wondrous works of God." Here, as from the minaret of a mosque, one may look out upon the landscape sleeping all fair and serenely in the sunlight of heaven—upon broad reaches of meadow-land dotted by patient cattle—upon close-clinging branches hung with a myriad leaves —upon the shimmering and shining waters of the far-off sea— upon the silver trail of tiny rivulets—upon gray church-tower, and many-gabled manor-house, and quiet hamlet—upon hill and dale, and grove, and garden—a goodly picture, designed and coloured by a hand Divine ! To the north and east spreads the Weald of Kent and Sussex, rich in a thousand changes of light and shade ; to the south-west rises the long bold line of the glorious Sussex downs ; to the south gleams and glitters the Channel, bounded in the distance by a low bank of clouds which denotes the position of the French coast. On the highest point of this elevation, and 646 feet above the sea-level, a neat Observatory stands—erected, some score of years ago, by S. Fuller, of Rose Hill Park. It is said to be visible from the neighbourhood of London, and the lofty columnar land-mark near it is necessarily of great service to the mariners of the Channel. The site of the ancient fire-beacon is curiously named " Browns Burgh."

In BRIGHTLING CHURCH there is nothing to interest the tourist. Its stained glass is not of special beauty. Its rectory, valued at £563, is in the patronage of the Rev. B. Hayley.

In this neighbourhood, and sheltered in a gap of the downs, lies ROSE HILL PARK (A. E. Fuller, Esq.).

A pleasant road from Brightling leads into the valley of the Rother, and on crossing that stream, winds up the hills to the Ticehurst Road Station. BURWASH lies about 1½ mile to the right.

The rail now carries us through a fertile country-side—hop-grounds and corn fields smiling abundantly around us—to the WADHURST STATION, 1 mile from WADHURST (population, 2802), and 52 miles from London. Observe, as you enter the village—the natives, by the way, call it "a town"—WADHURST CASTLE (E. W. Smyth, Esq.), a pleasant house in pleasant grounds. About 1 mile to the left, on the road to Frant, stands KNOLE HOUSE, an Elizabethan pile of some pretensions. WADHURST CHURCH, dedicated to Sts. Peter and Paul, is partly Early English and partly Decorated. It has a lofty shingled spire, and contains no less than 30 grave slabs of Sussex iron. Notice the memorial to *" John Legas, Gentleman."* The vicarage, valued at £659, is in the patronage of Wadham College, Oxon.

WADHURST, or WADE-HURST, indicates by its name its position on a branch of the Rother, in a wooded country. The prefix WADE is identical with the Latin *vadum,* a ford.

Between Wadhurst and Frant we pass through a tolerably long tunnel. FRANT (population, 2447) is a large and busy town, with a handsome church, situated on an eminence which overlooks one of the most glorious landscapes in Kent and Sussex—from the Sevenoaks hills to the heights of Dover ; from Chatham on the north-east to Leith Hill, south-west. Frant Church, Dungeness, and Beachy Head form the three points of one of the triangles of the Ordnance Survey.

The present CHURCH, a quasi-Gothic edifice, was built in 1821-2. The windows contain some good modern painted glass. The rector of Rotherfield has the patronage of the living, a vicarage, valued at £800.

SPERNFOLD PLACE (Hon. P. Ashburnham) and SAXONBURY LODGE (R. Davidson, Esq.) are situated in this vicinity. ERIDGE PARK (Earl of Abergavenny) skirts the high road to the Wells. BAYHAM ABBEY is about 3 miles distant. TUNBRIDGE WELLS, 3 miles by rail. (*See* p. 438).

MAIN ROUTE RESUMED—HASTINGS TO POLEGATE.

At ST LEONARD'S JUNCTION STATION we leave the London and South Eastern Company's carriages and jurisdiction, and commence our journeys upon that system of lines which is included in the comprehensive title of the London and South Coast Railway. The first station (3¾ miles) is called BEXHILL (population, 2148), but the village is nearly 1½ mile. distant ; a quiet, breezy, summery watering-place, in a fertile country, and looking

out upon the waters of the Channel, which are here gradually
retiring from the shore, and have recently given up to the curiosity of the geologist a singular submarine forest. The village is
situated upon high ground. The CHURCH, dedicated to St Mary,
has a Norman nave and Early English chancel. An ancient
east window of painted glass, containing representations of
Henry III. and his Queen Eleanor, was removed from the building by Horace Walpole, through the agency of the Earl of Ashburnham, and became, for a time, one of the glories of Strawberry
Hill. A similar window, with figures of Edward III. and Philippa
of Hainault, may now be examined in the CHURCH of HOOE
(population, 574), dedicated to St. James, and about 5 miles north-
west. The vicarage of Bexhill, valued at £1291 per annum, is
in the gift of the Bishop of Winchester. Hooe vicarage, worth
£235 yearly, is the property of the present incumbent.

The railway now runs along the shore, which is flat and uninteresting, to Pevensey Station, 6¾ miles. The long range of the
Martello Towers, chiefly occupied as coast-guard posts, will be
duly noticed by the traveller. Inland rises the venerable pile of
PEVENSEY CASTLE. PEVENSEY HARBOUR curves boldly to the
south-west, and terminates at LANGLEY POINT, beyond which is
EASTBOURNE BAY, bounded, in its turn, by the lofty chalk-heights
of BEACHY HEAD.

PEVENSEY—(*i. e.*, PEOFN'S EY, or ISLAND).

[Population, 412—*Inn :* The Royal Oak.   65 m. from London, by rail. ; 60 m. by
road ; 11¼ m. from Hastings.]

ANDERIDA, the modern PEVENSEY (*an* not, and *tred*, inhabited
—the uninhabited), was one of the great Roman strongholds which,
under the government of the *Comes Saxonici Littoris*, defended the
south-eastern' coast ; and derived its name from its position on
the borders of the vast ANDREDES-WEALD, or " uninhabited forest."
The Romans chose for the position of their camp one of the in-
sulated hills which then rose above the watery morasses, and
strengthened it with all the appliances suggested by their military
knowledge. In 477, Ælla and his Saxons effected a settlement
upon the coast near Chichester, and a few years later (A.D. 491)
attacked Anderida, captured it, and " slew all that dwelt therein,
nor was there one Briton left "—a simple but significant passage

(in the Saxon Chronicle), which Gibbon has commended for its impressive terseness. Anderida afterwards became an important Saxon settlement, and its area was considerably enlarged. The sea, now a mile distant, then beat against its cliffs on the south and east.

After the Conquest, Pevensey was bestowed by King William (who had chosen its bay for the disembarkation of his forces) upon Robert, Earl of Mortaigne and Cornwall, his half-brother, and one of the most potent of the Norman Barons. Recognizing the importance of its position " for one whose interests lay between England and Normandy," he founded here a Castle, at the southeast angle of the ancient town. From this point the conqueror embarked, in 1067, for his Norman dominions.

During his brief revolt (in 1089) against William Rufus, Pevensey castle was held by Odo of Bayeux, but famine threatening the besieged, and no succour arriving from Duke Robert, the warrior-priest was compelled to surrender. About 1104, Henry I. granted the manor and barony to Gilbert de Aquila, whence it acquired the name of the " Honour of the Eagle." It remained with his respresentatives about a century. Gilbert Earl of Clare, in 1144, defended it with extraordinary resolution against King Stephen, who was forced, after a wearisome siege, to withdraw his forces. It next passed into the hands of the Earls de Warrenne ; was granted in 1269, to Prince Edward (afterwards Edward I.) and his heirs ; remained with the Crown until Edward III. settled it on John of Gaunt, who conferred the governorship upon the Pelhams ; was threatened with destruction in the reign of Elizabeth ; sold, in 1650, by the Parliamentary Commissioners to John Warr, for £40 ; escaped these dangers, and partly survived the assaults of time ; and is now a venerable memorial of a long and chequered history, secure in the reverent care of the Duke of Devonshire.

Besides the sieges we have enumerated, the old castle was attacked, in 1265, by Simon de Montfort ; and, in 1399, by Richard the Second's forces, who were gallantly repulsed by the garrison under the command of the heroic Lady Pelham—her husband at the time serving under the flag of Bolingbroke. Edmund, Duke of York, found here a prison ; and at a later period, Queen Joanna of Navarre was confined within its walls for four wearisome years, on a charge of having subtilely plotted against the life of her step-son, Henry the Fifth.

2 K

With these few historical notes to assist us, let us turn to a survey of the ruined stronghold, adopting the results of the patient investigations of Mr. Lower (" Chronicles of Pevensey"), and Mr. Wright ("Wanderings of an Antiquary.")

The Castle is situated on gently rising ground, on the edge of Pevensey Level. Its walls are conspicuous from the railway station, whence a bye-lane leads into the road which leads up to the stately entrance towers, the " Decuman Gate" of the ancient Anderida. The width of the opening between them is now 27 feet. Probably, it was an approach to the narrower gateway of the town. The Roman masonry is still in wonderful preservation ; although it has been exposed to the changes of a great part of 2000 years, the mark of the trowel is still visible on the mortar, and many of the facing stones look as fresh as if they had been cut yesterday." The walls are generally 12 feet in thickness, and between 24 and 30 feet in height ; they enclosed an area of about 8½ acres, and on the southern and eastern sides "occupied a sort of low cliff, washed at every tide by the waters of the ocean, or at least a considerable arm of the sea."—(*Lower.*)

Taking the road to the left, outside the northern wall and its massive towers, and passing a modern house of no picturesque design, we reach a fine Roman tower, bearing on its summit a Norman superstructure, which appears to have been intended as a watch tower, and commands an extensive view of the principal approaches to this important fortress. " There is a striking contrast between the rough masonry of the Norman superstructure and the workmanlike finish of the Roman building below. The latter is here extremely well defined. It consists of a regular facing of squared stones, with the usual banding courses of bricks (a very peculiar characteristic of Roman masonry in this country). The interior is filled up with irregular materials, among which liquid mortar was thrown, and the latter (in which we observe at once the mixture of pounded tile so peculiar to the Roman mortar) has become harder than the stone itself." In one of the towers a large breach in the Norman masonry has been filled up with the usual Norman " herring-bone work."

At the south-east corner the Norman castle stands on what seems to have been an artificial mound, occupying an area of nearly an acre and a half, and forming an irregular pentagon round a large mound, so that the small interior court is much higher than the ground outside. The gateway, flanked by two towers, nearly faces the Decuman gate, and have evidently been imitated by the mediæval architect from the Roman models before him. The east tower formed the Keep ; the north-west may have been the governor's residence. Two sides were defended by a moat, over which was thrown a drawbridge. The ancient Chapel, excavated in 1852, stood within the court, to the right of the north-west tower. A rude Norman font, and three skeletons were found here. The castle well is 50 feet deep.

Some portions of Robert of Mortaigne's Castle may plainly be detected ; but most of the ruins exhibit the characteristics of the Transition Norman and Early English styles.

From the Castle we descend to PEVENSEY CHURCH (dedicated to St. Nicholas, the favourite Norman Saint), an Early English building, with a nave of Decorated character. The tower stands at the east end of the north aisle. There is a noble chancel-arch, and the clustered columns have richly foliated capitals, but the interior has been sadly disfigured by modern innovations, and is altogether in a painfully mutilated condition. It contains a monument and effigy for *John Wheatley, temp.* James I.

The vicarage, valued at £948, is in the patronage of the Bishop of Chichester.

PEVENSEY HARBOUR was formed by the estuary of the river Ashbourne, navigable for small vessels as high as Pevensey Bridge in 1720, but, in Pennant's time " quite choked a mile distant from the shore, and nothing left but a narrow drain, the receptacle of a few boats." Here the landing of Julius Cæsar has been fixed by Professor Airey, who has supported his theory by ingenious but unsatisfactory arguments. Here the disembarcation of William and his Normans *did* take place, his six hundred vessels filling all the coast from Pevensey to Hastings ; and he himself stumbling forward as he set his foot upon the shore. With what curious eyes must the bold adventurers have looked upon the glittering cliffs, the undulating downs, the vigorous woods, the already venerable walls of the ancient Anderida, as with glancing spear and glittering axe they prest forward towards that memorable plain where a nation's destiny was to be sealed in blood !

Pevensey was, and still is, a member of the Cinque Ports, and its corporation seal bears the usual Cinque Ports' escocheon. Here was born, or, at least, for some years resided, and practised as a physician, *Andrew Borde*, the original " Merry Andrew," and author of the famous " Tales of the Wise Men of Gotham." We owe to him the anecdotes of the humble-minded magistrate, who protested that " though Mayor of Pevensey he was but a man ;" of the " freeman of the port" who *drowned an eel* as a mode of capital punishment calculated to be highly effectual; and sundry other " merrie jestes" which our space forbids us to recapitulate.

With a curious extract from the " Custumal of Pevensey" we must close our notice :—" In judgments of the crown, if a man be condemned to death, the post-reeve, as coroner, shall pronounce judgment, and, being seated next the steward, shall say, ' *Sir, withdraw and axe for a priest ;*' and if the condemned be of the franchise, he shall be taken to the town bridge at high water and drowned in the harbour ; but if he be of the geldable (*i. e.*, liable to taxes, which the freemen were not), he shall be hung in the Lowy, at a place called the Wahztrew."

Near the Pevensey railway station, and, as its name indicates, west of the castle, is situated WESTHAM (population, 761), with a church, dedicated to St. Mary. The south wall of the nave and the south transept (now a schoolroom) have Norman characteristics, the rest of the building is Perpendicular. Some portion of the rood-loft remains, and in the east window glimmer a few fragments of stained glass. The vicarage, valued at £347, is in the patronage of the Duke of Devonshire.

At LANGLEY, 1½ mile south, moulder the desolate ruins of a grange-chapel formerly belonging to Lewes Priory. Two small forts have been erected at Langley Point.

The next station we reach is at POLEGATE, whence diverge short branches to Hailsham, on the north, and Eastbourne, south.

WILLINGDON (population, 678) is about 1 mile south of Polegate. The CHURCH is small and uninteresting. Beyond it, even to the very line of the rail, stretches the PARK. The vicarage, valued at £158, is in the patronage of the Dean and Chapter of Chichester.

EASTBOURNE (population, 3033) covers a much larger extent of ground than its population would seem to necessitate. In fact, it consists of four different portions,—the town, formed of four streets crossing each other almost at right angles ; SEA HOUSES, a terrace overlooking the sands ; SOUTHBOURNE, three quarters of a mile from the sea, to the west of the station ; and MEADS, a small cluster of cottages and cornfields, about a quarter of a mile beyond Southbourne. The station is about midway between the town and Sea Houses. The roads lie in the shadow of noble elms, and on each side stretch the green meadows and the smiling pasture. The walk along the sands to Beachy Head is one of unusual beauty.

EASTBOURNE CHURCH, dedicated to St. Mary, is a goodly Early English structure, measuring 124 feet by 50. The lofty tower contains a peal of six bells, of Sussex metal, cast at Chiddingly in 1651. There are three Perpendicular sedilia in the chancel, an Easter sepulchre (also Perpendicular), and a brass to *J. Hyng*, d. 1445. The chancel-arch is slightly pointed. The north chancel is divided from the south by Transition-Norman piers and arches. In the former stands a monument to *Gilbert Davies*, President of the Royal Society, who long resided at Eastbourne Place, beyond the village. In the east window glows some Flemish stained glass.

The vicarage, valued at £428, is in the gift of the Treasurer of Chichester Cathedral.

[A district church, dedicated to the Holy Trinity, stands near the SEA HOUSES. The Vicar of Eastbourne has the appointment of its curate. ST. GREGORY'S CHAPEL, the old PARSONAGE HOUSE, the curious vaulted room and subterranean passage at the LAMB INN, are things to be noticed by the tourist. A circular redoubt, erected in 1804, near the barracks on St. Anthony's Hill, mounts twelve guns, and will accommodate 400 men. Mortimer, the painter, was born at Eastbourne in 1741, and passed his early years in studying the wild scenery, and consorting with the bold smugglers, of this picturesque coast. Here the patela levis, crambe maritima, dropwort, and dwarf orchis, flourish in vigorous growth ; here the ring-dotterel deposits her three eggs, scarcely to be distinguished from the surrounding pebbles. "Many species of terns haunt it in great numbers during the summer months."]

In this neighbourhood the Romans had a settlement. On the road to Pevensey, 1½ mile east, a tesselated pavement and bath were discovered towards the close of the last century. South-east of Trinity Church the foundations of a Roman villa were excavated in 1858. Numerous tumuli and traces of circular encampments are visible on the downs.

BEACHY HEAD (575 feet above the level) raises its glowing wall of chalk about 3 miles south-west of Eastbourne, and is a favourite excursion-point of the Eastbourne tourists. The prospect is sublime : eastward it extends to Dover, westward to the Isle of Wight. The shores of France may also be seen, it is said, on a cloudless day. But not for the mariner does this precipitous cliff wear so goodly an aspect. It is associated in his mind with tales of fearful wrecks—not so frequent now that our charts are more skilfully constructed, and the science of navigation is better understood, but still numerous enough to render Beachy Head "a word of fear." The Dalhousie, a fine East Indiaman, was lost here, October 24, 1853, and only one life was saved.

Off Beachy Head, June 30, 1760, was fought the great fight between the combined English and Dutch fleets of 56 sail, under Arthur, Earl of Torrington, and the French, of 82, under the Comte de Tourville. The Dutch behaved with great valour, and were only saved from annihilation by Torrington's manœuvres, who contrived to interpose his fleet between them and the French. The combined fleets then took shelter in the mouth of the Thames. Torrington was tried by court-martial, but acquitted, and, hoisting his flag in his barge, went up the Medway in triumph. He was, however, deprived of his commission by King William,—wroth at the loss which his beloved Dutch had sustained,—and was never again employed.

A throng of wings immediately starts out of the chinks and crannies of this great ocean-wall at the sound of a bugle or musket. Guillemots, razor-bills, choughs, puffins, and other sea-fowl resort in vast numbers to this lonesome headland. Samphire grows here in profusion.

At BELLE-TOUTE, 1 mile west—a lofty promontory flung farther out into the sea than Beachy Head—stands a lighthouse, erected in 1831. Beneath the brink of the cliff are a staircase and a cavern, in two compartments, hollowed out of the solid rock, as a means of escape for shipwrecked seamen, by Jonathan Darby, a former vicar of East Dean (1715-28), who also found them, it is said, a convenient refuge for himself from the tongue of a shrewish wife. On one occasion a hurricane drove a Dutch galliot against this point, and fixed her bows in the mouth of one of the caverns (now known as "Parson Darby's Hole"). Twelve sailors were rescued by the intrepid pastor.

BIRLING GAP, 1½ mile west, was formerly defended by an arch and portcullis. Near this point Duguay Trouin, the bold French privateer, with 9 sail of the line, and some smaller vessels, captured the Hampton Court and Grafton men-of-war, and their convoy, and drove ashore the Royal Oak. At this "gate" or opening in the cliffs, the tourist may ascend to the high land.

.The beautiful Sussex downs stretch from Beachy Head to the Hampshire border in an undulating line, 53 miles in length.

[Just beyond Beachy Head, in a deep quiet valley, which is reputed to have been the scene of the first interview between King Alfred and the learned Asser, lies EAST DEAN (population, including Friston, 446). " Ibique illum," says Asser, "in villa regia, qua dicitur DENE, primitus vidi;" but some authorities place the scene of their meeting at East Dean, near Chichester. The vicarage, valued at £276, is in the patronage of the Bishop, Dean, and Chapter of Chichester.

FRISTON PLACE is a picturesque Tudor mansion. The cliffs, beyond this point, are broken into several conspicuous eminences, known as The Seven Sisters, haunted by the peregrine falcon, the raven, and the kestrel.

WEST DEAN (population, 129), is a pretty village at the head of a narrow chalk valley, which opens out upon the river Cuckmere. Its CHURCH is Norman, with Early English additions, and is cruciform in plan. The PARSONAGE HOUSE, a four-teenth century building, now divided into several small tenements, is partly built of oak and partly of timber. A newel staircase leads to the upper storey, where an ancient fire-place is built into the wall. The rectory is valued at £102, and is in the Duke of Devonshire's patronage.

At SEVINGTON (population, 325), a Norman Church, dedicated to St. Andrew, has a noble and massive square west tower. The rectory, valued at £309, is presented to by the Duke of Devonshire.]

From the POLEGATE STATION, a branch line, 3 miles to the north, conducts the tourist to the quiet market-town of HAILSHAM (population, 1825), one of the largest cattle-markets in Sussex. Its CHURCH is dedicated to St. Andrew, is mainly Perpendicular in style, and has a low pinnacled tower of more than ordinary interest. The vicarage is valued at £356. Hailsham is a place of considerable activity on Wednesday, the market-day, and can boast of three decent inns—the TERMINUS, the GEORGE, and the CROWN. The tourist will find it a convenient point from which to visit HELLINGLY, MICHELHAM, and HURSTMONCEUX.

☞ MICHELHAM, 2 miles west, is interesting from its ruined PRIORY,—a house of Augustinian canons founded by Gilbert de Aquila, *temp.* Henry III. It formed a stately quadrangle, which was encircled by a broad deep moat, fed by the river Cuckmere, and noted as a favourite resort of the stealthy otter. Three fish-stews, supplied by the moat, are still in good condition. A drawbridge, now replaced by a permanent bridge, was the only approach to the priory.

The remains of most importance are the square three-storied GATEWAY TOWER, the CRYPT, now made use of as a dairy, and the CANON'S ROOM, or, as it is usually called, the Prior's chamber. Observe in the latter a curious stone fire-place, with.

its projecting funnel, and a pair of andirons, of Sussex iron, terminating in human heads, *temp.* Henry VII. Near the back door of the present farm-house, some Early English arches seem to indicate the position of the Priory Chapel. The large parlour is Elizabethan. An arched passage, running parallel with the crypt—called ISAAC'S HOLE—may have been the monastic LATERNA, or place of punishment.

We may commend to the sketcher the old Priory-mill, with its background of venerable trees, as an exquisite "bit." The farmstead is abundantly favoured by the residence of a complete colony of the birds of Minerva.

☞ HELLINGLY (population, 1501), 2 miles to the north, on the left of the Mayfield road, is a pleasantly situated village, with a gray old church, and many picturesque cottages. The vicarage, valued at £344, is in the patronage of the Earl of Chichester.

HELLINGLY PARK, formerly in the possession of the Pelhams, was the scene of a hunting fray in the reign of Henry VIII., unhappily attended with fatal consequences. Holinshed relates the incident with his usual graphic simplicity:—" There was executed at St. Thomas Waterings three gentlemen—John Mantel, John Frowde, and George Roydon. They died for a murther committed in Sussex in company of Thomas Fiennes, Lord Dacre of the South ; the truth whereof was this. The said Lord Dacre, through the lewd persuasion of them, as hath been reported, meaning to hunt in the park of Nicholas Pelham, Esq. of Laughton, in the same county of Sussex, being accompanied with the said Mantel, Frowde, and Roydon, John Cheney and Thomas Isley, gentlemen, Richard Middleton and John Goldwell, yeomen, passed from his house of Hurstmonceux the last of April, in the night season, toward the same park, where they intended so to hunt ; and coming into a place called Pikehay in the parish of Hellingly, they found one John Busbrig, James Busbrig, and Richard Sumner standing together ; and as it fell out, through quarrelling, there ensued a fray betwixt the said Lord Dacre and his company on the one part, and the said John and James Busbrig and Richard Sumner on the other, insomuch that the said John Busbrig received such hurt that he died thereof the second of May next ensuing. Whereupon as well the said Lord Dacre as those that were with them, and divers others likewise that were appointed to go another way to meet them at the said

park, were indicted of murther ; and the seven and twentieth of
June the Lord Dacre himself was arraigned before the Lord
Audley of Walden, then Lord Chancellor, sitting that day as High
Steward of England, with other peers of the realm about him,
who then and there condemned the said Lord Dacre to die for
that transgression." He was executed at Tyburn June 29th, " sore
lamented by many," and not without suspicion that "his great estate,
which the greedy courtiers gaped after, caused them to hasten his destruction"—(*Camden*). The estates, however, were so closely entail-
ed that they did not fall into the hands of these rapacious cormorants.

An ancient boundary-stone, near Hellingly Park, is known as
the Amber-stone. " As *amber* is a word often found connected
with Druidical remains, this stone may have been held sacred by
our Celtic ancestors"—(*Lower*).

☞ A pleasant walk of about 4 miles will take the tourist from
Hellingly to HURSTMONCEUX (population, 1292), whose ver-
durous hill looks out upon a rich and fertile valley, while away
to the north and east sweep the glorious rounded Downs. Its
CHURCH, dedicated to All Saints, is Early English, and consists of
a nave, aisles, chancel, and north-western tower surmounted by a
shingled spire. Its principal memorials are—a fine brass to Sir
William Fiennes, d. 1402 ; a canopied tomb of Caen stone and
Petworth marble, finely sculptured, with recumbent effigies to
Thomas Fiennes, second Lord Dacre, d. 1534. The east window,
picturing scenes in the life of our Saviour, is a memorial to the
late learned and virtuous Archdeacon *Hare*, d. 1855, rector of
Hurstmonceux for many years, of active benevolence and unaffected piety. A monument by Kessels, a young Belgian sculptor,
commemorates Mrs. *Naylor* of Hurstmonceux Place, the mother of
Archdeacon Hare. The font is Decorated.

In the quiet shadowy churchyard sleep, under the dark-green
branches of a magnificent yew, Archdeacon Hare, his estimable
brother Marcus, and others of their kith and kin. Here the
tourist will do well to pause, and survey the glorious landscape
of dale, and down, and valley, and meadow, of lofty cliffs and
bright shimmering sea which spreads around and beneath him.

The rectory, valued at £920, is in the patronage of G. Jones
Esq. John Sterling was Archdeacon Hare's curate, in the earlier
years of his incumbency. Sterling died, and was buried, at Bon-
church, in the Isle of Wight.

A fine avenue, which no longer exists, formerly connected the church with HURSTMONCEUX CASTLE. The present path, however, is a sufficiently pleasant one, and, as the pedestrian pursues it, he may prepare himself for his visit by turning over Horace Walpole's lively account of a pilgrimage to Hurstmonceux in his correspondence with Mr. Bentley (vol. ii. p. 300, of Cunningham's edition).

HURSTMONCEUX derives its name from Waleran de *Monceux*, its first Norman proprietor, from whose representative it passed by marriage into the hands of Sir John de Fiennes. Sir Roger de Fiennes, one of the heroes of Agincourt, and treasurer to Henry II., built the castle in a quiet leafy hollow on the site of a camp formed here in 1162 by Henry II. It remained with the Dacres of the south until 1593 ; and passed from the Lennards early in the eighteenth century, to the Naylors, allied (by marriage) to the Hares. Having fallen into considerable decay, the Rev. Richard Hare, in 1777, called in that destructive architectural doctor, Mr Wyatt, who advised the demolition of the interior, and employed its materials in the repair and enlargement of the present mansion, situated on the west side of the Park, and known as HURSTMONCEUX PLACE (H. M. Curteis Esq.)

The position of Hurstmonceux is remarkable for its quiet beauty. It lies in a coombe or valley, from which, on every side, rise up low wooded hills. A dry moat surrounds it, and beyond flourishes a grand old grove of vigorous chesnuts. Everywhere a soft and fresh green sward springs, as it were, beneath the visitor's feet ; a luxuriant growth of ivy and hazel-bush lends to the gray walls an effective colouring. The building itself—one of the very first English edifices constructed of brick—is of singular interest. It retains the general form of a castle, with the battlemented towers, machicolations, drawbridges, moat, and other offensive and defensive appliances proper to one ; but having also something of comfort, and even ornament, combined with due regard to its belligerent character. It is, in fact, the intermediate link between the ancient castle and the modern manorhouse. It belonged to a transition state of society. It was strong enough, probably, to have withstood the casual attack of a wandering band of marauders, but would have been utterly incapable of enduring a regular siege—(*Thorne*). It encloses three courts ; a large, and two small ones. In the south front rises the MAIN-GATEWAY, a noble feature ; above it is sculptured the

Fiennes *escocheon*, and their device, the ALAUNE, or wolf-dog. At each angle stands an octagonal tower, 84 feet high, surmounted by beacon-turrets, which command a fine view of the distant channel. On the right side of the south front, beyond the gateway, stretches a LONG ROOM, which Grose represents as intended for a stable in case of a siege. The Hall measures 54 feet by 28 feet. The KITCHEN was placed on the west ; the great oven in the bake-house is 14 feet in diameter. The southeast front contained a small CHAPEL, whose stone-pillared oriel still remains. None of the coloured glass which Walpole saw is now in existence. The south-east tower was used as the DUNGEON, giving "one a delightful idea of living in the days of soccage, and under such goodly tenures"—(*Walpole*). The ancient drawbridge has been replaced by a rude wooden bridge. In a room over the PORTER'S LODGE, called "the Drummer's Hall," flourishes "the violet of a legend ;" shewing how, at midnight, the roll of a drum echoed through the silent ruins, and how that an invisible drummer guarded an invisible chest which was laden with an invisible treasure. The drum roll was, in fact, a rascally gardener's signal to certain smugglers who had made the castle their favourite haunt. Addison founded his indifferent comedy of "the Drummer" upon this tradition.

The plan of the castle is nearly a square, 200 feet on the north and south, and 214 feet on the east and west sides. Both hall and kitchen are lofty, and there is no upper storey above them.

The visitor to Hurstmonceux, desirous of fuller details than we have here afforded, may consult with advantage the interesting monograph by the Rev. E. Venables,—" Hurstmonceux and its Lords."

Some exquisite wood-carvings by Grinling Gibbons are preserved at HURSTMONCEUX PLACE. They were removed from the Castle, where they were seen and admired by Walpole.

MAIN ROUTE RESUMED—POLEGATE STATION
TO LEWES.

The railway now runs along a fertile country, with the noble heights of the Downs terminating the prospect to the south. Upon their slopes, at $3\frac{1}{2}$ miles from the Polegate station, and conspicuous from it, stand the gray old church and quiet village of WILMINGTON (population, 288). Upon the hills beyond are traces of the fosse and vallum of a semicircular camp, enclosing an area of about 12 acres. On the south-east side of the Downs may be traced the outline of a rude gigantic figure, popularly known as "the Long Man of Wilmington," 240 feet long, and holding in each hand a pole of the same length. "It appears that the outline was originally incised through the turf, leaving the chalk bare, but as it has not been kept *scoured*, like the famous White Horse in Berkshire, the depression has become so slight as to be invisible upon the spot, and it is only when the light falls upon it, at a particular angle, that it can be seen from a distance. At Cerne Abbas, in Dorsetshire, there is a similar figure, 180 feet long"—(*Lower*). As both these figures occupy a slope on a chalky down, and both lie immediately opposite to a religious house, we may conclude them to have been the work of some lazy mediæval monks. Some writers, however, consider them of Celtic origin.

WILMINGTON PRIORY was founded by Robert, Earl of Cornwall, lord of Pevensey, and bestowed upon the Benedictine Abbey of Grestein, near Honfleur. Its remains have been converted into a farm-house. The timbered roof is probably ancient ; the chapel has been secularized into a sitting-room ; the cellar is still supported by its old hexagonal pillar. At WELL HOLES, about 400 yards distant, is the monastic fish-pond.

The CHURCH is mainly Norman, and cruciform in plan. The arches and pillars of the south transept, and many of the windows, are fashioned out of the chalk of the district. A goodly yew, 20 feet in girth, adorns the churchyard. The vicarage, valued at £111, is in the patronage of the Duke of Devonshire.

[In the valley beyond Wilmington, and on the banks of the Cuckmere, is a complete cluster of villages, with gray old churches, and neatly ordered cottages,-- FOLKINGTON (population, 191); LULLINGTON (population, 26); and LITTLINGTON (population, 105), ancient Saxon settlements, which may probably afford the tourist much gratification, but of which, we confess, we know but little.]

☞ From the BENVICK STATION, 3½ miles beyond Polegate, we can best visit ALFRISTON and SEAFORD.

ALFRISTON (population, 576)—*i. e.*, Aluricestone, or *Aluric's town*—is about 3½ miles from the Benvick Station, and lies at the foot of the Downs, on the west bank of the small stream of the Cuckmere. Its ancient church is dedicated to St. Andrew. The Star Inn dates from the early part of the sixteenth century, and may have been resorted to by the devout on their way to the shrine of St. Richard of Chichester. Mitred figures of St.

Giles, with a hind, and St. Julian, the patron saint of wayfarers, are supported by wooden brackets on each side of the entrance. Other rude figures will reward the industrious investigation of the curious. A beam in the parlour bears a shield, lettered I.H.S.

The vicarage, valued at £135, is in the patronage of the Lord Chancellor.

SEAFORD (population, 997), a member of the Cinque Port of Hastings, is, probably, the ancient *Mercredesburn* (Mœr-cryd, the sea-ford), the site of Saxon Ella's victory in 485. It stands on the right bank of the Cuckmere. The old town was placed on the marge of the haven—formed by the junction of the Ouse with the Channel—which has been long filled up. The position, however, of the modern hamlet, with a bold sweep of sea before it, and lofty hills rearing their rounded crests behind it, is so picturesque that we may anticipate for it a long and prosperous career.

The last Martello-tower, No. 74, stands on the neighbouring shore, and one of Henry the Eighth's circular forts is placed under the cliff. Collins has made the scene the subject of one of his finest sea-scapes.

The history of Seaford is easily summed up : it was often attacked by the French, *temp.* Edward III., and was almost depopulated by " the black death." Claude d'Annebault, and his fleet, attempted to surprise it in 1545, but were repulsed by Sir Nicholas Pelham :—

" What time the French sought to have sackt Sea-ford
This Pelham did *repel 'em* back aboord."

On December 7, 1809, seven merchantmen and their convoy, H. M. Brig Harlequin, were wrecked upon this shore with a fearful loss of life.

The men of Seaford and the neighbouring villages were, in the bad old times, daring wreckers, and the unfortunates who escaped from the perils of the sea fell into a far more terrible danger. Congreve has alluded to their rapacity in bitter lines :—

" The Sussex men that dwell upon the shore
Look out when storms arise and billows roar,
Devoutly praying with uplifted hands,
That some well-laden ships may strike the sands,
To whose rich cargo they may make pretence,
And fatten on the spoils of Providence."

SEAFORD CHURCH is dedicated to St. Leonard, and is mainly Norman and Earl English in its architectural character. The central column of the south aisle is carved with a representation of the crucifixion, and above it stands a rude sculpture of St. Michael and the Serpent, found in the churchyard some years ago. A tombstone, graven with a cross, is inserted both in the north and south walls. The vicarage, worth £167, is in the patronage of the Bishop of Oxford.

A paper in the first volume of the " Sussex Archæological Collections " embodies a quaint story of a certain monk, Balger, of the priory of Bergue St. Winox, whose vessel having been forced by stress of weather into Seaford Harbour, he contrived to rifle the neighbouring monastery of St. Andrew of the bones of St. Lewuina, one the early Sussex apostles. The chronicler enthusiastically and antithetically extols him as " fidelis fur et latro bonus "—a faithful rogue and an honest thief !

PUCK CHURCH PARLOUR (from the popular Sussex " pharisee," the fairy Puck), a curious ledge of rock, jutting out beneath the brink of the cliff, east of the town, can only be reached by a dangerous path from above, and is now the sheltering-place of some wise old Reynards, who here have little reason to dread the huntsman or his hounds.

☞ From Seaford the tourist may keep along the coast to Newhaven, 2 miles, and thence, by the cliffs, proceed to Brighton.

The next station is at GLYNDE (population 323), lying, as its name—GLYN, Celtic—indicates, in a *vale* at the foot of the chalk-downs. The CHURCH was rebuilt, 1765, by Trevor, bishop of Durham, and in its frigid classicism is to be regarded as a warning by young architects. An obelisk in the churchyard is adorned with an inscription, from the pen of Mrs Hemans, to the two sons of Wedderburn, the great lawyer. The vicarage, worth £132, is in the patronage of the Dean and Chapter of Chichester.

On the left of the line, 1 mile north, spreads the fair estate of GLYNDE PLACE (Lord Dacre), and to the right, 1 mile south-east, stretches the woodland scenery of FIRLE PLACE (Viscount Gage). Both are picturesque Elizabethan houses, seated at the base of the Downs, which at Firle Beacon rise to an elevation of 820 feet. WEST FIRLE (population, 701) has a good sized church, on the left of the road to Alfriston. The vicarage is annexed to that of BEDDINGHAM (population, 321), is worth £345, and in the patronage, alternately, of the Bishop, and the Dean and Chapter of Chichester.

Passing swiftly through the valley which lies between the two walls of chalk-hills, separated by the Ouse—

> " Here Ouse, slow-winding through a level plain
> Of spacious meads, with cattle sprinkled o'er,
> Conducts the eye along his ruinous course,
> Delighted"—

we are borne onward to the beautiful and ever memorable town of

LEWES—(*i.e.* HLŒW, *Saxon*, a hill).

[Population, 9821.—*Inns :* The White Hart, the Star, the Bear, the Crown. 51 miles from London, by road ; 50 miles by rail.—26 miles, by rail, from Hastings ; 7 miles from Brighton ; 6½ miles from Newhaven, by road.]

☞ Communication with Brighton, Newhaven, Uckfield, Eastbourne, and Hastings by rail. With Ringmer by omnibus. There are also conveyances between the town and railway station, which is about ½ a mile distant.

LEWES is the county town of Sussex, though Chichester may be regarded as the capital of the western division. It lies chiefly on the right bank of the small river Ouse, on the slope of a chalk-hill, one of the glorious south downs, and others of that famous range are raised around it so as to shelter it, on almost every side. Its hilly uneven site gives to it a peculiarly picturesque appearance ; it seems an old town, though without many very old edifices, and is distinguished by an air of decorous respectability and sombre importance. Around its castle and priory it clusters, as if it felt that all its consequence was due to them ; and whether viewed from the Cliff, from the high ground of Southover, or from its own High Street, it presents a singular and romantic character, not, to our thinking, equalled by that of any other English town save Durham.

It principally consists of one street—the HIGH STREET— winding from St. Anne's Church, east, to the foot of Cliffe Hill, west, about three-quarters of a mile, where it throws out two branches. One, named SOUTH STREET, leads to Glynde, Firle, Alfriston, and Eastbourne ; the other, MALLING STREET, to Uck-field, East Grinstead, and so to London. Some smaller thorough-fares diverge from the High Street on each side. Of these we need only notice MARKET STREET, leading from the brow of School Hill into EAST STREET, which runs parallel to SCHOOL HILL, but with an easier descent, and is better adapted for equestrians and carriage-folk.

Quitting the railway terminus—the focus of trains from London, Hastings, Uckfield, and Newhaven—and turning to the right, we see the bold ascent of Cliffe Hill before us, forming the eastern boundary of the Ouse valley. The suburb of the Cliffe extends over the marshy plain on the opposite side of the river, and is connected with the High Street by a neat bridge of stone. Looking to the left, we notice School Hill connected with the central part of the High Street, "which is built on a nearly level terrace of inconsiderable breadth." Here are situated the Crown, Star, and White Hart inns ; the County Hall ; the Markets ; the Castle Gateway and Keep ; and St. Michael's Church. At the foot of School Hill formerly stood the east gate of the town, commemorated in a street to the right called EAST GATE STREET ; while that to the left, leading to Southover, is named FRIAR'S WALK, "in reference to the monastery of Grey Friars that anciently occupied the adjacent meadow."

Before we enter upon an examination of the notable antiquities that "do renown this city," let us, in accordance with our custom, glance rapidly at its interesting annals.

There is abundant proof of its early importance. The localities in its neighbourhood have chiefly British names. Roman urns and coins have been found here ; numerous earthworks and encampments ; and some antiquarians have supposed it to be the site of the mysterious *Mutuantonis* of the geographer Ravennas.

It was strongly fortified during the reign of Alfred, and in Athelstane's time possessed two mints. Specimens of Lewes coinage have been dug up at Milton Court 9 miles from Lewes, where they remain in Mr. Ade's possession. From Domesday Book we learn that the king's rent and tolls in Lewes amounted yearly to £6 : 13 : 1½, and he had 127 burgesses who were his immediate vassals ; and from the same authority we gather the following customs of the borough eight centuries agone :—

"The seller of a horse within the borough pays 1d. to the mayor, and the purchaser another ; if an ox, ½d. ; if a man, 4d., in whatever place he may be bought within the rape.

"A murderer forfeits 7s. 4d. ; a ravisher, 8s. 4d. ; an adulterer,

8s. 4d. ; an adulteress, the same. The king receives the adulterer's fine, the bishop the adulteress's.

"A runaway, or vagabond, that is recovered pays 8s. 4d."

After the Conquest, Lewes and numerous other estates belonging to the dead Harold—the "Last of the Saxon Kings," and not the unworthiest—were bestowed by the Conqueror upon Earl William de Warrenne, who had married his daughter Gundrada, and was potent in the royal councils. This famous earl built the Castle of Lewes (or largely repaired the old Saxon fortress), and, in conjunction with his wife, erected and endowed the Priory of St. Pancras. The fair Countess died in 1085, the wealthy baron in 1087.

With the De Warrennes this noble inheritance continued until the failure of the male line in 1347. The seventh Earl of Warrenne and Surrey joined the royal party against Simon de Montfort and the Barons, and was the stout noble who, when interrogated by the commissioners of Edward the First as to the titles by which he held his vast estates, drew forth his sword, and exclaimed, " By this instrument do I hold my lands, and by the same do I intend to protect them !"

The BATTLE OF LEWES was fought on Wednesday the 14th of May 1261. King Henry, accompanied by his son Prince Edward, and Richard, king of the Romans, arrived at Southover on Sunday, May 11, 1264, where he was sumptuously entertained by the Prior of St. Pancras, Prince Edward and his *suite* becoming the guests of Earl John de Warrenne in the Castle. The royal forces united with the earl's contingent, and encamped outside of the town.

De Montfort followed quickly in their footsteps. At Fletching Common, about 9 miles from Lewes, he halted his troops, and despatched the Bishops of London and Worcester with the view of effecting, if possible, an amicable arrangement. They reached Lewes on the 13th, and were received by the king in the Refectory of the Priory ; but their mission was utterly fruitless, and the barons found that there was no resource but the sword.

By break of day on the 14th the barons' army was in motion, and winding through the narrow glades of the leafy Weald, advanced towards the Downs by Newick and Hamsey, and ascended the hill by the road which winds along the steep northern escarpment overhanging Coombe Place (about two miles

2 L

north-west of Lewes). " They arrived on the Downs at so early
an hour that the king's army was unsuspicious of their approach,
and would have fallen an easy prey had not *such villanie*,'
as the old chronicler indignantly terms it, been inconsistent with
the chivalrous spirit of those times. De Montfort immediately
drew up his forces on the plain [just beyond the Lewes race-
course], and having addressed them on the righteousness of their
cause, and exhorted them to be valiant and steadfast in the glorious struggle in which they were about to engage, he alighted
from his horse, and prostrating himself on the ground, again
implored Heaven to bless them with victory. He then conferred
knighthood on several of his chiefs, and advanced towards the
town, which was seen at about a mile and a half distant, reposing
in the balmy dews of a bright May morning. A foraging party
of the royalists was soon descried and intercepted ; and some of
them escaping, fled to Lewes with intelligence of its approach."

The ridges, divided by three deep coombes, jut out from
Mount Harry (so called, it is said, in remembrance of Henry the
Third) across the country to Lewes, a distance of 3 miles. Along
these ridges pressed forward the barons' army in three divisions,
—the right wing commanded by De Montfort's sons, Hugh and
Guido ; the left, chiefly composed of London volunteers, led by
Nicholas de Segrave ; and the van by the Earl of Gloucester.
The reserve was under the immediate command of Leicester.
" The centre of the army was therefore posted on that ridge of
the hill which descends with a gradual and uninterrupted slope
to St. Anne's ; the left wing occupied the north branch of the
Downs, that extends to the WALLENDS ; and the right wing was
on the southern slope, which stretches towards Southover"—
(*Mantell*).

The royal forces were also divided into three bodies : the
centre commanded by the king, the right wing by Prince
Edward, and the left by the king of the Romans. Bearing down
upon De Montfort's army they hoisted the royal standard, the
" dragon full austere," and King Henry, elate with hope of an
easy triumph, exclaimed, as he neared his rebellious subjects,
" Simon, je vous defie !" And so the great fight began.

Prince Edward was speedily assaulted by Segrave's division,
but he repulsed them immediately, and pursued them for four
miles without ever checking the speed of his horsemen. This
was much to the discomfort of the barons' host ; " but the

barons," says Grafton the chronicler, "encouraged and comforted their men in such wise, that not all onely the fresh and lustye knights fought eagerly, but also such as before were discomfited gathered a newe courage unto them, and fought without feare, insomuch that the king's vaward lost their places. Then was the field covered with dead bodyes, and gasping and groning was heard on every syde ; for eyther of them was desyrous to bring others out of lyfe. And the father spared not the sonne, neyther yet the sonne spared the father! Alliance at that time was bound to defiaunce, and Christian blood that day was shed without pitie. Lastly the victory fell to the barons ; so that there was taken the king, and the king of Romaynes, Sir Edward, the king's sonne, with many other noblemen, to the number of fifteen barons and bannerets ; and of the common people that were slain, about twenty thousand. For their safe keeping the prisoners were sent unto dyverse castellis and prisons, except the king, his brother the king of Almayne, and Sir Edwarde, his sonne ; the which the barons helde with them vntill they came to London."

A dreadful slaughter took place south of the town, where a bridge crossed the river Ouse. Numbers were drowned, and others were suffocated in the mud. "From the swampy nature of the ground, many knights who perished there were discovered after the battle, still sitting on their horses in complete armour, and with drawn swords in their lifeless hands." The king of the Romans at first took shelter in a windmill which then stood on the site of the present Black Horse Inn—

> "The Kyng of Alemaigne wende do full well;
> He saisede the mulne for a castèl,"

but he was soon compelled to surrender. Prince Edward retired to the Priory, and was hotly beset by the barons, who set fire to the magnificent church. Fortunately, the monks succeeded in extinguishing the flames ; and Prince Edward gave himself up to the victorious Leicester.

The immediate consequence of this great triumph was the treaty of peace, historically known as "the Mise of Lewes." Its grander effects our limits will not permit us to trace. He who with earnest eye looks around England as it is, will easily recognize them, and in that recognition will see sufficient cause for grateful recollection of the genius and wisdom of Simon de Montfort !

There is little else of historical interest associated with Lewes, which, indeed, may be well content to rest its claims to remembrance as an English shrine upon the memorable battle which we have so briefly recorded. John, eighth Earl de Warrenne, married Joan the grand-daughter of Edward I., and figures as the hero of a mediæval romance. He had found, it appears, " one fairer and dearer, who occupied all his thoughts, and for whose sake he braved the anger of royalty, and the thunders of the church. It might have been that he had formed a contract with the beautiful *Maud de Nerford* before his fate was sealed to Joan. Such he asserted to be the case ; and in spite of all remonstrances he persisted in keeping her near him, and openly acknowledging her children ; while his wife sought, with an indignant mien, counsel from the ecclesiastics, who taking up her cause and that of morality, excommunicated the noble lover of Maud "—(*Costello*). Edward I. and his Queen Eleanor were entertained by the monks of Lewes for four days, in January 1276, on their way from Chichester—where they had been present at the translation of the body of the holy St. Richard de la Wych—to Canterbury.

LEWES CASTLE is gained from the High Street by a lane which turns off below St. Michael's Church. The GATEWAY, a fine old structure of great strength, in the early Edwardian style, is about 50 feet high, with machicolated battlements, and a circular tower at each angle. The staples for the hinges of the gates, and the grooves for a double portcullis still remain. The front wall is of squared flints, with fire-stone facings. Within, the old Norman gateway and plain semicircular arch will attract observation.

We now enter the outer BALLIUM, or BASE-COURT, irregular oval in shape, extending north-east and south-west for nearly 300 yards, and 130 yards in diameter. An artificial mound has been raised at each extremity, and surmounted by a keep. Of one of these the remains are considerable ; of the other, which crowned the Brack Mount, there exists but, some. slight traces of the foundations.

We reach the existing KEEP by a narrow winding path, closely overshadowed by trees. It was originally quadrangular, and strengthened by four hexagonal towers, about 54 feet in height from the base. The south and west towers alone remain, and time has adorned them with its wonted garniture of glossy foliage. The principal tower is occupied by the MUSEUM of the

SUSSEX ARCHÆOLOGICAL SOCIETY, and a fee of sixpence is required for the privilege of admission—a sixpence well bestowed, since it enables the visitor who mounts to " the leads " to enjoy an extensive and magnificent view of Lewes and the surrounding country. The picturesque old town, with its roofs, and spires, and winding columns of smoke, lies immediately beneath us, and away to the north and south stretches the deep river-valley—the Ouse trailing its somewhat sluggish current through a gap in the chalk-hills to join the gleaming waters of the Channel at New-haven. Northward, the eye ranges over the leafy groves and tree-encompassed meadows of the Weald, to the blue line of the Surrey-downs. From the terrace, known as the CASTLE BANKS, there is also a charming prospect which includes a portion of the river-valley, the chalk-pits of Offham, the villages of Malling and Barcombe.

We now descend the hill to examine the interesting ruins of the PRIORY of ST. PANCRAS, which, in their desolate solitude excited the regret of the poet Bowles. " All," he exclaims,

> " All, all is silent now ; silent the bell,
> Which, heard from yonder ivied turret high,
> Warned the cowled brother from his midnight cell ;
> Silent the vesper chants, the litany,
> Responsive to the organ ; scattered lie
> The wrecks of the proud pile, mid arches gray,
> Whilst hollow winds through mantling foliage sigh,
> And e'en the mouldering shrine is rent away,
> Where, in his Warrior-weeds, the Norman founder lay."

The ruins are private property, and there is some difficulty in procuring permission to view them, but from MOUNT CALVARY a sufficiently good position can be obtained. Over the site of the once magnificent PRIORY CHURCH the railway passes, and it was during the excavations here necessitated that the discovery was made of the coffins of William de Warrenne and his wife Gun-drada.

Lewes Priory was erected by the great Norman baron on the site of a small wooden chapel, dedicated to St. Pancras, and colonized with Benedictine monks from Clugni, where the founder and his Countess had been splendidly entertained on their route to Italy in 1070. The edifice was completed in 1077, and was the first Cluniac priory in England, and the *only one* for a period of nearly 150 years. It rapidly rose into importance, and gained in wealth, and was esteemed one of "the five chief daughters" of the mother-abbey of Clugni. Thirty-two priors ruled over it from the time of its foundation to its dissolution in 1537. Hugh, the second prior, became Archbishop of Rouen ; John de Courtenay resigned an earldom for the abbot's mitre ; and John de Cariloco, in 1377, led his retainers and vassals against the French at Rottingdean, and was taken prisoner. Here were interred the founder and his Countess, Peter de Warrenne, John de Braose of Bramber Castle, many of the Earls and Countesses de Warrenne, and other notable personages, whose names are recorded in Mr. Horsfield's History of Lewes. The magnificent church of St. Pancras was founded in the reign of Henry II., and at the time of the Dissolution was rich in gold and purple, in stately turrets, in gorgeous shrines, in windows glowing with the figures of saints, apostles, priests, and barons. The revenues of the priory were then estimated at a sum equal to £20,000 of the present currency. The pigeon-house, which, until about 60 years ago, stood south-west of the present ruins, " equalled in magnitude many a parish church, and contained 3228 pigeon-holes. The fish-ponds, of which some traces are still discernible, were on a corresponding scale of grandeur. The refectory was worthy of so splendid an establishment. The garden probably occupied the large hollow area called "the Dripping Pan," and the Mount Calvary was perhaps the artificial mound near the cricket-field, where the tourist is now supposed to be standing. The "lantern," or prison of the priory, a circular building underground, stands in a private garden.

Some notion of the general extent and splendour of the priory buildings may be gathered from a letter addressed to Cromwell— on whom, at the Dissolution, its demesnes were conferred—by his agent, John Portmari. It is curious enough to deserve a place in these pages :—

" My Lord—I humbly commend me to your Lordship. The last I wrote to your Lordship was the 20th instant (March), by the hands of Mr. Williamson, by which I advertised your Lordship of the length and greatness of this church, and the sale, how we had begun to pull down the whole to the ground, and what manner of fashion they used in pulling down. I told your Lordship of a vault on the right of the altar that was borne with four pillars, having about it five chapels, which were compassed with the vaults, 70 steps in length, that is, 210 feet. All this is down Thursday and Friday last. Now we are pulling down a higher vault, borne up by four thick and lofty pillars, 14 feet from side to side, and in circumference 45 feet, this shall be done for our second work ; as it goes forward I will advertise your Lordship from time to time. And that your Lordship may know with how many men we have done this, we brought from London 17 men,—3 carpenters, 2 smiths, 2 plumbers, and 1 that keeps the furnace,—every one of these keeps to his own office. Ten of them hew the walls, among which are 3 carpenters ; these make props to underset, where the others cut away. The others cut the walls. These are men exercised much better than the men we find here in the country, wherefore we must have men, and other things also that we have need of, the which I shall in a few days show your Lordship by mouth. They began to cast the lead, and it shall be done with such diligence and saving as may be. So, as our trust is that your Lordship will be much satisfied with what we do, when I must most heartily commend myself, much desiring God to maintain your health, and your heart's ease,

" Your Lordship's servant,

" JOHN PORTMARI.

" *At Lewes*, March 24, 1538.

" Underneath, your Lordship shall see a just measure of the wide abbey.

" Length of the church, 150 feet ; height, 63 feet ; the circumference, 1558 feet.

" The wall of the front, 10 feet thick.

" Thickness of the steeple-wall, 10 feet.

" There be in the church 32 pillars standing equally from the walls ; a high roof made for the bells ; 8 pillars very high, 13 feet thick, and 45 feet about. The height of the greatest sort is 43 feet ; of the other, 28 feet.

" The height of the roof before the great altar is 93 feet ; in the middle of the church where the bells did hang, 105 feet ; the height of the steeple in the front is 90 feet."

Some of the monastic buildings, however, were converted into a stately residence for Gregory Cromwell, the great statesman's son, who had married Elizabeth Seymour, sister to the Lady Jane, Queen of Henry VIII., and the king meditated paying them a visit, but was dissuaded by the younger Cromwell because the plague was raging terribly at Lewes.

The monastic lands afterwards reverted to the Crown ; were bestowed on Sackville, Earl of Dorset ; and have since undergone more mutations of proprietorship than it would interest the tourist to recount.

In the cloister school, attached to the priory in its palmy days, were educated Archbishop Peckham, and Edmund Dudley, Henry the Seventh's unscrupulous agent, whose father was, it is said, the monastic carpenter-in-chief.

The coffins of William de Warrenne and his Countess were discovered in October 1845, during the works carried on for the construction of the London and Brighton Railway. A cutting 40 feet wide, and 12 feet deep was required, and this cutting was made across the site, as it proved, of part of the ancient Priory church, and the adjoining Chapter-house. Here, about 2 feet beneath the turf, were discovered the coffins of the Earl and Countess, now preserved at Southover Church ; and other remains of considerable interest, to which we shall hereafter more particularly allude.

Close to the principal entrance of the Priory stands SOUTH-OVER CHURCH, dedicated to St. John the Baptist, a curious composition of many styles, repaired and improved some fifteen years ago. The chancel (at one time much larger than it is now), is Perpendicular ; the nave is Early Norman ; and there are also Early English insertions. The Norman chapel which encloses the remains of William de Warrenne and Gundrada was erected by subscription in 1847, from the designs of a local architect. The material employed is Caen stone. Figures of the Count and Countess, and the patron saint St. Pancras, are emblazoned on the richly painted windows. The floor is paved with tiles which glow with the escocheons of many a potent baron. Arcades relieve the monotony of the walls. The leaden coffins of the Count and Countess, respectively lettered " GUNDRADA " and " WILLELM," are preserved in two deep arched recesses in the south wall. The great Baron's coffin is 2 feet 11 inches in length, that of the Countess, 2 feet 9 inches. " From their small size it is clear that they were constructed to receive the bones long after their first interment, in consequence of the decay of the original coffins ; and it is probable that this took place in the time of Henry II., when the remains of William and Gundrada were transferred from their tombs in the original church of the Priory, to the chapter house of the new and more splendid edifice, styled by the old chronicler the ' great church of St. Pancras ;' the building of which was begun on the anniversary of the founder's death, in 1243"—(*Mantell*).

Of these coffins Mr. Lower supplies some interesting particulars :—" The lids do not appear to have been soldered or otherwise fastened to the coffins, but merely flanged over the edges. The ornamentation of both is very singular, though simple. ' The plates composing them are evidently cast. A cord of loose texture seems to have been impressed in the sand at regular intervals, and then crossed in the opposite direction, so as to produce on the plates a lozengy or network pattern, *in relievo*, with interstices averaging 5 inches by 3." From measurements made by Mr. Pickford, Earl William's stature was probably 6 feet 2 inches ; Gundrada's, 5 feet 8 inches.

Nearly seven centuries after the death of Gundrada, a slab of black Norman marble, richly sculptured, was discovered by Dr. Clarke, rector of Buxted, in the Shirley chancel of Isfield church, where it formed the table part of the mural monument of Edward Shirley, cofferer to Henry VIII., who appears to have rescued it from the ruins of the Priory, and converted it into a memorial for himself. At the expense of Sir William Burrell it was removed to Southover church, where, curiously enough, after so many changes, it has been restored to its original destination. The English version of the inscription is here adapted from one by Dr. Mantell :—

> " Gundrad, a noble branch of ducal race,
> Pour'd out on English shrines balsamic grace ;
> Like Mary holy, and like Martha kind,
> In her were truth and charity combin'd.
> Though death the part of Martha now receives,
> The better part of Mary ever lives,
> Then, holy Pancras, whom she made her heir,
> Still genial listen to our mother's prayer !
> On June's sixth kalend, nature's struggle came,
> And chill'd the life-blood in her tender frame ;
> Her spirit burst its marble shrine and gave
> The fragrance of her virtues to her grave."

In a recess in the north wall is placed an effigy, *temp.* Henry III., which, from some dim outlines of the Braose armorial bearings on the surcoat, has been supposed to personate *John de Braose*, lord of Bramber, d. 1232. Over the altar is a picture of the Last Supper by Mortimer.

The rectory of St. John's, Southover, is only valued at £35 per annum, and is in the patronage of the Lord Chancellor. It is generally held in conjunction with the rectory of All Saints. The other churches of Lewes are St. Michael's, St. Anne's, St. John's (*sub castro*), All Saints', and St. Thomas-at-Cliffe.

Sᴛ. Mɪᴄʜᴀᴇʟ's ɪɴ Fᴏʀᴏ stands in the High Street—conspicuous enough with its circular tower surmounted by a picturesque shingle spire. The body of the church was rebuilt in 1755, with the usual Georgian characteristics of plainness and deformity. There are two fine brasses, however, to afford the tourist some slight compensation ; one to *John Braydforde*, rector, d. 1457, and another to a nameless knight, *temp.* 1380-1400, apparently a member of the proud race of the De Warrennes. The tomb underneath was opened in 1828, and a leaden coffin discovered, enclosing " a tall slender corpse."

A fine mural monument on the north wall represents a knight and his lady in the costume of the sixteenth century, with figures of their ten children. A helmet hangs above it. The following inscription will interest the reader :—

" Hereunder lye buried the bodies of Sir Nicholas Pelham, Knt. (son of Sir Wm. Pelham of Laughton), and Dame Anne his wife, daughter of John Sackvile, Esq., grandfather of the Right Hon͠ble Thomas (late) Earl of Dorset. They had issue six sonnes and four daughters.

" His valrs. proofe, his manlie vertues prayse,
Cannot be marshall'd in this narrow roome ;
His brave exploit in great King Henry's days,
Among the worthye hath a worthier tombe ;
What time the French sought to have sack't Sea-Foord
This Pelham did repel 'em back aboord.
" Obiit 15 Decembris anno Dno. 1559.
Ætatis suæ 44."

The rectory, valued at £116, is in the Lord Chancellor's patronage.

Sᴛ. Aɴɴᴇ's Cʜᴜʀᴄʜ, a neat Early English edifice, stands on the summit of the hill to which it gives its name. It consists of a nave, chancel, and tower, surmounted by a shingled spire. The porch doorway is enriched with the usual Norman zigzag moulding. A cylindrical font, richly ornamented, is ancient. A small brass, affixed to the east wall of the chancel, bears a Latin epitaph to *Dr. Twyne,* a famous physician, d. 1613, who is extolled as " the flower and ornament of his age," and posterity is warned that it must not hope to produce " so great a physician and so renowned a man."

To the west of the church, in the old days, stood the ill-omened PEST HOUSE, and an hospital dedicated to St. Nicholas.

The Lord Chancellor presents to the rectory, which is valued at £190 per annum.

ST. JOHN'S SUB-CASTRO is a modern building, which unhappily occupies the site of an ancient church of more than usual interest. The arch of one doorway has, however, been preserved, and a curious Latin inscription, of four hexameters, divided into two rhyming hemistichs, " deeply and rudely cut on blocks of lime-stone," may easily be read. Dr. Mantell thus translates it,—

> " Here lies a knight of royal Danish birth,
> Mangnus his name, and great alike his worth ;
> Who, contrite for his sins, and spurning fame,
> A lowly, lamb-like Anchorite became."

The Magnus so highly extolled, and whose name has been misspelt by his panegyrist, was, according to tradition, a son of King Harold by his second wife Githa, sister of the Dane-King Sweyn.

The site of the churchyard is remarkable ; it occupies the brink of an abrupt cliff of chalk, on the south side of the river-valley, and was originally an oblong encampment, enclosing two conical mounds, one at the west angle, the other at the east. A deep vallum surrounded it on three sides. East of the church stands the tomb of Mr. *Thomas Blount,* " an eminent Lewes barber," d. 1611, who bequeathed a silver cup to the dignitaries, and certain sums of money to the charities of the town which he adorned.

The rectory of St. John Sub-Castro, valued at £250, is in the gift of the Rev. P. G. Crofts.

ALL SAINTS' CHURCH, in the Friars' Walk, at a short distance beyond the spring called PINWELL, has a fine Perpendicular tower, with a curious and many-windowed excrescence, built by Wylde, in 1807. It contains a memorial to *John Stanfield,* and a good painting of St John the Baptist in prison, presented by the Earl of Chichester, who purchased it in Italy.

The rectory, valued at £198, is in the gift of C. Goring, Esq.. Among the incumbents have been—Robert Cecil, the eminent divine ; and Thomas Aquila Dale, father of the Rev. Canon Dale.

St. Thomas-at-Cliffe, dedicated to St. Thomas the Martyr, stands in the High Street of the Cliffe,—a' venerable Perpendicular building, which occupies the site of a religious house established in honour of Thomas à Becket, shortly after the Archbishop's murder. The altar-piece is a picture of the Ascension, by Van der Gucht. The organ is said to be the instrument with which Handel delighted the lordly owner of Canons.

The rectory, valued at £130, is in the patronage of the Archbishop of Canterbury.

Let us now proceed to summarize, as briefly as may be, the principal objects of interest in Lewes, since the limits to which we are necessarily confined will not permit us to luxuriate, as we could wish, among the historical and legendary details connected with them. We may commend the tourist who desires to dwell at greater length upon the history and romance of Lewes to Mr. Dunran's, and Mr. Horsfield's elaborate histories ; to Mr. M. C. Lower's excellent handbook ; to Mr. Blauuw's valuable essay on " the Barons' War ;" Dr. Mantell's " Day's Ramble in and about Lewes ;" and, finally, to Miss Costello's " Legendary Towns."

[MEMORABLE PLACES and NOTABLE HOUSES.—The Star Inn contains a fine old staircase of carved oak, removed from Slaugham Place, the family seat of the Coverts ; and an ancient vaulted cellar which, it is said, in the days of the Marian persecution served as a prison for the martyrs, many of whom were burnt at the stake in the street opposite the house.

The Old House, near Southover Church, is traditionally reputed to have been the residence of that much-wandering Queen, Anne of Cleves. The great gate of the Priory formerly stood near the east end of the church, but was pulled down, we believe, in 1832. The side portal, however, still remains at the end of Southover Crescent.

The County Hall, in High Street, built in 1812 at a cost of £10,000, contains a Shakspearian picture by Northcote, and a portrait of General Elliot, Lord Heathfield, the gallant defender of Gibraltar.

Sireh Chapel, in the Cliffe, was erected by a fanatic, S. Jenkins, who distinguished himself as W. A.—or Welsh Ambassador—and its graveyard contains the tomb of William Huntington, S.S., or " Sinner Saved," a religious enthusiast of remarkable character. His epitaph, written by himself, runs as follows :—" Here lies the COAL-HEAVER : beloved of God, but abhorred of men : the omniscient Judge at the grand assize shall ratify and confirm this to the confusion of many thousands ; for England and its metropolis shall know that there hath been a prophet among them. W. H. S. S."

On the Downs, between the windmill and the great chalk-pit on Offham Hill, are the *mounds* of those who fell in the sanguinary battle of Lewes.

The BULL LANE MEETING-HOUSE was built by the Gorings, *temp.* King Henry VIII. In the house adjoining, Tom Paine for a time resided, while acting as a Lewes exciseman.

SOUTHOVER HOUSE was erected, in the sixteenth century, by a Mr. Newton, a steward of Lord Buckhurst's, out of the ruins of the desecrated priory. It contains some curiously inlaid doors. In a neighbouring field are the scanty ruins—a gothic window, and a fragment of a chancel-wall—of an ancient Alms House, or Hospital for thirteen poor brethren and sisters, dedicated to St. James.

The deep abrupt valley, known as THE COOMBE, should certainly be visited for the sake of the marvellous effects of light and shade which it presents at sunrise.

POINTS OF VIEW.—From Plumpton Plain, Mount Harry, St. Anne's Church-yard, and Lewes Race Course, on the west ; from Baldy's Garden, Cliffe Hill, Mount Caburn, Malling Hill, and Southeram Corner, on the east ; from Offham-road, Malling Deanery, and Malling Mill, on the west ; from Mount Calvary, Winterbourne Bridge, and road near Southover Church on the north.

GEOLOGICAL LOCALITIES (as pointed out by Dr. Mantell) :—The Chalk-pits at Offham ; Malling Hill, Bridgwick, on the Ringmer road ; in South Street ; Southeram Corner ; Marlpits on the Glynde road, Chalk Cliffs on each side of the Coombe, and the Coombe itself.

DISTANCES OF PLACES.—East Hoathly, 7 m. ; East Tarring, 4 m. ; Glynde, 5 m. ; Mount Caburn, 4 m. ; Offham, 2 m. ; Ringmer, 3 m. ; South Malling, 1½ m. ; Stanmer Park, 1 m. ; Willingham, 2 m. ; and West Firle, 3¾ m.

HINTS FOR RAMBLES.—1. Through the Friars' Walk, so named from a House of Grey Friars, fl. *temp.* Henry III., and thence to Southover. Visit the Church, and proceed to the Priory ruins. Observe the view from Mount Calvary. Return to South-over, and cross to the hills west of Lewes. Visit St. Anne's Church, and afterwards the Castle.—2. Through Malling Street to Ringmer. Take the road to Glyndbourne, and cross the Downs, by the base of Mount Caburn, to Glynde. Return by Raus-combe to Southeram, and thence to Lewes by road.—3. Through Iford, Rodmill and Southease to Newhaven. Cross the Ouse, and return by Denton, East Tarring, and Beddingham, about 14 m.—4. Through Ringmer to Laughton, and thence to East Hoathly. Cross to Little Horsted and return by the road, leaving Ifield, Barcombe and Hamsey, on the right ; or from Little Horsted proceed to Uckfield, and return by rail.—5. From Lewes to Charby. Cross to Wivelsfield. Keep southward to Ditch-ling, and return along the Downs by way of Plumpton, entering Lewes through Offham.—6. To Brighton by rail, and return by road.—7. Or to Brighton by rail, and then by the cliffs to Rottingdean and Southampton. Return to Lewes by rail, or by way of Rodmill, Southease, and Iford.]

BRANCH ROUTE FROM LEWES TO BATTLE.

We leave Lewes by way of MALLING (population, 730)— an ancient settlement of the Saxon *Mallingas*—and pause to ex-amine the CHURCH, founded in 1628 by John Evelyn, the author of ".Sylva," who was educated at Southover school. The site of an old collegiate church, called the " Deanery of Malling," lies at an inconsiderable distance west. Having been founded by Cead-walla, King of Wessex, about 680, it must be regarded as one of the earliest Christian churches in Sussex. It was attached to the see of Canterbury, whose Bishop had here an archiepiscopal palace. It was to South Malling the four knightly murderers of Thomas à Becket rode with whip and spur, after their dreadful deed. " On entering the house, they threw off their arms and trappings on the large dining-table which stood in the hall, and after supper gathered round the blazing hearth ; suddenly the table started back, and threw its burden on the ground. The attendants, roused by the crash, rushed in with lights and replaced the arms. But soon a second still louder crash was heard, and the various articles were thrown still further off. Soldiers and servants with torches searched in vain under the solid table to find the cause of its convulsions, till one of the conscience-stricken knights suggested that it was indignantly refusing to bear the sacrilegious burden of their arms. So ran the popular story ; and as late as the fourteenth century it was still shewn in the same place—the earliest and most memorable instance of a ' rap-ping,' ' leaping,' and ' turning table ' "—(*Stanley*). All that now remains to recall to the tourist " the stormy days of yore " is a foliated capital in the farm-house kitchen, and a " bit " of Early Norman wall in the garden.

The perpetual curacy of South Malling, valued at £117, is in Mrs Courthope's patronage.

About 2 miles beyond Malling we arrive at RINGMER (po-pulation, 1374), a village rendered interesting by its associations with White of Selbourne, who was accustomed from this point to pursue his delightful labours in the grand laboratory of nature. Though he had travelled the Sussex downs for upwards of 30 years, yet he could still investigate " that chain of majestic mountains with fresh admiration year by year." Ringmer lies at the base of Mount Caburn, whose entrenched summit and ver-durous slopes are things of fame all round this countryside. Here the soft green sward, and the deep shadowy coombes, and the patches of fragrant thyme, will fill the soul of the spectator with delight. The green paths that wind across these downs are called " Borstalls "—from BEORH-STEGELE, hill-paths, according to Kemble. From every point is commanded a breadth of glorious scenery of the richest and most varied character.

RINGMER CHURCH is a low but venerable building, with a tower, nave, chancel, and north and south chapels, containing numerous monuments and inscriptions of the seventeenth century. The vicarage of Ringmer, valued at £400, is in the patronage of the Archbishop of Canterbury.

LAUGHTON (population, 812) is a pleasant, breezy village, interesting from its association with the knightly Pelhams, who had here a large moated mansion, built about 1534. The ruins are of no great importance, but a tower of brick, now rising out of the shapeless mass of a modern farm-house, and a gabled building at the south angle, may interest the tourist. The Pelham buckle is frequently introduced among the ornaments.

The vicarage, valued at £224, is in the patronage of the Earl of Chichester.

Our route now takes us through a romantic and, generally, a well-wooded country, with broad patches of heath, wide sweeps of cornfield, and fresh green reaches of meadow land. Just beyond the eighth milestone, a road on the left leads to CHIDDINGLY (population, 1053), where there are some ruins of the picturesque Elizabethan mansion of the Jefferays, and a goodly Early English church, with a tower surmounted by a tall stone spire. Observe here the remarkable memorial, with recumbent effigies, to Sir *John Jefferay*, Chief Baron of the Exchequer, *temp.* Elizabeth. In niches on either side are placed the figures of Sir Edward Montague and his wife, a daughter of Sir John.

Earl Amherst has the patronage of the vicarage, which is valued at £158 per annum.

Our road to Battle passes through other villages of little interest to the tourist. At 4 miles from Lewes he reaches HELLINGLY, already described (see p. 504), while, 2 miles to the south, lies HURSTMONCEUX (see p. 505). After crossing Boreham Bridge (18 miles), he will observe a turning on the left,—a green and leafy lane—a true Kentish lane, tree-shadowed, and meadowbordered,—which leads to ASHBURNHAM PLACE (Earl of Ashburnham), a tabooed locality to the tourist, for whom neither gold nor silver key will unlock the magic gates. The causes of this illiberal seclusion we have been unable to ascertain, but such is the fact ; into Ashburnham Place there is no admission for the archæological inquirer or historical student.

The family mansion of the Ashburnhams is a towered and gabled structure of red brick, situated on a gentle ascent which swells out of a broad deep hollow, and reposes in the shadow of a background of dense and venerable woods.   The park is full of beauty ; there are sudden ascents, and wide stretches of springy turf, and clusters of dark brown trees, and dells of romantic loveliness.   A path, open to the public, crosses the demesne, and opens up some rare rich prospects of the distant cliffs and the everchangeful sea.

Here is preserved a remarkable collection of rare MSS. and valuable printed books, chiefly Latin, French, and Flemish, with some exquisite specimens of the burins of the early German artists. Armour of the knights of old ; a mass of antique and valuable plate ; and some fine specimens of Cuyp, Teniers, Rembrandt, and Rubens, are among the Ashburnham treasures.   Scarcely less interesting, perhaps, are the Carolian relics ;—Charles the First's watch, his white silk drawers, the blood-spotted shirt which he wore upon the scaffold, and the sheet flung over his corpse after the cruel axe had done its worst,—relics treasured up by the pious devotion of John Ashburnham, the king's faithful attendant. " For some years they were carefully preserved at Wick-Rising-ton, near Stow-on-the-Wold, Gloucestershire.   In 1743, they were bequeathed to the clerk of the parish of Ashburnham, Sussex, and his successors for ever, to be kept in the church," whence they have been removed, on what grounds we know not, to Ashburnham Place.

The Ashburnhams trace their descent from Bertram de Eshburnham, Vice-comes of Kent and Sussex under Harold, the last of the Saxon kings.   Fuller's panegyric of them, therefore, is not undeserved, as " a family of stupendous antiquity, wherein the eminency hath equalled the antiquity."

ASHBURNHAM CHURCH stands in the park, at no great distance from the house.   It was rebuilt by John Ashburnham, d. 1671, gentleman of the bed-chamber to Charles I. and Charles II., and contains a memorial to that worthy and his wives, and to his brother, Sir William Ashburnham.   There are some other monuments of an interesting character.   The vicarage of Ashburnham (population, 865), valued at £307, and in the patronage of the Earl of Ashburnham, is associated with the rectory of Penhurst. PENHURST (population, 120)—*i. e.*, the wooded hill—lies a short distance beyond Ashburnham Place.

From this point the road leads, through a fair and open country, to Battle and its historic ruins.

BRANCH ROUTE—LEWES TO FRANT.

After passing Ringmer, and its pleasant coppices, the first place of any interest on the road to Frant is EAST HOATHLY (population, 667), a picturesque village, situated on the borders of HOLLAND PARK, a former residence of the Pelhams. There are some remains of the Tudor mansion. The CHURCH is a Perpendicular structure, with a fine old tower, ornamented with the Pelham device of "the buckle." The rectory, valued at £261, is in the patronage of the Earl of Abergavenny.

WALDRON (1106), is a large and populous village, in a luxuriantly wooded country. The rectory, valued at £455, is attached to the patronage of Exeter College, Oxon.

Our road now runs along a branch of the great Forest Ridge of the Hastings sand, climbing short steep hills, descending into shadowy valleys, passing under the interweaving branches of ash and elm, skirting smiling meadows which are rich in blossom and verdure, running through clusters of quaint old cottages, crossing "brawling brooks," and plunging deep into leafy hollows ; winding, in fact, through landscapes of the most marvellous and unexpected beauty. Here and there we meet with a rustic inn, where we may obtain the homely refreshment of home-brewed ale, and bread and cheese, or, haply, of eggs and bacon, or we come to a sequestered farmstead, reposing under its ancestral trees, and seeing itself unchanged, and apparently unchangeable, in the pond which glimmers somewhat fitfully before it. The highest point of the ridge is at CROSS-IN-HAND (where there is a tolerable "hostel"), the point of divergence of the Mayfield road.

[About 4 miles beyond lies HEATHFIELD (population, 2200), with its pretty little church, and its noble PARK (G. E. Towery, Esq.), the residence for many years of General Elliot, the Gibraltar hero, who obtained his barony from this place. The grounds, and *not* the house, will obtain the visitor's approval. HEATHFIELD TOWER, 590 feet above the sea level, was erected as a memorial to the gallant Elliot by Francis Newbery, Esq., to whom the estate was sold by that hero's successor. The view from the tower is of great extent, and includes a circle of some 30 miles in diameter.

Of the vicarage, valued at £349, the Bishop of Chichester has the patronage.
Returning from Heathfield Church into the Lewes road, we pass through the
little hamlet of CADE STREET, associated, of course, with traditions of that gross
" disturber of the Commonwealth." The column here was erected by Mr. Newbery
to mark the legendary site of his death by the hands of Alexander Eden, the Kentish
sheriff, who, it is said, surprised him while playing at bowls in the garden of the
village ale-house. Cade was certainly a retainer of Lord Dacres, then owner of
Heathfield, but the weight of evidence would seem to be in favour of his death having taken place in Kent.

Heathfield was the seat of one of the most considerable of the Sussex iron works,
especially famous for its production of superior iron ordnance. " When the late
Major Fuller entered on his first campaign in India, he found, with mingled pleasure
and surprise, some of the old artillery inscribed with the name of his native village
—' Heathfield'"—(*Lower.*)

Three miles south is situated WARBLETON (population, 1509), where the remains
of a house of Augustinian canons, removed from Hastings by Sir John Pelham,
temp. Henry IV., are, as was apparently usual in Sussex, embodied in a farm-house.
The CHURCH contains a fine brass to *William Prestwick,* d. 1436, prior of Battle
Abbey. The pelican crest of the canopy, and the inscription on the priestly apparel
—" Credo quod redemptor meus vivit"—should be remarked. A loft in the church
tower was used as a prison for heretics during Queen Mary's "reign of terror," and
here Richard Woodman was confined previous to his auto-da-fè at Lewes.

The present incumbent of Warbleton holds the advowson of the living, a rectory,
valued at £663 per annum.]

At Cross-in-Hand branches off the road to MAYFIELD (population, 2370), rapidly descending the northern slope of the sandstone ridge, and running through a rich and glowing landscape.
The town of MAGAVELDA is seated on high ground, overlooking
an extensive breadth of country, and is one of the pleasantest in
northern Sussex. It was one of the " peculiars" of the Archbishops of Canterbury, who had here a famous palace. St. Dunstan built the first church at Mayfield ; a wooden building, which,
when he was dedicating it, he found not canonically placed due
east and west, and putting his saintly shoulder to it, speedily
pushed it into its proper position. It was here that his famous
contest with the devil took place, and it was from this point that
the fiend sprang at one leap to Tunbridge Wells, to cool his in-
flamed nose in the pleasant waters.

St. Dunstan is said to have also founded here an archiepiscopal palace, but the present ruins are evidently of no greater
antiquity than the fourteenth century. Archbishop Islip erected
the principal pórtion in the Decorated style, and cut down so
much of the Weald timber as to incur censure for his rapacity,
and to bring down upon himself " a signal judgment." While
riding from Sevenoaks to Tunbridge he was thrown by his horse,
repaired to Mayfield, and after dinner was seized with paralysis

—a warning to all sacrilegious meddlers with the sacred oàk ! Archbishops Stratford and Islip also died at Mayfield. A great council was held here by the former in 1332, for the regulation of the feasts and fasts of the church. Cranmer exchanged Mayfield with Henry the Eighth for other estates, and it afterwards passed through a long succession of proprietors. Sir Thomas Gresham resided here, and splendidly received under his roof the great Gloriana. Towards the end of the eighteenth century the despoiler, as usual, stepped in, and despoiled and shattered into ruins the stately pile hallowed by so many interesting associations.

The principal, and the most ancient portion of the ruins, is the GREAT HALL, 70 feet long, 39 feet wide, and 50 feet high, erected by Archbishop Islip about the middle of the fourteenth century. The three arches which formerly supported the open roof remain entire. They are turned above the windows and between the buttresses, so as to sustain a longitudinal as well as an outward pressure. The tracery of the windows is beautiful, and of that kind which is known as " Kentish." It is to be lamented that the timber roof should have been destroyed, for " it was probably unique." A niche formed of roses, carved in stone, at the upper end of the hall, indicates the position of the archiepiscopal chair.

The GREAT DINING-ROOM occupies one side of the quadrangle. Observe its hooded chimney-piece of stone, and the iron chimney-back, dated " 1663." The GRAND STAIRCASE now leads into a large wainscoted room, the receptacle of the St. Dunstan relics— his anvil, hammer, and tongs. The iron handled hammer is ancient, but the tongs and anvil cannot boast of a very great age. An old sword is also said to be St. Dunstan's. The iron rail of the staircase, and these notable relics, were all manufactured at the Mayfield furnaces—formerly of great repute.

On each side of the door of the ante-room are obliterated armorial bearings, probably those of the See of Canterbury. North of the hall some steps descend to a doorway, which opens upon a subterranean passage to Mayfield Church. The kitchen and buttery were at the lower end of the hall, and the servants' apartments in a projecting square tower—[See the description of Mayfield in Parker's Domestic Architecture."] The gate-house still remains entire. St. Dunstan's Well, reputed to be 300 feet in depth, adjoins the kitchen apartments, and has been walled round.

Thomas May, the eloquent historian of the great deeds of the Long Parliament, was born at Mayfield Palace in 1595.

MAYFIELD CHURCH, dedicated to St. Dunstan, occupies the site of the ancient wooden structure, destroyed by fire in 1389. It is a large and goodly Early English building, recently restored. The vicarage, valued at £151, is in the patronage of Mrs. Greaves.

Both at BUTTERTON and CALTON there are small churches, pleasantly situated, but of no particular interest.

About 4 miles to the north-east lies ROTHERFIELD (population, 3531), the ancient " Ville of Redrefeld," where the ealdorman Berhtwald, having been restored from a severe illness by a visit to the shrine of St. Denis, built a church in honour of that saint, and deposited in it the precious relics he had brought back from the Norman abbey. He afterwards bestowed the church on its monks (A.D. 792), who founded here a small cell. The present structure is principally Early English, with a tall, tapering spire of much elegance. Its arched roof is of chestnut-wood. The rectory, one of the wealthiest in Sussex, is valued at £1434, and is in the patronage of the Earl of Abergavenny.

The old manor-house of WALSHES, with its original porch and two or three antique windows, is about 2 miles east of the church.

Hence the tourist will proceed, by way of Mark's Cross and Sockbury, to FRANT.

BRANCH ROUTE—LEWES, *viâ* UCKFIELD, TO TUNBRIDGE WELLS.

We shall avail ourselves, on our way to " the Wells," of the branch railway to Uckfield, which, at about 2 miles from Lewes, passes to the west of HAMSEY (population, 529), a village bordering on " the sad-coloured Ouse," with a Perpendicular church, situated on a considerable ascent. In the north wall is placed a richly sculptured Easter sepulchre. The rectory, valued at £570, is in the patronage of Sir George Shiffner, Bart.

Still speeding through the fertile river-valley, we reach, at 2 miles farther north, BARCOMBE (population, 1075), a busy and populous hamlet, in a good agricultural district. The rectory, valued at £719, is included in the Lord Chancellor's patronage.

ISFIELD (population, 508), is the next station, but the village itself stretches away along the road to Baresfield for some distance, with its CHURCH at its northern extremity, on the right bank of a small offshoot of the Ouse. This is a building in the Decorated style, with some Perpendicular insertions. The SHIRLEY or SHURLEY CHAPEL, on the south side, contains some memorials of interest ; a stately altar-tomb, with recumbent effigies to Sir *John Shurley*, d. 1631, and his two wives, and small kneeling figures of their children. The brasses commemorate *Edward Shurley*, d. 1558, and his wife, and *Thomas Shurley*, d. 1571. The rectory, worth £340, is in the Archbishop of Canterbury's patronage.

ISFIELD PLACE still retains some traces of its ancient splendour, and over the entrance are preserved the escocheons and mottoes of the Shurleys. A high and massive wall, strengthened at each angle by a watch-tower, formerly encircled it, and is still in tolerable repair. The mansion has been *diminished* into a farm-house.

[On the north bank of a tributary of the Ouse, and to the right of the Tunbridge road—about 2 m. east of Isfield—is seated LITTLE HORSTED (population, 283), a picturesque village, with a Norman church, which the tourist should examine. It consists of a nave, chancel, and turret. The rectory, valued at £356, is in the patronage of J. Barchard, Esq.]

At 8 miles (by road) from Lewes we reach UCKFIELD (population 1590), the terminus of this short branch-line of railway, and an agricultural centre of some importance. It mainly consists of one long street, lining the high road to Tunbridge Wells, and on " market day " presents a lively and attractive scene—Sussex lasses, fresh and blooming, Sussex farmers, many of them retaining the traditional top-boots and " cut-away coats " of the Georgian era, London contractors, and staring villagers gathering here on their divers errands. The neighbourhood is rich in attractive landscapes—woodland, and meadow, and cornfield, and brown ridges of heathy hills—combining in pictorial effects of great interest and beauty.

The church is modern, and contains nothing worthy of special notice. The living is a perpetual curacy, valued at £315, of which the Archbishop of Canterbury has the patronage.

At COPWOOD (Mrs. Streatfield), on the marge of a picturesque sheet of water, lie some masses of rock of similar character to those which are scattered in the neighbourhood of Tunbridge Wells.

We now abandon the rail and return to the road, proceeding through a country of unusual interest, and enjoying a succession of bold and varied landscapes. As a whole, this district will be found but thinly populated, and to retain much of its primitive character, for the locomotive has not yet sped through its glades, or penetrated into its thick woodlands, and the village inn is as humble now as " in the days when George III. was king,"— its *cuisine* limited to bread and cheese, or bacon and eggs—and its cellars innocent of French vintages.

☞ At 2 miles from Uckfield the road diverges to Mayfield, and crosses a branch of the Ouse, at BUXTED (population, 1313), —the "village of the beech-trees." BUXTED CHURCH, Early English, stands on an ascent, with a low shingled spire, a decorated chancel, nave, and aisles—an interesting and, indeed, a handsome building. Here is a brass to *Butellus Avenel*, rector, d. 1375, with the figure of a priest ; and *Christopher Savage*, " both flesh and bone," lies interred in the chancel. The figure of a female holding in her hands a large churn—a rebus for the name of Alchurn, Alchorn, or Allchorn—and flanked by warriors, each with a shield on his breast, should be noticed over the north porch. She was possibly a benefactor to the church or village. The value of the rectory is £403 yearly, and the Archbishop of Canterbury has the patronage. The Rev. Edward Clarke, father of Dr. Samuel Clarke, the adventurous traveller, held this quiet Sussex incumbency for some years. George Watson, the Sussex calculator, was born here. His dexterity in arithmetical operations and his powers of memory were extraordinary ; in other respects he was almost imbecile. Richard Woodman, one of the ten protestant martyrs burnt at Lewes in 1557, was a native of Buxted.

BUXTED PLACE (Colonel Vernon Harcourt) was the seat of the late Earl of Liverpool, whose daughter brought it by marriage to its present proprietor—formerly M.P. for the Isle of Wight, and the third son of the late Archbishop of York. The house is commodious and pleasantly situated. The park is of considerable extent, and rendered specially attractive by its' rich masses of vigorous foliage.

Buxted was one of the great " iron-towns " of the Weald whose noble trees—

" Jove's oak, the warlike ash, veined elm, the softer beech,
    Short hazel, maple, plane, light asp, the bending wych,
    Tough holly, and smooth birch, must altogether burn,"—

to supply its famous furnaces, before the introduction of coal for
manufacturing purposes, removed them to the busy northern
counties. An interesting relic of the iron-times is still extant at
HOWBOURNE, in this parish—an old hammer-post, on the marge
of the once extensive but now drained pond. It is formed of an
oak tree, and in excellent preservation. Its height above ground is
9½ feet.

The first iron cannons cast in England were manufactured
at Buxted, in 1543, by Ralph Hoge, or Hogge, assisted by Peter
Baude, a Frenchman, and Peter Van Collet, a Flemish gunsmith.
Bombs, fawconets, fawcons, nimions, and sakers, and other kinds
of ordnance, were here produced. Hogge's house is still standing,
near Buxted Church, and from their rebus, or " name-device,"
a hog, carved over the doorway, is called the Hog-house. " The
name of Hogge or Hoggé seems to have been confounded with
that of Huggett ; and there is a place on the confines of Buxted
and Mayfield, called Huggett's furnace, where, according to tradition, the first iron ordnance was cast. The traditionary distich that

'Master Huggett and his man John,
    They did cast the first can-non,'

is firmly believed in the locality "—(*Lower*). Many persons of the
name of Huggett still carry on the trade of blacksmith in east
Sussex.

The decline of the Sussex iron-manufacture dates from the production of iron in the northern coal-fields. In 1740 there were
59 furnaces in England, and 10 of these were in Sussex ; in 1788,
there were 77, but only 2 in Sussex ; and in 1796, while England
possessed 104, Sussex had but *one !* Many of the great Sussex
families owed their prosperity to this now extinct staple. " In
the days of Elizabeth, the Ashburnhams, the Pelhams, the Montagues, the Nevilles, the Sidneys, the Sackvilles, the Dacres, the
Stanleys, the Finches, the Gages, and even the Percys and the
Howards, did not disdain such lucre, but pursued it to the destruction of old ancestral oak and beech, and with all the apparent
ardour of Birmingham and Wolverhampton men of these times.
We may add after these the Culpepers, the Dykes, the Darrels,
the Apsleys, the Coverts, the Merleys, the Shirleys, the Burrells,

the Greshams, the Bullens (kinsmen of royalty), the Grativekes, the Bakers, and the Fullers. Concerning the last mentioned, there is a foolish tradition that the first of the name and family in Sussex gained his wealth by hawking nails about the country on the backs of donkeys. This is absurd ; but at the same time it is generally understood that the family were greatly enriched by the manufacture—a fact which is indeed frankly avowed in their singular motto ; ' *Carbone et forcipibus.*' "

Returning into the high road, we see to our left the populous village of MARESFIELD (population, 1805), where, through the researches of the rector, the Rev. Edward Turner, have been discovered the remains of extensive Roman iron-works. Some Roman coins, a considerable quantity of pottery, fragments of glass, pieces of sheet-lead, a stylus, and several skeletons, have here at various times been excavated.

MARESFIELD PARK (J. V. Shelley, Esq.), is a demesne of goodly proportions and picturesque beauty. It lies between the East Grimstead and Tunbridge roads. MARESFIELD CHURCH is a small Decorated structure, containing some good ancient woodwork. The rectory, valued at £645, is in the patronage of Viscount Gage. There is a small district church at Nutley Green, 3 miles north, on the East Grimstead road.

The road now winds through "the tufty friths" and "mossy fells" of the Weald country,—still rich in masses of leafy shadow, though the glorious old forest has been shorn of almost all its ancient grandeur,—and ascends a steep ridge of the Hastings sand to CROWBOROUGH, 804 feet above the level of the sea, which may be discerned from this lofty elevation, though distant from it some five and twenty miles. The prospects enjoyable on every side are such as can barely be realized in words. Especially so towards the south, where the Downs rear their magnificent crests like crowned giants, and now glow in the golden sunshine, now loom all grandly and solemnly through the passing shadows.

Crowborough was one of the beacon-stations of Sussex, where the ball-fire was lighted on all occasions of impending peril, and shot up its warning flames to the awakening of the entire Weald. The place where it stood may be seen at a short distance from the wayside inn, on the opposite side of the road.

The road now skirts the remains of Ashdown Forest as far as

BOAR'S HEAD STREET,—a name* which has a veritable woodland flavour,—and, passing through the romantic charms of ERIDGE PARK, again ascends the rising ground before it reaches TUNBRIDGE WELLS, at 22 miles from Lewes.

☞ From Crowborough the tourist may descend by a most picturesque and delectable route to WITHYHAM (population, 1692), a route which, if his time will permit, he must not fail to undertake, as it traverses a country side of extraordinary and romantic interest. Whether he be a sketcher, intent on transferring to his tablets the outlines of a magnificent landscape ; a botanist, eager to investigate the treasures of the Sussex flora ; a geologist, learned in strata ; or an idler, in search of the picturesque,—he will do well to adopt our recommendation.

Withyham itself is a village of more than ordinary interest, and the tourist may provide himself with the Hon. and Rev. Sackville West's " *Historical Notices of the Parish of Withyham,*" if he care for fuller details than our plan permits us to afford. The CHURCH, dedicated to St. Michael, is situated upon rising ground, near the rectory,—where application must be made for permission to view the chancel and Sackville Chapel,—and is a large and goodly Early English building, with additions made in the seventeenth century, after it had severely suffered in a terrible storm of lightning and thunder (June 16th, 1663). The repairs were not completed until 1672, the date now upon the porch, where it was replaced after some careful restorations made about 20 years ago. In the chancel windows there is some good stained glass, and the north windows of the nave are emblazoned with armorial bearings. The Dorset chancel, or Sackville Chapel, was rebuilt in 1624. The south aisle is a modern addition, and the Sackville Chapel itself has been thoroughly restored by the present incumbent of Withyham. The ceiling is a reproduction of the Tudor style. A genealogical emblazonment of the Sackvilles, from the time of the Norman William, in richly coloured glass, and several interesting memorials, including two fine sculptures by Flaxman and Nollekens, will repay the visitor's careful examination. In the vaults beneath lie many of the famous Sackvilles—knights, poets, statesmen—the " true men of

* Some authorities pretend that the village is named from a curious rock placed in a garden on the right of the road, in which they see a resemblance to " a monstrous head."

old," whose names are among the cherished memories of our glorious England, and among them the great *Thomas Lord Buckhurst*, Lord High Treasurer to Gloriana and her successor, the pedant James, and the author of "Gorboduc." His monument was destroyed in the fire of 1663.

The chapel is decorated with the Sackville banners. Observe the white marble altar-tomb to *Richard Earl of Dorset*, d. 1677, representing his infant son, recumbent, between the standing figures of his countess and himself. It was originally designed for the infant, but the Earl died before its completion. Observe, too, the monuments already referred to, by Nollekens and Flaxman respectively, to the first *Duke of Dorset*, d. 1749, and the second Duke of Dorset, killed by a fall from his horse in 1815. The Earl of Dorset, d. 1705, commemorated by Pope as

"Dorset, the grace of courts, the muse's pride,"

is buried in this church, but the monument on which the poet's panegyric was to have been engraved has never been erected.

Both church and churchyard are maintained in admirable order, and the tourist will find no difficulty in obtaining admission.

The rectory, valued at £717, is in the patronage of Earl Delawarr, the proprietor of BUCKHURST PARK, which passed to him upon his marriage with the Countess,—a lineal descendant of the Sackvilles.

Of BUCKHURST, the ancient seat of this ancient family, situated at a short distance south-east of the church, only the gate-tower remains. It was originally a pile of unusual magnificence, and appears—from the ground-plan preserved in Horace Walpole's "Anecdotes of Painters,"—to have occupied an area of 260 feet by 200. The HALL was 55 feet long and 40 feet wide, the TENNIS COURT was 55 feet in length, and the other apartments were constructed on the same scale of grandeur. There were eight towers besides the gate-tower, and the surrounding park was of noble dimensions and admirable beauty. But such were the "extreme bad ways" and miry roads by which the Sackvilles alone could reach their Sussex-palace, that they represented their miserable condition to the Crown, and obtained, about 1630, a grant of Knole, near Sevenoaks, and removing thither, permitted Buckhurst to fall into ruins. Some portion of it was broken up, and made use of in the erection of Sackville College, at East Grinstead.

The present house, a noble Tudor building, stands at a short distance from the old tower, in a park of great extent, famous for its rich masses of beech-trees. On the death of John Frederick, third Duke of Dorset, it fell to the share of one of his daughters and co-heiresses, Elizabeth, who married the Earl Delawarr.

One mile beyond Withyham, on the north boundary of the once famous Ashdown Forest, is situated HARTFIELD (population, 1573), a pleasant village, with some leafy copses round about it. The CHURCH, dedicated to St. Mary, stands on rising ground. It is partly Early English, and partly decorated. The vicarage, valued at £452, is in the nomination of Earl Delawarr, who is one of the largest land proprietors in this part of Sussex. BOLEBROOK, an old house of the Sackvilles, which passed to them, by marriage, from the Dalyngrugges, about 1400, is now included in the Buckhurst estates. It was built in the fifteenth century, and was one of the earliest brick-built houses in England. A gate-tower is the principal portion extant.

[4 m. north of Hartfield, and across the Kentish boundary—here formed by the river Medway, is situated COWDEN (population, 712), with its old church on the brink of a hill, overlooking a wide and varied landscape. The pulpit bears the date of 1628, and one of those old hour-glasses which were a warning to prolix preachers and a comfort to inattentive congregations. The present incumbent holds the advowson of the rectory, valued at £347.

A pleasant walk may be taken from this starting-point passing HOLTY HOUSE (R. M. Whatley, Esq.), and thence, by way of Holt Common, across Blackham Common, and through Ashurst to Tunbridge Wells.]

The tourist may penetrate from Hartfield or Withyham into the depths of the romantic district still known as ASHDOWN FOREST. It lies within the manor of Maresfield, and was included in the Honour of the Eagle of Pevensey. The Earl Delawarr is, at present, lord of this extensive chase. About 13,000 acres were formerly enclosed within a fence, and well stocked with deer; but during the troublous times of the Civil Wars, the fences were uprooted, and the deer slain. The thick woods which were once the boast of this sylvan country side, are now represented by clumps of trees crowning the higher ground.

The north-west extremity is FOREST Row, a pretty village, built, it is said, for the accommodation of those nobles and their retainers who pursued the chase in the adjoining forest. Near it is KIDBROOK, the seat of Lord Colchester. A new district-church, Early English in style, was erected at Forest Row in 1835.

Its south boundary was formed by the Downs, which extend from Uckfield to Etchingham. Withyham was its north-east point, and Crowborough, on the east, overlooked the entire tract of rank and luxuriant woodland.

BRANCH ROUTE—LEWES TO EAST GRINSTEAD.

The direct East Grinstead road, at about 3 miles from Lewes, leaves the COOK'S BRIDGE STATION on the left, and CONEYBAR-ROW PARK on the right. About 5 miles further, after passing the village of CHAILEY, it is crossed by the road from Cuckfield to Etchingham. Following the latter for 2½ miles we should reach NEWICK, and crossing the Ouse at Gold Bridge, and turning to the left at Pitt Down, visit FLETCHING, and, by way of SHEFFIELD PARK, regain the high road near the 39th milestone. From this point the route lies through a thinly populated and romantic country, skirting Ashdown Forest, crossing Dane Hill, and by way of Chelwood, Kidbrook, and BRAMBLETYE PLACE, entering East Grinstead.

If at the cross road already alluded to we took a westerly direction, we should proceed by Pelling Bridge to LINDFIELD, and thence, by the main road, with HORSTED-KEYNES and WEST HOATHLY on the right, and Ardingley on the left. At Sidlesfield Common a road branches off to East Grinstead—the main road continuing by way of Godstone and Croydon to London. For the convenience of the tourist, we notice the places particularized in capitals in the order in which we have named them :—

CHAILEY (population, 1268) is a large agricultural district. The rectory, valued at £505, is in the hands of Mrs. Blencowe and Mrs. Hepburn, as patrons. The church is not a very interesting building. NEWICK has a population of 966. The Rev. J. Powell holds the advowson of the rectory, which is valued at £327. FLETCHING (population, 2132) is an extensive and populous parish. The village lies to the south-east of SHEFFIELD PARK (Earl of Sheffield), a noble and well-wooded demesne. The stately mansion was greatly enlarged and completely renovated by the late Earl. The walls are decorated with carvings of the armorial bearings of the different lords of the manor, from the days of William the Norman. A fine portrait, by Sir Joshua

Reynolds, of Gibbon, who spent many years at Sheffield Place, then in the hands of his friend, John Holroyd, first Earl of Sheffield, is preserved here.

FLETCHING CHURCH, dedicated to St. Mary and St. Andrew, is a large Early English building, with a nave, chancel, aisles, transepts, and tower surmounted by a spire. The tower is Norman, and the double windows are divided by Norman balusters. An altar-tomb in the south transept bears a brass for a Sir *Walter Dalyngrugge*, d. 1395, and his wife. Observe, also, the altar-tomb, with figures, of *Richard Leche*, d. 1596.

Gibbon lies interred in the Sheffield mausoleum. The inscription, in sonorous Latin, is from the pen of Dr. Parr.

The vicarage of Fletching, valued at £300 per annum, is in the patronage of the Earl of Sheffield.

Sir T. Maryon Wilson, Bart. of Charlton, has a pleasant house and grounds at SEILES, adjoining Sheffield Park.

The reader will remember that the night before the battle of Lewes, May 13, 1264, Simon de Montfort and the Barons' army encamped in the woods of Fletching, then a dense and almost impenetrable mass ; and it was from this point he moved forward to Mount Harry, after the failure of his attempt to negotiate with the king.

Regaining the high road beyond Sheffield Park, we proceed through a hilly and sparsely cultivated country, by way of Kidbrook and Forest Row, to East Grinstead (9½ miles). Just beyond Forest Row, a turning on the left leads to the ruins of BRAMBLETYE HOUSE, associated in the memory of veteran novel-readers with the scenes of Horace Smith's best romance. It was built, *temp.* James I., by Sir Henry Compton, whose armorial bearings quartered with those of his second wife, Mary Browne, are sculptured over the entrance. It was captured by the Roundheads during the Civil War, and in 1683, while its then owner, Sir James Rickards, was rousing the deer in the great forest-depths of Ashdown, it was searched by the royal messengers, and considerable quantities of arms and ammunition were found. Sir James fortunately obtained information of the movements of his foes in time to make his escape and retire to Spain. The house was thus left without a lord, and speedily fell into decay. The existing ruins consist of the chief gateway, one square turret, and portion of another. Underneath the building are the domestic offices and vaulted cellars, displaying some good pointed arches.

The valley where Brambletye House is situated is of great beauty and is still clothed with a fresh and vigorous verdure. It is watered by the infant stream of the Medway, which has its source at Turner's Hill, west of East Grinstead Church, and about 4 miles distant.

Returning to Chailey, and taking the Cuckfield road instead of the route we have just described, we first arrive (7 miles) at LINDFIELD (population, 1814), a village romantically situated in a luxuriantly wooded, " deep-bowered and happy-meadowed " country-side. Its CHURCH, dedicated to St. Michael, has an Early English tower—a nave, chancel, and aisles, Perpendicular. The wall of the aisle is enriched with a curious fresco of great antiquity, dating from, perhaps, the fourteenth century. The Virgin is pictured with a glittering nimbus round her head—a small figure kneeling at her feet—and with a staff in her hand which she aims at a six-headed dragon, whose heads, however, have already been severed by her companion, St. Michael. The robes of the archangel are spotted with the letter M. ; he stands upon the conquered dragon, and weighs souls in a pair of scales.

Observe, too, the remarkable effigy engraved upon three glazed tiles which each measure 15 inches square—2 feet 9 inches in all. The date is 1520.

The Archbishop of Canterbury holds the right of presentation to the perpetual curacy of Lindfield.

In the neighbourhood of this quaint, old-fashioned, and secluded village—secluded, though it is scarcely 3 miles from the Hayward's Heath Station on the London and Brighton railway, and about 5 miles from Cuckfield—are some most delectable bits of scenery, some nooks and corners of enchanting beauty, which the tourist should leisurely explore. There are some old houses, too, which deserve examination ; old Elizabethan mansions, with many gables, and twisted chimneys, and curious effects of light and shade :—PAX HILL, EAST MAXALLS (the ancient seat of the Newtons), KENWARDS (of the Challoners), and LUNT (of the Hamlyns).

A pleasantly leafy road, by way of Pax Hill, leads to HORSTED-KEYNES (population, 715), lying in a picturesque hollow brightened by the waters of the Ouse. Its small Early English church should be visited for the sake of its effigy, 27 inches in length, of a knight templar—possibly one of the *Keynes* or *Cheyney* (from Cahaignes in Normandy) family, who may have fought against the Saracens under the banner of Edward I.　Archbishop *Leighton*, d. 1684, the virtuous primate of Glasgow, who resided for ten years—after his resignation of his mitre—at Broadhurst in this parish, and preached constantly by word and example in the neighbouring villages, lies interred in the south chancel.

The rectory, valued at £342, is in the patronage of Thomas Austen, Esq.

Some curious illustrations of Sussex life will be found in the DIARY of Giles Moore, rector of this parish from 1655 to 1679, printed in the first volume of the "Sussex Archæological Collections." For a companion-picture the reader may turn to the JOURNAL kept by one Timothy Burrell, Esq. of Ockendon House, near Cuckfield, from 1683 to 1714, and preserved in the third volume of the same work.

A road which passes the church of Horsted-Keynes, crosses a branch of the Ouse, and soon ascends to higher ground, conducts us (4 miles) to WEST HOATHLY (population, 1068).　Its Early English CHURCH is large and interesting, and consists of a Perpendicular tower, nave, chancel, and aisles.　At the entrance lie two iron slabs, memorials to members of the Infield family. The fort is ancient.　The Lord Chancellor presents to this vicarage, valued at £150 per annum.

To the left of the church, about ½ mile distant, and on the very brink of a sandstone cliff, are placed two rocks—one, a mass of about 350 tons weight, being exactly poised on the other, which is a much smaller rock.　The villagers expressively call them "Great-upon-Little." According to some authorities they are connected with the old Druidic rites, but the grounds for this opinion seem very unsatisfactory.

[ARDINGLEY (population, 666) lies about 3 miles south-west of Hoathly, on the eastern slope of a sandstone-ridge of picturesque character. The landscapes here are reproductions, in their general outlines, of the Tunbridge Wells scenery. The CHURCH, chiefly decorated, has an ancient wooden porch, a good oaken screen, stone effigies of an unknown knight and a nameless lady, and several *brasses*, memorials of the Culpepers of Wakehurst, a branch of the Great Kentish family. Observe the altar-tomb and brass to *Richard Wakehurst*, d. 1464, and his wife *Elizabeth*, with their figures in the costume of the period.—The rectory, valued at £498, is in the gift of J. F. W. Peyton, Esq.

WAKEHURST PLACE (Sir Alexander Cockburn, L.C.J.) lies in the bosom of much agreeable leafiness, about 1 mile north of Ardingley village, and near the East Grinstead road.   It was formerly the seat of a family of the same name, and after- wards passed to the Culpepers, one of whom, in 1590, erected the present house—a quaint, old-fashioned, and goodly pile.]

From West Hoathly we cross the high ground of SIDLES- FIELD or SILSFIELD COMMON—one of the ancient beacon-stations, and overlooking an extensive prospect—to

EAST GRINSTEAD (population of the parish, 3820—*Inn :* Dorset Arms), an irregularly-built, but pleasant market-town, situated on an ascent which commands a good view of Kent, Surrey, and Sussex.   It contains some old timbered houses, and some modern ones of tolerable pretensions, and may probably become the great agricultural depot of northern Sussex.

The CHURCH, dedicated to St. Swithin, is, from its lofty position, a conspicuous object from many points in the surrounding land- scape.   It is the third that has existed in the short space of a century and a half.   The old building was destroyed by fire in 1684.   The tower of the second fell in 1785, and demolished a considerable portion of the church.   The present tower is of great height, and adorned with pinnacles.   The nave, aisles, and chancel are all of good dimensions.   Observe the brass (from the ancient building) of *Catherine Lewkner*, of Brambletye, d. 1505, and the stately monument to the first Lord *Colchester* (better known as " Speaker Abbott "), d. 1829.   A brass, and monu- ment of Sussex marble, commemorate Dame *Elizabeth Gray*, and her two husbands.   She was one of the ladies in attendance upon the Queen of Henry VII., and, in conjunction with her second husband, " founded, indued, inorned this present church to the lawde and honore of God with dyvers ornaments, and an alms- house for three persons."   Lord *Abergavenny*, d. 1744, is com- memorated by a tablet in the south aisle.

East Amhurst has the patronage of the vicarage, which is valued at £350 per annum.

East Grinstead formerly returned two members to Parliament, and is now one of the polling-places for the electors of East Sussex.   It is 29 miles from London by road ; and connected with the London and Brighton railway by a branch line, 7 miles in length, from the Three Bridges' station.   The neighbour- hood is rich in scenery of a somewhat wild and picturesque character.

BRANCH ROUTE, BY RAILWAY, FROM LEWES TO BURGESS HILL.

At first we are rapidly borne through the fertile valley of the Ouse—the lofty crests of the South Downs looming magnificently to the south west, against the distant and misty skies.   At about 3 miles from Lewes we pass on the right, Coneybarrow Park, and reach the COOK'S BRIDGE STATION, on a branch of the Ouse. PLUMPTON *(population, 383), a pretty village built upon a pleasant green, lies nearly 2 miles west.   There are here a small, and not peculiarly interesting CHURCH, and an old moated house, PLUMPTON PLACE, the ancient residence of the Maxalls—one of whom, Leonard Maxall, *temp.* Henry VIII., first introduced carp, it is said, into this country by domesticating some *Cyprinidæ* of the Danube in the moat which encircled his house.   He is also reputed to have brought "the Golden Pippin" into Sussex, but some authorities pronounce it indigenous to the county.

The rectory (worth £221 yearly) is in the patronage of the present incumbent.

[STREET PLACE is another interesting old house, 1¼ mile north of Plumpton. It was the seat of the Dobells, and dates from *temp.* James I.   The library, now converted to "baser uses," is adorned with carved pilasters, and with a cornice which is elaborately lettered with quaint Latin mottoes.   Behind the great chimney-place of the hall was a deep recess, used for purposes of concealment, and there exists a tradition that a cavalier horseman, hotly pursued by some "malignant" troopers, broke into the hall, spurred his horse into the recess, and disappeared for ever.   STREET (population, 170) has a small Early English church.   The rectory, valued at £172, is in the gift of H. C. Lane, Esq.]

PLUMPTON GREEN now lies on our right, and DITCHLING on our left.   We soon cross the main road, *via* Lancefield, to London, and through a hilly and undulating country, reach the BURGESS HILL STATION, 41¼ m. from London, and 9 m. from Lewes.   Here the main line diverges to Brighton, and passes through a country which we shall hereafter describe [See Route XI.]

ROUTE XI.—LEWES, via BRIGHTON, to CHICHESTER.

[Lewes to Falmer, 4 m. ; Brighton, 4 m. ; New Shoreham, 6 m. ; Worthing, 4¼ m. ; Angmering, 5 m. ; Arundel, 8 m. ; Woodgate (for Bognor), 5 m. ; Chichester, 5 m.]

"That palace or China shop, Brighton which is it ?

With lanterns, and dragons, and things round the dome."—MOORE.

We leave Lewes for Brighton by the branch line which runs through an open country to FALMER (population, 537), a small and pleasant village where we need not linger, and underneath which we are carried, by means of a tunnel 200 yards in length. Shortly afterwards we skirt the fair' demesne of STANMER PARK (Ear of Chichester), a well-wooded and pleasantly-diversified estate, some 1500 acres in extent—and enter a deep cutting three quarters of a mile in length. We next pass through two short tunnels, and enter Brighton over the PRESTON VIADUCT—a noble structure of 27 arches, elevated 67 feet above the Preston road (observe, on the right, the cavalry barracks.) We here obtain a good view of the north-eastern suburb of Brighton—pleasant, populous, agreeable Brighton. The monster "watering-place" of England—indeed, the largest in the world—to which we shall be constrained to devote a considerable number of our pages.

BRIGHTON (*i. e.*, BRIGHTHELM'S TOWN.)

[Population, including Hove, 69,726.—Average number of visitors, 80,000.—*Hotels and Inns* :—1st class, Bedford, Old Ship, Royal York, Royal Albion, Bristol ; 2d class, New Ship, New Steyne, Norfolk ; 3d class, White Hart, Post Office, Pier, Clarence, etc., etc.

50½ m. from London, by rail.—53 m. by road ; 8 m. from Lewes ; 9 m. from New-haven ; 6 m. from Shoreham ; 4¼ m. from Rottingdean ; 5½ m. from the Devil's Dyke ; 9¼ m. from Bramber ; 28 m. from Chichester.

☞ *Omnibuses*, to meet the trains, between Hove, Brighton, and the Railway Station (on the north of the town.) *Conveyances*, daily, to Lewes and Shoreham. *Flys*, 1s. 6d. per mile.—*Post Office* ; 3 arrivals and 5 departures daily. *Baths* : Brill's, Creale's, Hobden's, and Mahomed's—*Bathing Machines*, 1s. each person—Railway Journey to London occupies 1 hour 20 minutes by express, and 2 hours by ordinary trains.]

"Brighton," says Hazlitt, "stands facing the sea, on the bare cliffs, with glazed windows to reflect the glaring sun, and black pitchy bricks shining like the scales of fishes. The town is, however gay with the influx of London visitors—happy as the conscious abode of its sovereign ! everything here appears in motion— coming or going. People at a watering place may be compared to the flies of a summer ; or to fashionable dresses, or suits of clothes, walking about the streets. The only idea you gain is, of finery and motion." Thackeray, in THE NEWCOMES, writes of it more eulogistically :—" It is the fashion," he says, " to run down George IV. ; but what myriads of Londoners ought to thank him for inventing Brighton ! One of the best physicians our city has ever known, is kind, cheerful, merry doctor Brighton. Hail, thou purveyor of shrimps, and honest prescriber of South Down mutton ; no fly so pleasant as Brighton flys ; nor any cliffs so pleasant to ride on ; no shops so beautiful to look at as the Brighton gimcrack shops, and the fruit shops, and the market. " Mr Thorne's graphic description will interest the reader :—" If some daring engineer were to lift the line of houses facing Park Lane, place them upon the south-coast railway, convey them to the seaside, and plant them directly alongside the beach, he would make an almost exact resemblance to Brighton as viewed from the sea. So much does the line of houses facing the cliff resemble some parts of the West-end, that the spectator who has been shot down from town in an hour by the express-train, finds a difficulty in believing that he is far away removed from his old haunts, until he turns to the bright sea, which lies before him like a flat and polished mirror, and champing and frothing upon the pebbly beach below. The western extremity of the town, which is bounded by Adelaide Crescent and Brunswick Terrace and Square, lies comparatively low : and from. this point to Kemp Town, which is fully 3 miles to the east, runs a splendid promenade. The life and variety which everywhere meet the eye along this pleasant walk, is perhaps unequalled." The great drawback of Brighton, however, is its *want of shade.* It has no trees to afford a coolsome shadow—no obscure groves, no romantic bowers—though, indeed, Hood has protested " that of all the trees he ever saw, none could be mentioned in the same breath with the magnificent BEACH at Brighton."

But now a-days everybody goes to Brighton. It is brought so near to London by the agency of the rail ; the excursion fares are so moderate ; there is such a *reality of sea* about it—not like that shrimp-abounding town—yclept Gravesend, which is simply *brackish*—that we marvel not the eager Londoner starts away, fifteen minutes before eight, to enjoy " six hours " at this city of chalk. There are grand, lofty cliffs, glittering like ramparts of silver or walls of pearl. There is a glorious expanse of ocean-waters, ever varying from blue to green, and green to purple, as they surge and seethe in sunshine or in shadow ; aye, ocean waters, only bounded by the dim circle of the distant sky. And there is a pebbly beach, with huge clusters of dank seaweed, and trim fishing boats hauled up above the tide-mark, and—yes, we must proclaim it—most loveable groups of dark eyes and blue eyes, bent, apparently, upon their sketch-books, or the pages of the last new novel. "A day out," if spent at Brighton, is a day to be remembered. We once heard a mechanic, in an excursion train, describe this favourite town in language quaint, but not elegant : "It's a stunning sight," said our emphatic friend ; " for all the world like Piccadilly gone out to sea !"

Certainly, there is little sign of antiquity about the good town at present, and yet its annals begin at a period not within the memory of even " the oldest inhabitant." It was, probably, a British settlement, for in its vicinity are numerous traces of the rude fortifications or " earthworks " of our ancestors. That it existed during the Saxon period of English history is indisputable. Its name is Saxon, derived, it is said from Brihthelm, a Bishop of Selsay, and we know that it paid a rent, or " gablum," to Earl Godwin, the great Saxon noble. In 1081, this rental was paid in herrings (4000 halices) yearly—equivalent, in our money, to something like £300. There were then two distinct settlements here—one upon the heights, " a colony of landsmen ; " one upon the shore, a village of *jugs* or fishermen. It was then called Brighthelmstone, a name it retained until very recently ; and was numbered among the rich manors bestowed by William the Conqueror on his loyal adherent, Earl de Warrenne, who exercised almost a sovereign sway over the fair county of Sussex.

The French attacked the town, and burnt it, in the reign of Richard II. In 1513, they again made a descent upon the coast, under " Prior Jehan," but were compelled to retreat, with considerable loss. During the war between Henry VIII. and Francis I., in 1545, they harassed the whole southern coast, under their high admiral, Claude d'Annebault, who, says the old chronicler, Holinshed, " hoisted up sails, and with his whole navie came foorth into the seas, and arrived on the coast of Sussex before Bright-Hamsted (Brighton), and set certain of his soldiers on land to burne and spoile the countrie ; but the beacons were fired, and the inhabitants thereabouts came down so thick, that the Frenchmen were driven to flie, with losse of diverse of their numbers, so that they did little hurt there."

Shortly after this event, considerable fortifications were erected. There was a circular fort, called the Block House, and a battery called the Gun Garden, and a flint wall, 400 feet long, " from the east gate westward, where the cliff was lowest ; and from that point a parapet three feet high, with embrasures for cannon, was continued to the west gate." These no longer exist.

There was, also, a small battery at the verge of the cliff, on the King's Road, which mounted six forty-two pounders ; but Brighton's present defences are England's " wooden walls," well manned by " hearts of oak."

Amongst the interesting events of Brighton history, we must not omit to record the escape of Charles II. from Cromwell's troopers. After the fatal battle of Worcester—which Cromwell might well speak of as his " crowning mercy," for it placed the English sceptre virtually in his hands—the unfortunate king made his way, in disguise, to Brighton, where he arrived on the 13th of October. He passed the night at an inn (*The King's Head*) in West Street ; and the following morning moved to Shoreham, whence he immediately departed for the French coast, in a small boat belonging to a gallant loyalist, named Tattersall. After the restoration, the Brighton mariner, perceiving that the king's memory was very treacherous, sailed in his little craft to the River Thames, and moored it opposite Whitehall. Charles ordered it to be entered in the Royal Navy as the " Royal Escape," settled upon the gallant mariner and his heirs an annuity of £100, and presented him with a ring, which is now in the possession of a descendant—Sir Henry Shiffner.

During the seventeenth century the town suffered severely from the raids of the sea, and in Defoe's time, could only boast of six decent streets. The women employed themselves in weaving nets ; the boatmen were glad to obtain employment from the Yarmouth merchants in the herring-fishery. In 1703 and 1706 it was further desolated by violent storms. In the latter year no less than 130 houses were swept away, and £40,000 worth of property destroyed by the inundations which accompanied the tempest. In a few years all traces of ancient Brighton were lost under an accumulation of shingle. In 1818, during some excavations between Middle and Ship Streets, the walls of one of the streets of the lower town, called South Street, were discovered under a layer of beach, 15 feet in depth.

Brighton, like Ventnor, owes its present prosperity, in the first place, to a physician, Dr. Russell, who removed here from Malling, in 1750, and resided in a house on the Steyne,—*i. e.*, stane, a rock—where the Albion now stands. His portrait, by Zoffany, is preserved in the Old Ship Hotel. He published a treatise on the advantages of sea-bathing, and drew several patients from London to test the soundness of his theory. The Duke of

Cumberland, the victor of Culloden, was one of Brighton's earliest patrons, and lived in a house north of the Pavilion. The Duke and Duchess of Marlborough also sought the Brighton physician, and resided at Elm Grove. Dr. Johnson accompanied hither Mr. and Mrs. Thrale and Fanny Burney, in 1770, and declared the country " so desolate, that if one had a mind to hang one's self for desperation at being obliged to live there, it would be difficult to find a tree on which to fasten a rope." Miss Fanny visited the " King's Head Inn" (originally the George), in West Street, and gazed with loyal satisfaction on its sign — a head of his " black-wigged Majesty" Charles II., who slept there the night before his escape from Shoreham. The Thrales and their friends resided at No. 75 in the same street. George IV., then Prince of Wales, paid his first visit to Brighton in 1782, and built a house here in 1784—an epoch in the fortunes of the town duly remembered by all loyal Brightonians. It was not completed until 1817, when it was taken to pieces, remodelled, repaired, gilded, decorated, and moulded into the present bizarre architectural model—the PAVILION. The THEATRE was opened in 1807. BEDFORD SQUARE was commenced in 1810. The CHAIN PIER was begun in 1822 and completed in 1823. KEMP TOWN, on the estate of Mr. Thomas Kemp, rose into existence between 1821 and 1830. The MARINE WALL, 23 feet thick at the base and 60 feet in height, was built in 1827-8 at a cost of £100,000. In 1841 the BRIGHTON RAILWAY was opened throughout, having cost £2,569,359, and occupied two years and a half in its construction. Among the attractions of Brighton can scarcely be included its public buildings, and yet there are two or three points of interest to which the tourist must be formally introduced.

The CHAIN PIER, " where for the sum of 2d. you can go out to sea, and pace the vast deep without need of a steward with a basin," deserves the celebrity it has acquired, and is unequalled as a marine promenade. From this point the entire " sea-face" of Brighton is seen in a striking manner. It was commenced in 1822, and completed in the following year, under the direction of Captain Sir S. Brown, R.N., and at a cost of £30,000. It is 1136 feet in length and 15 feet in width, is supported by four piers which stand upon piles of oak driven 10 feet into the solid chalk, and by four cast-iron towers, 25 feet high, over which are carried the wrought-iron suspending chains, four deep, and two inches in diameter. Each of these four divisions or bridges is 258 feet in length, and has 117 links of one foot each. A fearful storm in November 1836 overthrew this fragile structure, snapping the suspending rods and breaking the central bridges, and necessitating repairs which cost £2000. Some injuries were done by a gale during the night of October 15, 1838, but, since that event, it has withstood in security the heaviest tempests which have visited our shores.

The PAVILION cannot be visited by the tourist without recalling to his mind the luxurious days when George, Prince Regent, was eulogized as " the finest gentleman in Europe," and Mrs. Fitzherbert, " fat, fair, and forty," was the cynosure of admiring eyes. Among his companions were Lord Barrymore and his two brothers—a trio, known by the expressive nick-names of " Hellgate," " Cripplegate," and " Newgate ;" Sir John Ladd, of four-in-hand memory ; and Colonel Hanger, renowned as " the Knight of the Black Diamond." Well might Lord Thurlow reply to the Prince's query, " Thurlow, how is it you have not called on me ? You must find a day for dining with me."—" I cannot, your Royal Highness, until you keep better company." On another occasion, when Thurlow *had* consented to dine with the Prince, he was informed that Sir John Ladd would also be a guest. The Prince apologized to the surly Lord Chancellor, but with little effect. " I do not object," said Thurlow, " to Sir John Ladd in his proper place, but that I take to be your Royal Highness's coach-box, and not your table."

The Pavilion occupies with its gardens about eleven acres and a half, and is a curious combination of domes, minarets, and cupolas, looking, according to Sidney Smith, " as if the dome of St. Paul's had come to Brighton and pupped." Cobbett suggests that " a good idea of the building may be formed by placing the pointed half of a large turnip upon the middle of a board, with four smaller ones at the corner." Nor is this description exaggerated in its ridicule, and he who gazes upon the monstrous pile can well understand " the intensity," of Sir Walter Scott's feelings when he wrote to his friend Morritt, then residing at Brighton (A.D. 1826) :—" Set fire to the Chinese stables, and if it embrace the whole of the Pavilion, it will rid me of a great eyesore."

The original Pavilion was commenced for the Prince Regent by the architect Holland in 1784, but was entirely reconstructed by Nash in 1818 under the immediate direction of the Prince, who had fallen " China-mad" through reading the accounts of Lord Amherst's Chinese embassy. The royal stables, for sixty-three horses, now converted into a winter garden, cost £70,000. The circumference of the great dome is 250 feet. The Chinese gallery measures 162 feet by 17 ; the banqueting-hall, 60 by 42 ; the music-room, 62 by 41 ; and the rotunda is 55 feet in diameter. These, and several other apartments, elaborately decorated after the Chinese manner, may now be inspected by the curious at 1s. admission.

William IV. sometimes resided here, and Queen Victoria occasionally visited it before she purchased Osborne. Her refined taste, however, was disgusted at its semi-Chinese monstrosities, and she intimated her intention of abandoning it as a royal residence. It was then (1849) purchased by the town for £53,000 —not a fourth of the sum originally lavished upon it—and has since been adapted for concerts, public meetings, balls, and general entertainments, remaining a building of no ordinary interest, though of more than ordinary architectural deformity.

In the QUEEN'S PARK, a pleasant plantation north of the town, is situated the ROYAL GERMAN SPA, where chemical imitations of the different German mineral waters are manufactured— to the great benefit of those who are unable to patronize the springs of Marienbad, Pyrmont, Seidschütz, and Seltzer.

The only relic of ancient Brighton is ST. NICHOLAS' CHURCH, situated on the hill north-west of the town. It is mainly Perpendicular in style, was built in the reign of Henry VII., and restored, in 1853, in memory of the Duke of Wellington, who often worshipped within its walls, and was for some time a pupil of the vicar. The memorial then erected is a richly decorated Cross, by Carpenter, 18 feet high, in the south chancel. A scroll, entwined about the shaft, bears the magic words, " Assaye, Torres Vedras, Vittoria, and Waterloo." A figure of St. George is inserted in the canopied niche at the top. The east window represents, in rich colours, the miraculous draught of fishes. The perpendicular screen, of painted oak, has been painted and gilded. The Norman circular font, brought, it is said, from Normandy, has its sides adorned with sculptures representing the Lord's Supper, and its base disfigured with the names of the church-wardens who officiated in the church in 1745.

In the churchyard are placed the memorial-stones of Captain

Nicholas Tattersall, " through whose prudence, valour, and loyalty, Charles II. was faithfully preserved and conveyed to France, 1651 ;"—*Phœbe Hessell,* panegyrized by George IV., from whom she received a yearly pension of £18, as " a jolly old fellow," and who, according to her epitaph, " served for many years as a private soldier in the 5th Regiment of Foot in different parts of Europe, and in the year 1745 fought, under the command of the Duke of Cumberland, at the battle of Fontenoy, where she received a bayonet wound in the arm. Her long life, which commenced in the reign of Queen Anne, extended to George IV., by whose munificence she received comfort and support in her latter years. She died in Brighton, where she had long resided, December 12, 1821, aged 108 years." There is also a memorial to Mrs. *Crouch,* the actress ; and the base of the old churchyard cross is still extant.

The Bishop of Chichester has the right of presentation to the vicarage of St. Nicholas. The vicar himself nominates to eight incumbencies—1. ST. PETER's (perpetual curacy), at the end of the Steyne, built in the Late Perpendicular style, by the late Sir Charles Barry, at a cost of £20,000 ; 2. ST. PAUL's, in West Street, built by Carpenter in 1847 ; 3. ALL-SOULS ; 4. CHRIST CHURCH (perpetual curacy, valued at £420), built in 1838 ; 5. ST. JOHN THE EVANGELIST ; 6. ALL SAINTS' CHURCH (perpetual curacy, £200) ; 7. CHAPEL ROYAL, in Prince's Place, built by Saunders in 1793 ; and 8. ST. STEPHEN's. There are, besides, ST. JAMES's CHAPEL, belonging to the trustees of the late P. Kemp, Esq. ; ST. MARY's CHAPEL, Rev. H. Venn Elliot ; ST. GEORGE's, TRINITY, and ST. MARGARET's CHAPELS, and ST. MARK's CHURCH.

In the way of public buildings, Brighton can boast of the SUSSEX COUNTY HOSPITAL, founded in 1828, and built by the late Sir Charles Barry at a cost of £10,000,—the Victoria wing was added in 1839, and the Adelaide wing in 1841. It is " open to the sick and lame poor of every country and nation." The BRIGHTON COLLEGE, a proprietary school established in 1847, occupies a handsome Tudor building. ST. MARY's HALL, in Kemp Town, is an institution for educating the daughters of poor clergymen, and preparing them for governesses. The TOWN HALL, a large and imposing structure, 144 feet long and 113 feet deep, was erected at a cost of no less than £50,000. Here the magistrates meet ; the market is held ; offenders are imprisoned ; and

the borough elections (Brighton returns two members to Parliament) transacted with a due amount of noise and bustle.

Let us now take a WALK THROUGH THE TOWN previous to
resuming our rural rambles, and cursorily glance at those points
of interest which have hitherto escaped our critical notice. We
start from the west extremity of the town, and pass through the
populous suburb of HOVE, and near Brunswick Square descend
upon the beach. Here we may gaze upon a scene as full of life
as the greatest London thoroughfare,—and fuller, perhaps, of
contrast,—for fishermen hauling up the dingy boats—bathing
machines dipping their grotesque hoods into the brine—coils of
old cable—fragments of spars—a net or two, and half a dozen
oars— are combined with novel-reading ladies in the amplest of
crinoline and the gayest of bonnets, with invalids in Bath-chairs,
with pedestrians eager to indulge their locomotive propensities,
with worn-out age seeking new vigour and fresh energy from the
sea-breeze, and amateur artists outlining sundry picturesque and
uncouth objects upon their tablets. Such is the scene presented
until the Chain Pier is reached. " The land side is equally alive
with carriages and equestrians, Bath-chairs, goat carriages, donkeys,
and promenaders. The King's Road, which forms the western-
most portion of the Promenade, or Esplanade, is terminated by
the open space called the Steyne, over the trees of whose enclosure
the minarets and domes of the Pavilion rise against the sky. From
this spot the Marine Parade commences, and the ground rises
until the roadway is full 60 feet above the level of the beach"—
(*Thorne*).

We pass Brill's Bath, leaving the Town Hall to our left, and
continue our road to Kemp Town. On the beach here we may
notice the GROYNES or jetties,—rows of piles running down into
the water, and planked on one side—intended to prevent the loose
shingle from being tide-driven out to the east. "For centuries
this process has been going on along the south coast of England,
and within the memory of man vast tracts of land have been
swept away by the sea. In the time of Elizabeth a great part of
Brighton stood where the Chain Pier now stretches its iron arm
across the sea. So constant and energetic is the action of the
ocean that Sir Charles Lyell, the eminent geologist, anticipates
that in a few centuries the alluvial deposit lying between the
South Downs and the sea, and forming so fertile a plain to the

west of Brighton, will be swept away, leaving the bare and steep hill-side as the coast line."

Returning along the promenade, from the easternmost extremity of the town, we may notice Sussex Square and the Crescent —the latter 200 feet wider than the famous Crescent at Bath. A tunnel here leads underneath the road to an esplanade formed upon the beach.

Arrived at the Steyne we may visit the Pavilion—and the Steyne Gardens, where Mrs. Honeyman resided (*See* " The Newcomes"), and thence proceed in a northerly direction into the heart of the town. The Western Road is a thoroughfare deserving notice. The Hospital may next be visited, and afterwards St. Nicholas Church, whence we may once more return to the beach, satisfied with our survey of Brighton.

[HINTS FOR RAMBLES.—1. By rail to Lewes; visit the Castle and Priory, and Mount Harry. Return by road, *viâ* Falmer. 2. Across the Downs to Rottingdean, and thence to Newhaven. Keep along the bank of the Ouse to Lewes, and return by rail. 3. To the Devil's Dyke, and thence descend into the plains at Kingston. Visit Shoreham, and return by rail. 4. To Worthing, thence to Sompting, and descend into Lancing. Return by rail. 5. Keep northward to Patching. Cross the hills to Stanmer, and thence to Falmer. Walk over the Downs to Ovingdean, and return to Brighton by way of the race-course.]

BRANCH ROUTE—BRIGHTON TO NEWHAVEN.

The walk to Newhaven, along the crest of the glorious South Downs, is one not easily to be forgotten, but rather to be remembered as " a joy for ever." Their crisp green sward, their swelling lines of beauty, their shadowy *coombes* and *denes*, whether seen in the gray light of early morning, or reddening with the retiring glory of the sunset, have an inexpressible attraction—a charm and a character of their own. And from these lofty heights the eye surveys a wonderful expanse of country ; quiet leafy villages with a gray old church-tower or so ; a picturesque many-gabled house, dating from the stormy days of Tudor and Stuart ; broad reaches of verdurous pasture ; ample stretches of yellow cornfields ; a whirling, sweeping mill, on the brink of a bubbling rivulet ; a noble mansion, crowning a gentle knoll which rises above a mass of vigorous foliage. Then, too, far away to the south glimmers the broad mirror of the Channel ;—its rolling waves seem fixed in repose from the elevation at which we stand, and only a dim, faint echo of its music falls upon the attentive ear. If we descend to the shore by one of those gaps in the cliffs, always to be met with near a Coastguard station, we shall find a scarcely less interesting scene. Above us towers a wall of glittering chalk, 300 feet in height,—spotted with layers of flint which incline southward to the sea. Observe the broad masses of calcareous strata, 50 feet thick, in which are frequently found the bones and teeth of the fossil elephant,—brought hither, it may be, from a far off land by floating icebergs during some great natural convulsion in the pre-historic period. On the shore are frequently discovered fossil sponges of rare beauty, huge ammonites, and those lumps of black bitumen mixed with salt and sulphur, which are known as *stromballen*, or stream-balls,—the name given to them by the Early Flemish fishermen.

The epicure's delicacy, the *wheat-ear*, is an inhabitant of the Downs. The shepherds entrap him in this wise : they incise the turf in the shape of the letter T, cover over the hollow, and place at the mouth a horse-hair springe, into which the wheat-ear flutters at the slightest cry or movement, and is consequently caught. "Wheat-ears," says Fuller, "is a bird peculiar to this country—hardly found out of it. It is so called because fattest when the wheat is ripe, being no better than a lark, which it equalled in the fineness of the flesh, and far exceeded in the fatness thereof. The worst is, that being only seasonable in the heat of summer, and naturally larded with lumps of fat, it is soon subject to corrupt, so that (though abounding within 40 miles) London poulterers have no mind to meddle with them, which no care in carriage can keep from putrefaction. That palate-man shall pass in silence, who being seriously demanded his judgment concerning the abilities of a great lord, concluded him a man of very weak parts, ' because he saw him at a great feast feed on chickens when there were wheat-ears on the table.' "

The numerous *fairy-rings* and *hay-tracks* upon the green slopes of the Downs will not fail to attract the tourist's attention. It is now generally admitted that they originate in the growth of various species of *fungi*, but the Sussex shepherds believe them to be formed by the feet of dancing fairies, or, as they are locally called, *Pharisees*, who,

> " In their courses make that round
> In meadows and in marshes found,
> Of them so call'd the fairy ground,
> Of which they have the keeping"—(*Drayton*).

OVINGDEAN (Population 149), the sheep valley, has a picturesque little CHURCH, partly Norman in style, and partly Early English. The rectory, valued at £355, is in the patronage of the present incumbent.

ROTTINGDEAN (population, 1084) is one of the prettiest watering-places on the south coast, and lies in a sheltered hollow which opens pleasantly upon the sea. Its neat cottages are embowered in trim gardens. Its Early English CHURCH, dedicated to St. Margaret, is maintained in decorous neatness. Here, at a school kept by Dr. Hooker, the author of " The Caxtons" received his early education. Here, too, a band of marauders was bravely repulsed, in September 1377, by Prior John de Cariloco, of Lewes, and his retainers, though the priest militant was unfortunately taken prisoner.

The Earl of Abergavenny has the patronage of the vicarage, which is valued at £332 per annum.

☞ BALSDEAN, another hamlet sequestered in a hollow of the downs, lies about two miles inland. An ancient Decorated CHAPEL is now used as a barn. Remark its thatched roof.

The tourist, at 7 miles from Brighton, descends the hills to NEWHAVEN (population, 1358), lying in a deep valley, at the junction of the Ouse with the Channel. A swing-bridge is thrown across the river. The railway station is on the opposite bank, and communicates with a pier, whence the steamers for Dieppe start daily in connection with certain London trains. The harbour is held in considerable estimation from its position on the exposed coast of the Channel, and is defended by a battery on the hill above. The depth at the mouth in spring-tides varies from 18 to 20 feet ; in neap tides, from 13 to 15 feet. Two wooden piers protect the entrance, which is 106 feet in width.

Since the establishment of the Dieppe packet-service, Newhaven has risen into a place of some importance. The entries of coasting ships, *inwards,* average 280 vessels of 30,000 tons— *outwards,* 65 vessels, of 7000 tons ; of foreign vessels, *inwards,* 135 vessels of 20,000 tons, and *outwards,* 120 of 18,000 tons.

On a hill above the town—which consists of one long street, crossed by two smaller ones—stands the CHURCH, dedicated to 'St. Michael, a Roman building, with a nave, north aisle, central tower ornamented by a single spire, and apsidal chancel. The nave and aisle are of recent erection. An obelisk, near the graveyard, commemorates the loss of the war-brig, Brazen, stranded off the port, on the 6th of January 1860, with the loss of her commander and 104 men. Only one life was saved.

The rectory, valued at £186, is in the patronage of the Lord Chancellor.

It was at Newhaven Louis Philippe and his queen landed, as Mr. and Mrs. Smith, in 1840, after crossing from Triport in a small fishing-smack. Among those who welcomed him on his arrival was a Mr. Smith ; much to the astonishment of the deposed sovereign, who naïvely remarked, in ignorance of the myriads of Smiths existing in England—that " he thought he had heard the name before ! "

The passage from Newhaven to Dieppe is effected in about five hours. The steam-packets start according to the changes of the tide.

In the neighbourhood are some Celtic earthworks ; the nearest is an oval encampment on the summit of Castle Hill.

[Between Newhaven and Lewes are the Norman churches of SOUTHEASE (population, 102), and PIDDINGHOE (population, 253), which have a strong family-likeness, as Mr. Lower has pointed out, to the churches in Normandy. Piddinghoe, according to a local saying, is the place where "they shoe magpies." On the opposite bank of the Ouse are the villages of EAST TARRING (population 75), or Tarring-Neville ; HEIGHTON (population, 84), and DENTON (population, 195), commemorated by the jesters of the Downs as " Heighton, Denton, and Tarring all begin with an A." BISHOPSTONE (population, 328), which may be easily reached from Newhaven, has a remarkable CHURCH. The tower rises in four stages, each gradually diminishing in diameter. In the first and second stories is a single round-headed window ; in the third, a circular moulded window ; in the fourth, a double window with balusters. The tower-arch is low, but there are traces of an earlier and loftier one. A small spire surmounts the tower. The chancel is in two divisions, with Norman and English arches. The present windows are all English. Observe the curious porch, and the stone dial and crown over the door, lettered with the name of some Saxon king, Eadric, who was probably its builder. A stone slab, inscribed with a cross, bearing in circular compartments the Agnus Dei, and the symbol of two doves drinking, should be carefully examined. It appears to be the work of some Norman sculptor, who, however, was not ignorant of the spirit and influences of Italian Art.

A monument in the chancel commemorates the Rev. *John Hurdis*, Oxford Professor of Poetry, and an agreeable didactic rhymester, d. 1801. The epitaph is by Hayley.

The vicarage, valued at £88, is in the patronage of the Bishop of London.]

BRANCH ROUTE from BRIGHTON to THREE BRIDGES.

[By the London and South Coast Railway.]

Let us fancy ourselves borne, with all the speed of a Brighton express train, across the Preston viaduct, scarcely able to distinguish the features of the magnificent landscape which spreads away to the eastward, and afterwards through the PATCHAM TUNNEL, 2 furlongs and 2½ chains in length, taking its name from the pretty village of PATCHAM (population, 490), which lies to our right, upon the old London and Brighton road. We then run through a deep cutting, and enter the CLAYTON TUNNEL (cost £90,000, and 1 mile 2 furlongs 4 chains in length), piercing the chalk mass of the Downs, and opening out upon the meadows of KEYMER (population, 1001), whose Saxon and Norman Church lies about 1 mile east of HASSOCK'S GATE (*hassock*, a small wood or coppice) STATION. The curacy of CLAYTON (population, 645), is attached to the rectory of KEYMER, in the patronage of Brazennose Coll., Oxon.

☞ Beyond Keymer is situated, on the slope of the hills, DITCHLING (population, 1069), whose CHURCH is an eminently interesting structure. The nave and aisle are Transition-Norman ; the tower, chancel, and transepts, Early English. The vicarage, valued at £200, is in the Lord Chancellor's gift.

Passing through the village, we climb the steep and lofty Downs to their highest elevation, DITCHLING BEACON, about 858 feet above the sea level. What a landscape spreads beneath and around ! The rich and leafy plains of the Weald, the vales and groves of southern Sussex, and the bright waters of the boundless sea, lie before us in a light as magical as that which floats over a picture by Turner. The remains of a Roman encampment crown the summit, and recall to the memory the grand old times when yonder rich and fertile Weald was an impenetrable forest, when tidal waters seethed and fretted in the broad valley of the Cuse, when Lucullus built his villa on the grassy slopes, and Aglaia wandered in love-musing upon the pebbly shore. The Roman road up the ascent, trod 1500 years ago by the stalwart legionaries of imperial Rome, may still in many places be distinctly followed. Here, on this breezy peak, they kept watch and ward over the subject-land, and here, it may be—as their gaze rested upon the distant channel—they dreamed of the blue skies and myrtle bowers of their beautiful Italia.

☞ West of Hassock's Gate, and nearly 3 miles from the station, on a clayey soil, and belted round with oak, beech, and ash, lies HURST-PIER-POINT (population, 2219),—the wood (*hurst*) of the Pier-points,—its Early Norman lords. The CHURCH was carefully restored and rebuilt, in the Decorated style, by the late Sir Charles Barry, some twenty years ago, and its interior is one of unusual interest. Observe the defaced effigy of a templar, *temp.* Henry III., in the south transept, and another of a nameless knight, *temp.* Edward III., in the north aisle. The view from the well-kept churchyard extends to the Surrey hills on the north, Ashdown forest on the north-east, the South Downs on the south, and the forest ridge on the east.

DANNY PARK (W. J. Campion, Esq.), the seat of the Dacres, into whose hands it passed from the Pierripoint family, lies under the hills, south of the village, a pleasant breadth of green sward and venerable oaks, and an Elizabethan brick mansion, dating from 1595. WOLSTANBURY HILL (Wolstan's byrig?), in the rear of the house, is crowned with a Celtic encampment of a circular form.

To the left of the road, between the village and the station, stands ST. JOHN'S COLLEGE, an educational establishment in connection with St. Nicholas' College, Shoreham, providing board and education for the sons of farmers at £23, or £18 : 18s. per annum. It can accommodate 300 boarders, and is carefully superintended by able and zealous masters, under Episcopal supervision.

The rectory, valued at £1000 per annum, is in the patronage of N. Borrer, Esq.

Resuming our railway journey, we speedily pass the Burgess Hill Station, 41½ miles, and there the point of divergence of the Lewes line. To the right may be descried the village of WIVELSFIELD (population, 608)—*i.e.*, Wifl's field—with its Early English Church, and masses of trees, and smiling meadows. The perpetual curacy, worth £94, is in the gift of R. Tanner, Esq. Just beyond is MORE HALL, Mr. Tanner's ancient and picturesque family seat.

Crossing Hayward's Heath, and the main road from Cuckfield to Maresfield, we reach the HAYWARD'S HEATH STATION, 37½ miles from London, and 22¼ miles from Brighton. About 2 miles to our left lies

☞ CUCKFIELD (population, 3196 ; *Inn :* The King's Head), a busier town now than in the pre-railway period, and situated in a charming country, all cornfield, and pasture, and grove, and richly cultivated lands. Its goodly Early English CHURCH (with a Perpendicular tower), contains some interesting memorials, and monuments by Flaxman and Westmacott. The vicarage, valued at £613, is in the Bishop of Chichester's patronage. There is a district church, dedicated to St. Mark, at Staplefield Common.

CUCKFIELD PLACE (W. Sergison, Esq.) is situated west of the town, and is not only interesting as a fine Elizabethan mansion, but as having suggested to Ainsworth the "Rookwood Hall" of his striking romance. "The supernatural occurrence," he says, "forming the groundwork of one of the ballads which I have made the harbinger of doom to the house of Rookwood, is ascribed, by popular superstition, to a family resident in Sussex, upon whose estate the fatal tree (a gigantic lime, with mighty arms and huge girth of trunk) is still carefully preserved. Cuckfield Place, to which this singular piece of timber is attached, is, I may state, for the benefit of the curious, the real Rookwood Hall ; for I have not drawn upon imagination, but upon memory, in describing the seat and domains of that fated family. The general features of the venerable structure, several of its chambers, the old garden, and, in particular, the noble park, with its spreading prospects, its picturesque bits of the hall, 'like bits of Mrs. Radcliffe' (as the poet Shelley once observed of the same scene), its deep glades, through which the deer come lightly tripping down, its uplands, slopes, brooks, brakes, coverts, and groves are carefully delineated." In the avenue that winds towards the house the Doom-Tree still stands :—

" And whether gale or calm prevail, or threatening cloud hath fled,
By hand of Fate, predestinate, a limb that tree will shed ;
A verdant bough, untouched, I trow, by axe or tempest's breath,
To Rookwood's head, an omen dread of fast approaching death."

In this neighbourhood are OCKENDON HOUSE, TYE, SLOUGH, and BOARD HILL, all seats of some importance and considerable antiquity ; and LEIGH POND (50 acres in extent), a fen haunt of the wild-fowl during the winter months.

[On the Croydon road, about 1¼ m. north-east of the station, is situated LIND-FIELD (population, 1814). HORSTED-KEYNES is 3½ m. north-east ; FLETCHING, 6¼ m. east ; BOLNEY, 2¼ m. south-west.]

We resume our journey through a country side of exquisite luxuriance, and in a few minutes cross the valley of the Ouse by means of the OUSE VIADUCT, a magnificent specimen of engineering skill, 1437 feet long, and supported by 37 arches, each 30 feet in span, and about 60 feet high. It was constructed at a cost of £58,000, and is one of the finest in the world. Noble prospects of the surrounding landscapes are here commanded.

At 4½ miles from Hayward's Heath, 26¼ miles from Brighton, and 33¾ miles from London, we arrive at BALCOMBE (population, 851), with its Early English CHURCH, and quiet village lying at the foot of the clay hills, on the southern skirts of the great Tilgate Forest. This district was formerly the delta of a mighty river, and offers to the persevering geologist the remains of enormous reptiles, palms and tree-ferns of an oriental character. Dr. Mantell here discovered the first bones of the huge Iguanodon, and the earliest traces of the mighty Hylæo-saurus. Tilgate Forest covers about 1500 acres, and presents some pleasant woodland pictures at various points. WAKEHURST PLACE (Sir Alexander Cockburn) is situated 2 miles east. SLANGHAM (population, 1418), with SLANGHAM PLACE, 3 miles west. The latter is a Tudor house of some interest, the ancient seat of the Coverts, whose landed supremacy, in the days of Elizabeth and her successor, extended " from Southwark to the sea." SLANG-HAM CHURCH is Early English, and contains some richly-coloured glass, and brasses for *John Covert*, d. 1503 ; and *Richard Covert*, d. 1547, and his three wives ; *Jane Covert* d. 1586.

The rectory, valued at £460, is in the gift of W. Sergison, Esq.

After leaving the Balcombe Station we quietly enter the BALCOMBE TUNNEL, 6 furlongs and 3 chains in length. The line then skirts the eastern boundary of Tilgate Forest, and crossing an open country, reaches the THREE BRIDGES Junction Station, so named from the intersection of the main roads by the river Mole. These branch lines diverge to EAST GRINSTEAD. 7 miles east, and CRAWLEY, 1½ mile, HORSHAM, 8½ miles west.

☞ The village of WORTH (population, 2475) lies about '1½ mile east of the station, and should be visited for the sake of its curious CHURCH, the only perfect ground-plan of a Saxon church extant in England. It is seated on a knoll, and embowered in trees, and approached by an ancient lich-gate which opens into a quiet and picturesque yard. The plan of the building is cruciform, —the chancel and nave intersected by north and south transepts. The chancel is apsidal. The walls, of roughly-hewn stones and rubble, are obscured with modern plaster. Round the building and half-way between the ground and the roof, is carried a string-course of stone, and bands of stone at various places diversify the surface. On a double course of stone rise pilasters of irregular long and short work, which support the string-course. The outer buttresses are recent, and the west and south sides are Decorated insertions. In the window over the west door are the De War-renne arms. The transept arches are unornamented ; the chancel-arch has a rude moulding. A small Saxon window remains in the east wall of the north transept. The font is ancient, and consists of two basins, one placed above the other.

This interesting church may have been built (as a writer in the Sussex Archæological Collections suggests) by a Saxon " earl " who had settled down in the wild forest of Worth—some traces of which still linger in the high ground—for the sake of hunting the deer. It afterwards belonged to the barony of Lewes, and passed from the De Warrennes in 1347 to the Fitzalans.

The rectory, valued at £608, is in the patronage of the Rev. G. C. Bethune.

At Worth, and in 'Tilgate Forest, flourishes the *scyphophorus microphyllus*, a lichen of great rarity ; *rhynchospora alba, heliocharis acicularis, carex curta*, and *epilobium angustifolium*. The sandstone dug here, " of a white, pale fawn, or yellow colour," often affords the leaves and stems of ferns and other plants.

After leaving the Three Bridges' Station, a ride of about 2 miles carries us over the county-border into Surrey. We cross the Mole, and at 25½ miles from London reach the Horley Station. But this portion of the line will be found described in the " Guide to the History, Topography, and Antiquities of Surrey," issued by the publishers of the present volume.

RRANCH ROUTE—BRIGHTON TO HORSHAM.

[A coach leaves Brighton for Horsham every Monday, Wednesday, and Friday.

The road at first skirts the base of the South Downs, and passes the sequestered village of PRESTON (population, 625)—*i. e.*, Priest's town, because it formed a part of the possessions of the see of Chichester—where the little Early English CHURCH, dedicated to St. Peter, and consisting of nave, chancel, and tower, is worthy of a patient examination. On the walls of the nave are some rude frescoes, in red and yellow, of the murder of Thomas à Becket, shewing the four knights, and the monk Grim protecting the Archbishop with his arm. St. Michael, with his scales, is figured on the other side. In the nave lies the tomb-stone of *Francis Cheynel*, D.D., d. 1665, the bitter antagonist of Chillingworth, whose grave he profaned with his unseemly violence. Douglas, the erudite author of the "Nenia Britannica," and the father of Sussex archæology, lies interred in the churchyard.

The vicarage, valued at £306, is in the patronage of the Bishop of Chichester. Hove, and its two churches, St. Mark's and St. John the Baptist's, are within this parish. Anne of Cleves resided here for a short period.

From this point HOLLINGSBURY CASTLE (2 miles north), a square camp, five acres in extent ; WHITE HAWK HILL, a triple entrenchment, near the Brighton race-course, three quarters of a mile in circumference, and the camps on Ditchling Beacon may be visited, as the three points of a triangle which commanded the sea-coast, and overlooked the passes of the Weald.

The tourist should now leave the high road and ascend the downs to the DEVIL'S DYKE (5½ miles from Brighton), a remarkable natural fosse, steep, abrupt, and of unusual depth (300 feet), which looks as if the Titans had excavated it as a defence for some enormous stronghold. The legend attached to it is curious : —the Devil, or, as the Sussex hinds more sympathizingly call him, the Poor Man, wroth at the number of churches which sprang up yearly in this neighbourhood, resolved to dig a trench from this point down to the sea, and so to inundate the whole country side. But as he was toiling by night with assiduous energy, he was descried by an old woman from the cottage window, who held up a candle that she might the better comprehend his design, and frightening the devil into the belief that it was the sunrise, he immediately disappeared. When he found out his error, he was too ashamed of his folly to return, and the Dyke to this day remains—a witness to an old woman's curiosity and the devil's discomfiture !

On the brow of the hill beyond this immense verdurous fosse, the Romans formed, or rather adopted what the British formed, an oval encampment, defended by a wide ditch and huge vallum, about one mile in circumference. They also rendered the sides of the Dyke more precipitous, cutting them down at an angle of 45°.

A pleasant "hostelry," where reasonable "creature-comforts" may be obtained, stands on the brink of the down—a point from which the tourist will enjoy the most magnificent prospect in this part of Sussex. "If Nature had endeavoured to create a surprise for man, she could not have done it more effectually than by leading him over the gradual ascent of a vast down, and then suddenly sinking the earth 600 or 700 feet in a bold escarpment, until it formed a plain almost limitless to the eye, and rich in summer foliage and yellow corn. For miles on each side the Downs descend into this plain in an almost perpendicular manner. If you throw yourself down on the edge of this fearful descent on a fine summer's afternoon, and strain your eyes over the wonderful plain beneath, you gain a sensation of space that scarce another landscape in England can afford. The valley before you stretches north-east to south-west a space of no less than 120 miles, commencing at Maidstone, and only terminating at the Hampshire Downs, near Portsmouth. To the north and north-west the eye reaches, it is affirmed, but we confess to some misgivings, as far as Croydon and Norwood ; no fewer than six counties being rolled out, in this gigantic map, at the spectator's feet, and these, for the most part, garden or park-like in culture and appearance. Those who are curious about the matter may, it is said, count upwards of sixty churches dotted over the wide landscape. Turning to the southward, the spectator traces distinctly the extensive bay sweeping between Beachy Head and Selsey Bill, with Brighton in the centre. Looking over the ocean to the west, the Culver Cliffs of the Isle of Wight are, on a clear day, seen distinctly by the naked eye, although upwards of forty miles distant ; and a vast expanse of ocean stretches before you"—(*Thorne*).

Descending into the high road, beneath the Downs, we arrive at POYNINGS (population, 261), where the Perpendicular CHURCH, dedicated to the Holy Trinity, with its central tower, transepts, aisle, and nave, will remind us of that of ALFRESTON (see p.508), and induce us to accept Mr. Hussey's conclusion, that both were built by the same architect. The font is octagonal, and there are three sedilia in the chancel. The rectory, valued at £297, is in the gift of the representative of the late Viscount Montague.

NEWTIMBER (population, 161) lies about one mile east of the main road. The CHURCH, dedicated to St. John, has some good painted glass in the east window, and two grave-slabs despoiled of their brasses. NEWTIMBER PLACE (Lady Gordon) is a moated mansion of venerable age. To the north is situated DANNY PARK (W. T. Campion, Esq.), already described (see p. 560).

Beyond the 48th milestone (from London) we pass the parliamentary boundary of West Sussex, and one and a half mile further reach WOODMANCOTE (population, 326), in a well-wooded but thinly-populated district. The tree-embowered CHURCH is Early English, with nave, chancel, and turret. The rectory is in the Lord Chancellor's gift, and valued at £369.

[About two miles north lies ALBOURNE (population, 377), on a *bourne,* or branch of the Adur—it was formerly in the hands of the Juxon family, and ALBOURNE PLACE (Miss Long) is reputed to have been built by the good prelate who soothed the last hours of Charles the First.—The rectory, worth £225, is in the gift of John Goring, Esq.]

At nine miles from Brighton we gain the hill whereon the village of HENFIELD (population, 1669) clusters, some of its cottages quaint enough in aspect to merit a place in the sketcher's note book. The CHURCH, dedicated to St. Peter, is chiefly Perpendicular. The nave and south aisle are separated by elongated arches. There is a brass, on an altar tomb, for *Thomas Bisshopp,* d. 1552, and an epitaph upon *Meneleb Raynsford,* d. 1627, aged nine, of so ludicrous a character in its combination of the Pagan and Christian as to merit quotation :

" Great Jove hath lost his Ganymede, I know,
Which made him seek another here below ;

> And finding none, not one like unto this,
> Hath ta'en him hence unto eternal bliss.
> Cease, then, for thy dear Meneleb to weep;
> God's darling was too good for thee to keep;
> But rather joy in this great favour given,
> A child on earth is made a saint in heaven."

The Bishop of Chichester has the presentation to the vicarage, which is valued at £412 per annum.

At Chestlem's Bridge we cross a tributary of the Adur, and passing through a fertile country reach SHERMANBURY (population, 458), upon another branch of the same river. SHERMANBURY PLACE (S. Challen, Esq.), was erected, about fifty years ago, on the site of an Elizabethan mansion. The CHURCH, dedicated to St. Giles, is a small Early English building, close to the house. It contains a Perpendicular font, and some good modern painted glass. The Challen family hold the advowson of the rectory, worth £299 per annum.

A little to the west of the Place stand the venerable remains of the old moated mansion of EWHURST, the ancient seat of the Peverels. The arched gateway, with its pointed roof, dates from the reign of Edward I.

An open country lies before us, meadows and corn-fields spreading on either hand, and in due time we arrive at COW-FOLD (population, 975), whose very name savours of abundant and fertile pastures. The CHURCH stands on the left side of the road. The chancel is Edwardian, the nave and south aisle Tudor, and the tower at the west end Late Perpendicular. It contains a very fine brass for *Thomas Nelond*, prior of Lewes, d. 1433, with figures of the Virgin and Child, St. Pancras trampling on a sword-brandishing knight, and St. Thomas à Becket with mitre and crosier.

The vicarage, valued at £452, is in the patronage of the Bishop of London.

Our road now enters the woodlands, and passes " under the shade of melancholy boughs." We turn aside from the highway to visit the leafy hamlet of NUTHURST (population, 727), and as we penetrate the shady groves of Highhurst—a portion of the once extensive forest of St. Leonard's—from the hills we look back upon the fair landscapes of southern Sussex, bounded afar off

by the glowing waters of the Channel. Near NUTHURST LODGE
(J. Nelthorpe, Esq.) are the ivy-shrouded remains of an old moated
mansion, and a spring lined with large blocks of stone, and called
the Wren's Well. The CHURCH, dedicated to St. Andrew, is a
Decorated building, with panelled ceiling, and remains of ancient
painted glass. The Bishop of London is the patron of the rectory, valued at £480.

We regain the high road at Monk's Gate, and 3 miles further,
reach the ancient town of HORSHAM (population, 6056. *Inns :*
King's Head, Anchor), so named from *hors-ham*, the horses' meadow, and not, as some speculative antiquarians would pretend,
from Horsa, the Saxon chieftain, whom they slay at this place.
The town stands on the Adur, in the heart of much agreeable and
well-wooded scenery, and consists of two main streets intersecting
each other at right angles—a pleasant green to the north, and an
open area to the south wherein the court house is situated. Its
markets for corn, cattle, and poultry are held in high repute.
Until the Reform Act of 1832 it returned two members to Parliament ; it is now restricted to one.

The lordship of the borough has descended from William de
Braose to the Duke of Norfolk. To one of the wealthy and
powerful members of the De Braose family may be ascribed the
foundation of the CHURCH, which is a large and venerable Early
English building, dedicated to St. Mary, and consists of a nave,
chancel, two aisles, and lofty tower surmounted by a spire. The
east window is Perpendicular, and has five lights. There is a
note-worthy memorial to *Thomas, Lord Braose,* d. 1396, representing him in the armour of the period. Unfortunately it is
much mutilated. An altar-tomb of Sussex marble belongs, it is
said, to *Thomas, Lord Hoo,* Chancellor of France to Henry VI.,
d. 1455. A finely sculptured effigy and tomb of pure white
marble, commemorate *Elizabeth Delves,* d. 1654. Two brasses
remain,—one of a priest in his cope, the other of a man in a
furred gown and a woman in appropriate dress,—but their inscriptions have disappeared.

The vicarage, valued at £751, is in the patronage of the
Archbishop of Canterbury. The vicar himself presents to the
curacy of ST. MARK'S, and the perpetual curacy of SOUTHWATER,
(1½ mile south), two churches of recent erection.

The GRAMMAR SCHOOL, adjoining the churchyard, was founded

in 1532, by Richard Collier, for the support of a master and usher, and the instruction of sixty scholars. The *worthies* of Horsham are, Nicholas Hortresham, or Horsham, a physician of eminence in the reign of Henry VI. ; and Barnaby Lintot, born in 1675, the publisher of Pope's " Iliad," and Gay's " Trivia," and prose and verse by other " eminent hands."

South of the town lies DURNE PARK (C. G. Eversfield, Esq.) The ivy-decorated mansion stands on an elevated site, and overlooks a considerable portion of Sussex and Surrey. It is approached from the London road by a fine avenue of beech-trees. One mile east is COOLHURST (C. S. Dickens, Esq.), a picturesque Elizabethan house, with gabled roof and mullioned windows, partly rebuilt about thirty years ago. There are some remains of the ancient edifice at CHESWORTH, half a mile south-east, the residence of the De Braoses, lords of Bramber.

From Horsham we may conveniently penetrate into ST. LEONARD'S FOREST, a tract of about 9000 acres, which takes its name from a chapel, dedicated to St. Leonard, formerly situated in the north-eastern recesses. A great portion of the forest is included in the northern division of the parish of Beeding. It was formerly held by the De Braose family, but is now divided amongst various proprietors. The principal avenue contains nearly 16,000 trees, not one, however, of more than eighty years' growth, their predecessors having been uprooted in a violent storm,—is 1½ mile in length, and, from an unhappy athlete who ran the distance for a wager, and fell dead at the moment of victory, is called MIKE MILL'S RACE. The pleasant vistas in the wide woodland, through columned aisles of pine, and larch, and oak, and beech, are numerous, and there are many delightful little dells, and a running stream or so lends life, and light, and music to the scene. Nightingales occasionally fill the shadowy arcades with their " most musical, most melancholy " song, and disprove Andrew Borde's assertion that " they will never singe within the precincts of the foreste, as divers keepers and other credible parsons did show me."

" The violet of a legend" blows, as one might easily conclude, in these obscure and dreamy glades. The daring horseman who penetrates their mirky depths at night must prepare to ride with a headless phantom, which will not quit him until the forest shadows are past. St. Leonard engaged here in a fearful contest with a " mighty worm," struggling with him in many places before he conquered him, and clumps of lilies sprang up wherever the saint's pure blood was spilled—a sort of allegory, we fancy, if read aright, and a dim reflection evidently of the old "St. Michael and the Dragon" story.   As late as 1614, a dragon, we are told, haunted the forest glens ; and " a discourse" concerning this " strange monstrous serpent" was printed and published in London by one John Trundle.   " There is always left in his track or path," says the writer, " a glutinous and shine matter (as by a small similitude we may perceive in a snail's), which is very corrupt and offensive to the senses ; the serpent is reputed to be 9 feete, or rather more, in length, and shaped almost in the forme of an axeltree of a cart, a quantitie of thicknesse in the middest, and somewhat smaller at both ends.   The former part, which he shootes forth as a necke, is supposed to be an elle long, with a white ring, as it were, of scales about it.   There are likewise on either side of him discovered two greate bunches so big as a large foote-ball, and, as some think, will in time grow to wings ; but God, I hope, will so defend the poor people in the neighbourhood that he shall be destroyed before he grow so fledge."

Within a compass of three or four miles, near the south boundary of the forest, the Arun, Adur, and Ouse have their source ; and not far from Coolhurst are two of " the hammer ponds" formerly the indispensable adjuncts of the Sussex iron works.

☞ At FAYGATE, 3 miles north-east of Horsham, there is a station on the Horsham branch of the London and South Coast Railway.   It adjoins the large estate of Lord St. Leonards, who derives his title from his property in this neighbourhood.

About 3 miles further, and the railway traveller will see on his left the village of IFIELD (population, 1112), seated on a broad and pleasant green, and surrounded by a vigorous growth of oaks.   It was once the seat of a considerable iron trade, of which the disused " hammer ponds" are now the sole remains. Its CHURCH, dedicated to St. Margaret, is partly Early English and partly Decorated.   There are two tombs under the nave arches, bearing respectively the effigies of a cross-legged knight, and a lady in Edwardian costume, which are reputed to be those of Sir *John de Ifield*, and his wife, d. 1317.   The vicarage (£180) is in the gift of Mrs. Blaker.

[RUSPER (population, 533) lies about 4 miles to the east of Ifield.   The road across the hills is a pleasant one, and commands some good views of the Weald of

Surrey, Leith Hill, and the country about Dorking. Gervaise, Archbishop of Canterbury, founded here a Benedictine nunnery, *temp.* Richard I., of which there are
no remains. The farm of NORMANS has been held by a family named Multon, ever
since the Norman Conquest. "The present proprietor has the chest brought over
the water, as he terms it, by his ancestor, the Norman, who first settled at Rusper"
—(*Horsfield*).

The Early English CHURCH, dedicated to St. Mary, a small and antique building,
contains a brass for *John de Kyngesfold*, and *Agnes*, his wife ; and another for *Thomas
Challoner*, d. 1532, and *Margaret*, his wife. Mrs. Greene is the patron of the rectory,
valued at £202 yearly.]

We now arrive at the CRAWLEY STATION, adjoining the old
posting-town of CRAWLEY (population, 447), now shorn of all
its glories. The Brighton four-in-hand no longer rattles through
its streets, and instead of the blithe horn of " the guard," a shrill
railway whistle awakens its echoes. The neighbourhood is very
pleasant, and Tilgate Forest lies within a moderate distance.
On the high road stands a venerable elm, a well-known object,
which arrests the eye of the stranger at once by its tall and
straight stem, which ascends to the height of 70 feet, and by the
fantastic ruggedness of its widely-spreading roots. The trunk is
perforated to the very top, measuring 61 feet in circumference at
the ground, and 35 feet round the inside at 2 feet from the base."
An old and time-worn oak in the centre of the village is a remarkable object.

CRAWLEY CHURCH is chiefly Decorated in style, and has
recently undergone a careful restoration. One of the tie beams of
the roof is lettered—

" Man yr wele bewar ; for warldly good maketh man blynde.
Bewar for whate comyth behinde."

The living is a rectory, valued at £116. At VINE COTTAGE,
near the Station, resides Mark Lemon, Esq., the well-known editor
of " Punch."

After leaving Crawley a few minutes' ride brings us to the
junction-station at THREE BRIDGES.

MAIN ROUTE RESUMED—BRIGHTON TO SHOREHAM.

The road from Brighton to Shoreham lies along the coast, in
sight and hearing of the glorious sea. We cross a level of great
fertility, the downs rising up to the northward like a formidable
bulwark, and descend a slight incline into the valley of the

Adur. To our right we pass, in succession, HANKLETON (population, 57), a small hamlet 1 mile west, with an Early English
CHURCH, and a Tudor manor-house—the rectory (£209) in the
gift of Earl Amherst ; PORTSLADE (population, 733), where
there is an Early English CHURCH, dedicated to St. Nicholas,—the
vicarage (£171) in the Lord Chancellor's patronage; SOUTH-
WICK (population, 1190), 5 miles from Brighton, a populous village,
whose church, dedicated to St. Michael, is large and handsome ;
and KINGSTON-BY-SEA (population, 153), where goods are for-
warded for the Shoreham shipping.   " The tide once flowed by
this place, and brought large vessels as far as Bramber, 3 or 4
miles higher ; but the navigation has long since been choked up.
Before Old Shoreham is a marshy tract watered by the river
Adur ; its channel once ran on this side, but about thirty years
ago [1750] was diverted towards New Shoreham, not only for the
purpose of serving the harbour, but for gaining much good land
from the marshes.   As a proof that the sea had once occupied
this tract, anchors have been found very far from the present
shore"—(*Pennant*).   The CHURCH is uninteresting, and is but a
portion of the original edifice.   The Wyndham family have the
patronage of the living (a rectory, valued at £200).

The railway is carried across the Shoreham flat by a viaduct,
the Adur Viaduct, 550 yards in length.   OLD SHOREHAM lies to
the right, just beyond the Portsmouth road ; NEW SHOREHAM
occupies the banks of the Adur,—one long, squalid, and winding
street, irregularly crossed by other streets as squalid and " fish-
like," and chiefly inhabited by ship-builders, ship-chandlers,
fishermen, and those who go down to the sea in ships.

NEW SHOREHAM (population, 2590. *Inns :* Dolphin, Surrey Arms, Buckingham Arms, and Swiss Cottage) rose into importance
as Old Shoreham, owing to the gradual silting-up of its harbour,
fell into decay.   The ancient haven, formed by the estuary of the
Adur, was early regarded as of some maritime importance, from
its position with respect to the coast of Normandy, and to defend
this important pass a Norman stronghold was raised at BRAMBER,
up the river, just as Lewes commanded the Ouse, and Arundel
the Arun.   King John landed here in 1199, immediately after
the decease of Richard Cœur-de-Lion..   He also embarked from
hence in the following June on his way to France.   In 1346,
when Edward III. fitted out two large fleets of 706 ships, Old

Shoreham contributed 26, whilst London furnished but 25, Southampton 21, and Hull only 16. But early in the fifteenth century the sea made rapid encroachments upon its insecure marshes—the port was destroyed—and the town had fallen into so sad a decline, that in 1432 it could but number 36 inhabitants.

It was long before brighter fortunes dawned upon the natives of Shoreham, but, by degrees, a new town sprang up along the banks of the Adur, and in 1724, the population had increased to 640 souls, chiefly employed in " the building and fitting up of ships." The attention of the Government was at length directed to the condition of the harbour, and considerable improvements were effected. The entrance, however, continued to the eastward, at the rate of a mile in forty years, until the present substantial piers were erected by Clegram, in 1819, and a species of canal fenced in. The mouth is now 218 feet wide, and at spring tides has about twenty feet depth of water, fourteen feet at neap, and only four feet at low. A light-house has been erected for the convenience of mariners. The principal imports are corn, grain, coals, and Irish produce; the export, timber. About 1100 vessels, of 115,000 tons, enter the harbour yearly.

The handsome SUSPENSION BRIDGE, built in 1833 at the expense of the Duke of Norfolk, by Clarke, the architect of the Hammersmith Bridge, is not only an ornament but an advantage to the town. It shortens the distance between Brighton and Worthing by 2 miles.

The CUSTOM HOUSE was built in 1830, and designed by Smirke. Two Hospitals, and a Priory of Carmelite Friars, are said to have existed here, but Dryasdust himself could not discover the slightest trace of either. The timber bridge over the Adur (*dwr*, water), at Old Shoreham, 500 feet long and 12 feet wide, was erected in 1781.

The principal historical association of Shoreham is the escape of Charles II. after the defeat at Worcester, and his preservation at Boscobel. Crossing the country, attended by Lord Wilmot, he reached Brighton on the evening of October 14, 1651, and passed the night at the George (now the King's Head) Inn, in West Street. Early on the following morning they set out for Shoreham, where Captain Nicholas Tattersall had moored his bark, and when the tide served, effected their embarkation undetected. On the same day (October 15th) the Earl of Derby, one of Charles's stoutest adherents, was executed at Bolton.

The Churches, both at Old and New Shoreham, possess an unusual interest for the archæologist.

OLD SHOREHAM CHURCH (¾ mile west) is an Early Norman church, cruciform in plan, and " remarkable for the small number of windows, and the consequent darkness of the nave ; as also for possessing on the tie-beams of the chancel the tooth-moulding which is very rarely found carved in wood." The central tower is supported by four enriched circular arches of conspicuous beauty. An oblong window in the south transept has ·a zigzag moulding. Mr. Ferrey has " restored " this interesting edifice with commendable care—The vicarage, valued at £458, is in the gift of Magdalene College, Oxford.

NEW SHOREHAM CHURCH was probably erected about 1100. It contains some Norman portions, and additions in Transition-Norman and Early English. " When entire it was a stately and capacious edifice of a cruciform shape, having a tower 83 feet high, rising from the centre of the cross. The nave has been long destroyed, and what remains consists of a choir, with side aisles, transept, and tower. The walls of the choir, now used as the parish church, rise considerably higher than those of the transept ; two massive flying buttresses support the upper part "— (*Horsfield*). The windows in the aisles are semicircular ; in the south side they are of a later date. The choir is divided into five bays by Early English arches, springing from columns whose richly foliated capitals should receive a careful examination. The exterior mouldings of the arches are similarly enriched. The east end has a triple lancet window, surmounting three semicircular Norman windows. The transept and the tower are Norman and Transition-Norman. There is a brass of the time of Edward IV.

The vicarage, valued at £127, is in the patronage of Magdalene College, Oxford.

BRANCH ROUTE FROM SHOREHAM TO HORSHAM.

[A branch line of the Brighton Railway, to connect the Chichester line with the Horsham and Petworth branch, is projected. It will embrace much the same tract of country as is hereinunder described.]

As we ascend the Downs from Old Shoreham to Bramber, two quiet, secluded, but picturesque villages may be discerned in the valley beneath, and on the west bank of the Adur—COOMBES and ST. BOTOLPH'S.

COOMBES (population, 72), whose situation is indicated by its name, lies in a hollow, from which, on every side, rise the verdurous hills. A thick environment of trees is about it. Its CHURCH is Early English, and would, perhaps, accommodate, in an emergency, 150 persons. The Wyndham family hold the patronage of the rectory, which is valued at £201 per annum.

ST. BOTOLPH'S (population, 55) lies upon a ridge of chalk, which slopes somewhat abruptly into the valley of the Adur. The church is small, consisting of a nave, chancel, and low tower. The vicarage has long been annexed to the rectory of Bramber.

And it is at BRAMBER (population, 130), 5 miles from Shoreham, that, crossing the river, we next arrive. Bramber, the Saxon fortress (*Brynamburh*), the Norman stronghold, the considerable market-town, the corrupt parliamentary borough, the quiet old-world village—for such are the mutations it has undergone. Here, on the hill, against whose base the tidal waters of the Adur fretted, the Saxon kings, probably on the site of a Roman encampment, erected a castle, which commanded the narrow pass. After the conquest, castle and barony were bestowed upon William de Braose, the builder of the massive fortress whose scanty ruins still excite the tourist's admiration. It occupied an area of three acres (560 feet by 280), on the brink of a steep abrupt spur of chalk which jutted out into the morasses of the Adur. On the west, south, and north, the castle was defended by a stout vallum and deep fosse, on the east the river-marshes were sufficient protection. Only a fragment of the barbican tower, and some crumbling stones, remain as the solemn " Hic jacet " of the once powerful race of De Braose.

Beneath the castle ruins stands the old Norman Church, dedicated to St. Nicholas, the patron saint of the Anglo-Normans. It consists of a nave and chancel, divided by a Norman arch, but has evidently been of larger proportions. Magdalene College, Oxon, has the patronage of the rectory, which is valued at £160.

STEYNING (population, 1464. *Inn :* the White Horse)— from *stean*, a stone—a Roman *via*, or Stane Street, having formerly connected Arundel with Dorking, lies about half a mile beyond Bramber. An omnibus runs between it and Shoreham thrice a-week.

The tide anciently rose as high as Steyning, whose harbour was the well-known PORTUS CATHMANNI. It stands at the foot of a hill—one wide street running north-west, from which another diverges in a north-easterly direction to the Church. The chief traffic is in cattle, a market being held once a fortnight.

The ancient CHURCH (dedicated to St. Andrew) was founded by St. Cuthman, a saint whose life was one long series of miracles. When, as a youth, appointed to the care of his father's sheep, he defied all hostile influences, and saved himself " a world of trouble" by drawing around them a mysterious circle, into which none could break. He travelled with his widowed mother into " the far east," wheeling her in a sort of barrow, whose cords snapping asunder he made use of some elder twigs. At the expedient some haymakers sillily laughed, and lo ! the rain ever afterwards descended upon their fields when the hay was ready for the garner. At Steyning the elder twigs broke, and there he consequently resolved to locate himself. Having built a hut, he erected a wooden church, where he regularly worshipped, and where he was interred. To his grave in due time flocked the wayfaring devout, and around the little timbered sanctuary a town speedily arose, and St. Cuthman became a word of love and reverence for all the country side. The Saxon Ethelwulf, king Alfred's father, was afterwards buried here (?), and Edward the Confessor bestowed the church on the Benedictine Abbey of Fécamp (in Normandy), whose monks established a small cell.

The present CHURCH probably occupies the site of Cuthman's building, and is purely Norman, with additions in the Early English style. It appears to have been designed as a cruciform structure, and never completed. The nave is exquisitely beautiful. It has five bays, whose arches, as well as the capitals of the piers, are elaborately enriched. Each column is 3 feet 8 inches in diameter. The chancel was restored by the late Duke of Norfolk ; the chancel-arch is 38 feet in height. There is a large square Norman font. Most of the building and the ornamentation date from 1150.

The Duke of Norfolk is the patron of the vicarage; which is valued at £308.

In the Church Street stands an ancient house, called Brotherhood Hall, bestowed by Alderman Holland of Chichester upon the Grammar School which he founded here in 1614.

In this neighbourhood the ornithologist will meet with the

wood-warbler, purple heron, reed-warbler, and little bittern ; and the botanist with salicornia radicans, vicia lutea, spiridia fulmentosa, and polysiphonia fibrillosa.

One mile and a half east of Steyning lies WISTON (population, 256), a neighbourhood of the highest interest, from the picturesque character of its scenery, and the romantic nature of its associations. Just beyond the Church the Downs rise up to a noble elevation, inferior only to Ditchling and Firle, and the fir-crowned height of CHANCTONBURY RING, at 814 feet above the sea-level, becomes "a thing of wonder" to all West Sussex. The views from this glorious eminence are worthy of the Downs, and embrace all that vast variety of scenery—of dale and hill, and glen and grove ; of gabled farmhouse and ivied tower—which is peculiar to the landscapes of England.

The circular encampment called "the Ring" is British, but Roman coins have been discovered here, and the Roman *via* passes at the foot of the hill.

WISTON HOUSE (Rev. John Goring), with "its ancient and well-wooded park," lies below the Downs, and overlooks a valley of unusual beauty. The grounds are well arranged,—its "undulating surface" and "stately forest-trees" lending them all the charm of varying light and shade. The house is a goodly Tudor pile, erected by Sir Thomas Shirley about 1576, and much "improved upon" by his successors. The hall, 40 feet in length, breadth, and height, has a noble groined roof ; the dining-room retains the original oaken wainscot.

The manor passed, by marriage, from the family of De Braose to that of Shirley. Of the latter race came several Sussex worthies. Sir Hugh Shirley was one of the knights who, disguised as the King, fought with the Douglas on the field of Shrewsbury, 1403,—" the spirits of *Shirley*, Stafford, Blunt," alike unequal to cope with the valour of the Scot. Another Shirley fought at Agincourt. Sir Thomas, who built the Wiston manor-house, begat three extraordinary adventurers,—" The Three Brothers, Sir Thomas, Sir Anthony, and Mr. Robert"—whose romantic career was made the subject of a play, " written by a trinity of poets, John Day, William Rowley, and George Wilkins," in 1607.

Thomas, the eldest, fitted out three vessels, manned them with 500 choice spirits, cruised in the Greek Archipelago, was captured and imprisoned at Negropont, ransomed himself for 40,000

sequins, and died in the Isle of Wight. *Anthony* fought at Zut-
phen with Sir Philip Sidney, and against the Portuguese in
Africa; departed to Persia in 1598, on a mission of political importance ; drank at Aleppo of coffee—" a drink made of seed
that will soon intoxicate the brain ;" was created a Mirza by the
Shah; despatched to Europe with the powers of an ambassador ;
quarrelled with the Persian Court ; became Admiral of the
Venetian fleet in the Levant, and died in 1631. *Robert Shirley*
accompanied his brother to Persia ; obtained a distinguished
military command ; was sent as ambassador to Europe to form a
confederacy against the Turks ; married a Circassian lady, named
Teresià ; was received in Germany, Rome, and England with great
distinction ; deceived, and finally disavowed by the crafty Persian ; and died of chagrin and disappointment, at Kazveen, in
1628.   His adventures have been graphically narrated by
Stowe.

WISTON CHURCH, dedicated to St. Mary, is a Decorated building.   The manorial chapel, at the east end, contains a beautiful
brass, inlaid with the words " Jesu Mercy," for Sir *John de Braose,*
d. 1426, who is figured in full armour, a helmet on his head, and a
gorget round his neck.   The inscription runs—" Es testis Xte,
quod non jacet lapis iste corpus ut ornetur, sed spiritus ut me-
moretur. Hiñc tu qui transis, medius, magnus, puer an sis. Pro me
funde preces, quia   .   .   .   spes."   On the north side, under an
arch, lies the effigy of a child.   Sir *William Shirley* is commemorated by a monument which represents him standing on a rock,
in an attitude of prayer, and lifting his hands towards a dove—
the symbol of the Holy Spirit.   Against the wall are the effigies
of Sir *Thomas Shirley,* the builder of Wiston, and his wife *Anne,*
daughter of Sir Thomas Kempe of Ollantighe, in Kent.

As we continue our journey northward we pass, 3 miles from
Steyning, through the village of ASHURST (population, 441)—the
Ash-wood—whose Early English CHURCH stands at some slight
distance from the road, and consists of a nave, chancel, south
aisle, and low shingled spire.   The patronage of the rectory,
valued at £268, belongs to Magdalene College, Oxon.

Three miles further, we arrive at WEST GRINSTEAD (population, 1252), the centre of a great corn-growing district. The
CHURCH, dedicated to St. George, stands on the right side of the
road, at a small distance from the river Adur.   Its architecture

exhibits specimens of the Norman, Decorated, and Perpendicular styles. The projecting wooden porch has a niche above the entrance, wherein a figure of the Virgin formerly stood. The Burrell Chapel contains two large and fine brasses: one for a female, reported to be *Philippa*, wife of John Halsham, and one of the co-heiresses of David de Strabolge, Earl of Athol, d. 1385; the other for *Hugo Halsham*, d. 1441, and his wife *Joan*, d. 1421. A monument, with two figures in *Roman* costume, by *Rysbrach*, commemorates *William Powlett*, d. 1746, and his wife *Elizabeth*. Flaxman is said to have admired it—an extraordinary proof of the great sculptor's good nature! The sarcophagus and urn for *William Burrell*, d. 1796, the collector of the Burrell MSS. (British Museum) on points connected with Sussex history, were executed by Flaxman. The Wyndham family hold the patronage of the rectory, which is valued at £791.

WEST GRINSTEAD PARK (W. W. Burrell, Esq.) skirts the Horsham road, which divides it from Knepp Park for some distance. It was erected by Walter Burrell, Esq. in 1806, and if not designed in the purest form of Gothic architecture, is certainly an imposing and stately pile. Indeed its position would redeem from mediocrity a far inferior building. It stands near the site of an old mansion, which was long the residence of the Caryls, one of whom was the host and friend of Pope, and suggested to him the " Rape of the Lock:"—

" What dire offence from amorous causes springs;
    What mighty contests rise from trivial things,
    I sing.—This verse to Caryl, muse! is due :
    This even Belinda may vouchsafe to view :
    Slight is the subject, but not so the praise,
    If she inspire, and he approve my lays."

" Pope's Oak" is still pointed out in the park, which is luxuriantly wooded and charmingly diversified.

KNEPP PARK (Sir C. M. Burrell, Bart., M.P.) lies on our left. Its stately castellated mansion, built by the present proprietor, stands on an ascent overlooking some attractive scenery and a magnificent piece of water, whose banks are fringed with some noble trees. There is here a good collection of portraits:—

Anne of Cleves, by *Holbein ;* Cromwell, Earl of Essex, *Holbein ;* Stafford, Duke of Buckingham, *Holbein* (engraved by Hol-

lar) ; Sir Henry Guldeford, Comptroller of the Household to
Henry VIII., *Holbein* (engraved by Hollar) ; Lady Guldeford
(engraved by Hollar) ; Sir Richard Rich, Chancellor to Edward
VI., *Holbein;* Algidus, a learned person employed by Francis I.
to visit the East on a commercial mission, *Holbein;* a Woman of
rank, name unknown, *Holbein;* Sir Robert Cotton, founder of
the Cottonian Library, *Vansomer,* engraved by Vertue ; William
Herbert, Earl of Pembroke, *Vansomer,* engraved by Papæus in
1617 ; Loyens, Chancellor of Brabant, *Philip de Champagne;*
Cornelius Van Tromp, *Frank Hals;* Henrietta Maria, a whole
length, *Vandyke;* Charles II., *Sir Peter Lely;* Lord Lumley,
Vansomer; A Head, *Quintin Matsys;* Sir Merrik Burrell, *Opie;*
Sir William Burrell, who mainly formed this interesting collection, *Reinagle;* Lady Burrell, *Leslie;* and Sir C. M. Burrell,
Reinagle.   Observe, also, the sea-views by *Vandervelde,* a battle-
piece by *Bourguinon,* and two specimens of *Albert Durer.*

The ruin of KNEPP CASTLE—a part of a Norman inner tower
or keep—stands on a knoll about half a mile west of the present
mansion.   It was erected as a " hunting-box" by one of the De
Braoses, who here maintained a numerous establishment and a
large kennel, and often " roused the hart" in the neighbouring
woodlands.   KNEPP is derived from the Saxon *cnæp,* a hillock,
indicative of its position.   It is situated in the parish of SHIP-
LEY (population, 1160)—*i.e.,* the sheep meadow—whose Norman CHURCH, dedicated to St. Mary, stands to the left of a lane
which joins the Horsham road near Southwater.   The tower is
two stories in height, and surmounted by a low shingled spire.
The flat oaken ceiling has been enriched with colours.   A curious
reliquary of wood is preserved in the church chest.   It is 7 inches
long and 6 inches high, enamelled, and gilt on the sides and ends
with the subject of the Crucifixion and angelic figures.   The letters X P S, in Greek characters, surmount the Cross.   It was
possibly brought from Byzantium by the Knight Templars, to
whom the church formerly belonged.   Remark the altar-tomb
and effigies, in vari-coloured marble, and restored about thirty
years ago by Carew, for Sir *Thomas Caryll,* d. 1616, and his
Margaret.   The epitaph is very quaint :—

> " Aske not who lyes entombed, that crime
> Argues you lived not in his time ;

His virtues answer, and to fate,
Outliving him, express their hate,
For stealing away the life of one
Who (but for fashion) needs no stone
To seek his praise. His worst did dye,
But best part outlives memorie.
Then view, reade, trace his tombe, praise deeds
Which teares, joy, love-strains causeth, breeds."

☞ From Shipley to Horsham is about 7 miles. The road lies through a pleasant agricultural district, but passes no object of particular interest. At 3 miles from Horsham we pass through SOUTHWATER, a pretty well-wooded hamlet, with a new district church, and afterwards skirt the grounds of DANNY PLACE (see p. 560), turning to the right out of the main road, and entering Horsham at a point near the Church.

ITCHINGFIELD (population, 371) lies to the east, in the heart of numerous leafy *shaws*, and surrounded by many fine old oaks. At almost every point the sketcher will find a charming woodland landscape. The rude Decorated CHURCH, dedicated to St. Nicholas, consists of a nave, chancel, low oaken spire and tower. An old font of Sussex marble was dug up in the churchyard some years ago. Miss Louisa Scott is the patron of the rectory, which is valued at £280.

BRANCH ROUTE—SHOREHAM TO PETWORTH.

The Petworth road, as far as Steyning and Wiston, has been already described. After leaving Wiston Place it skirts the base of the chalk downs until at Storrington it makes a sudden curve, and strikes inland towards the hills of Pulborough.

Our first halting-place is at WASHINGTON (population, 884), whose small CHURCH is mainly Early English. It consists of a nave, chancel, north aisle, and low embattled tower, and contains a monument to *Johannes Byne*, with two figures in the costume of the sixteenth century. The vicarage, valued at £63, is in the patronage of Magdalene College, Oxon.

A grave-slab in the churchyard bears the following curious epitaph upon one *Carolus Goring*, d. 1821 :—

" Ab orienti redux incorruptus.
   Optimatibus improbusque invisus,
   Divitiarum honorumque spretus,
   Populi salutis et potentiæ vindex."

SULLINGTON (population, 243), a settlement of the Saxon Syllingas (so Angmering of the Angmeringas, Poling of the Polingas, Beeding of the Bedingas ;—see Kemble's " Saxons in England "), lies about 1 mile south of the turnpike road. The Downs, which are spotted with numerous Saxon tumuli, form the southern boundary—a glorious swarded rampart, which seems to reach the very skies !   Ascend them, and before you stretches the valley of the Adur—the third of the great passes or defiles in the huge chalk range which runs across Sussex in a line parallel with the coast—and beyond it the glittering expanse of the Channel, while far away to the south-east rises the gleaming cliffs of the Isle of Wight.   The view to the north embraces a considerable portion of the verdurous and leafy Weald, watered by the Adur, the Arun, and their numerous tributaries :—

" A land of streams ! some, like a downward smoke,
   Slow-dropping veils of thinnest lawn, did go ;
   And some through wavering lights and shadows broke,
   Rolling a slumbrous sheet of foam below."

Sullington has an Early English church, dedicated to St. Mary, which contains the mutilated effigy of a knight, *temp.* Henry III., said to be that of Sir William de Covert.   The Rev. J. Palmer has the patronage of the rectory, which is worth £296 yearly.

Not above 1½ mile beyond Sullington we pass through the village of STORRINGTON (population, 1038).   The common (on the right) is a favourite resort of the rabbit tribe.   The village consists of two long streets, intersecting each other at right angles.

The CHURCH has a nave, chancel, north aisle, and low square western tower.   The chancel alone is ancient ; the rest of the building was rebuilt in 1731.   It contains two sculptures by Westmacott ; a sarcophagus, with military emblems, for Sir *Henry Bradford*, d. 1816 ; and a female figure for Major *Falconer*, d. 1827, and his daughter.   There is an inlaid slab commemorative of *Henricus Wilshe*, a priest, d. 1591.

The Duke of Norfolk is patron of the rectory, which is valued at £600 yearly.

The road now bends to the north, and brings us to the PARK and VILLAGE of PARHAM (population, 55), the latter a mere cluster of cottages on the outskirts of the Hon. Mr. Curzon's noble domain.

PARHAM HOUSE, a *picquant* Elizabethan structure, nestles in the shadow of the Downs, and looks out upon a luxuriantly wooded breadth of hill and dale, and glen and lawn. Under the leafy branches of the vigorous trees repose a fine herd of deer. Rare plants and glorious blossoms brighten and enrich the well-ordered parterres.

The house was built by Sir Thomas Palmer about 1540, and, in 1597, passed into the hands of the Bisshopp family, afterwards Lords de la Zouch. The present representative is the Baroness de la Zouch, who married, in 1802, the Hon. Robert Curzon, the well-known traveller, and author of an interesting work on the "Levantine Monasteries." Mr. Curzon has formed here a most valuable library, rich in MSS. and early printed books, as well as a collection of works of art of the most *recherché* character. Permission is readily given to the tourist to inspect the greater portion of these costly treasures, and we shall briefly indicate the objects of the highest interest.

In the HALL, remark the escocheon of Queen Elizabeth pointing out the spot where the great lady sat at dinner, in 1592, when she visited Parham on her way to Cowdlay. Remark, too, the interesting collection of armour, principally of the fifteenth century, brought from the church of St. Irene at Constantinople by Mr. Curzon, and carefully arranged in veritable *armoires*. These helms, and gorgets, and hauberks encased the stout frames of the gallant Christian knights who, in 1652, defended Constantinople against Mahomet II. Here, too, are the sword of a German *Heidenmauer*, or headsman, beneath whose sharp edge many a chivalrous life has gasped out ; a thumb-screw, and an old iron lock from a house which formerly stood in Chichester High Street ; two ancient helmets (one Etruscan), recovered from a tomb at Bari in Calabria ; a shield which was borne by the handsome and ill-fated Courtenay, Earl of Devon, whose misfortune it was to attract the favour both of Mary and Elizabeth ; some pieces of armour engraved by Hans Burgmais for Maximilian of Austria ; the garniture of the Mameluke horse ; an English helmet of the twelfth, and some Venetian helmets of the fifteenth centuries ; a model of a Greek casque, discovered at Delphi, and probably "the *salve* (or offering) of some ingenious Greek who had vowed a helmet to Apollo," and cheated the god in this subtle fashion ; some richly ornamented oriental armour ; and a copper-gilt chamfron and gauntlet, which appear, from the purport of their Arabic inscriptions, to have belonged to the chivalrous Saladin

Remark, in the SMALL DRAWING-ROOM, two Interiors by *Ostade ;* four pictures of the Seasons, finely enamelled on copper, by *Pierre Courtois* of Limoges ; and a Holy Family, *Pontormo,* purchased in Italy by Mr. Curzon.

In the DINING-ROOM, a portrait of Lady Wilmot Horton, with Lord Byron's verses, in his own handwriting,—" She walks in beauty, like the night of cloudless climes and starry skies ;" and a portrait, by *Gainsborough,* of Lady Frederick Campbell, widow of the Earl Ferrers, who was hanged at Tyburn with a silken cord for the murder of his steward.

The DRAWING-ROOM contains—Sir Philip Sidney, Lady Sidney, and Robert, Earl of Leicester, by *Zucchero ;* Mary Curzon, gouvernante of Charles the First's children, *Vandyke ;* the great Constable Bourbon, *Titian ;* St. John the Evangelist, a sketch, *Raffaelle ;* two landscapes on copper, *Ricci ;* the Holy Family, *Jacobello Flores ;* a Holy Family, *Carlo Maratti ;* and numerous portraits by unknown masters, including those of Sir Francis Walsingham, Lord Crewe, bishop of Durham, and the Prince of Orange, father of William the Third.

The GALLERY, 150 feet long, is a noble room, full of valuable relics and interesting portraits. Observe the Egyptian ark, of sycamore, brought from Thebes by Mr. Curzon, and adorned with hieroglyphics, indicating its construction during the reign of Amunoph, 1550 B.C. Its dimensions, compared with those of the ark of the covenant (see Exodus, chap. 25), which is generally dated from 1500 B.C., are as follow :—

	Length.	Width.	Height.
Parham Ark,	2 ft. 9 in.	1 ft. 1 in.	1 ft. 4 in.
Ark of the Covenant,	4 ft. 6 in.	2 ft. 3 in.	2 ft. 3 in.

When discovered, numerous figures of the Egyptian gods were in its interior.

Observe the collections of rare china, and literary antiquities, equally unique in their way.   The pen-case of Henry VI. is among the latter.

Among the portraits are Charles Paget, brother to the Lord Paget, implicated in Babington's conspiracy ; Sir Henry Wotton, by *Jansen ;* and Queen Elizabeth at the age of 25.   A Roman pig of lead, excavated at Pulborough, lies upon the floor.

The CHAPEL, at the end of the Gallery, contains figures of St. John and two monks, by *Andrea della Robbia ;* some good stained glass, a curious Elizabethan font, and much admirable wood-carving.

The picturesqueness of the Park will enchant the artist. Clumps of venerable trees chequer with floating shadows the crisp green sward, while the soft swell of the Downs is seen through a frame-work of the richest foliage.   A famous heronry is located in the depth of the pine wood.   Its history is curious : From Coity Castle, in Wales, the birds were removed, *temp.* James I., by Lord Leicester's steward, to Penshurst.   Two hundred years later they emigrated to Michel Grove, near Arundel, whence, twenty years ago, disturbed by some meditated improvements of the Duke of Norfolk's, they transported themselves to Parham. They assemble early in February, repair their nests, lay early in March, and watch over the young fledglings through the summer. " The trees are never entirely deserted during the winter months, a few birds, probably some of the more backward of the preceding season, roosting among their boughs every night." There are now fifty-eight nests.

PARHAM CHURCH, repaired and modernized in 1800, adjoins the house.   The leaden font bears the armorial distinctions of Andrew Purcell, 1351, and the inscription, in Lombardic letters, Ih'C NAZAR (*Jesus Nazarenus*).

Lady de la Zouch is the patron of the rectory, which is valued at £120.

After leaving Parham, the road crosses Wiggonholt Common, and leaves WIGGONHOLT (population, 39), or rather its church, for half-a-dozen houses can scarcely be termed a village, on the left.   Just beyond is GREATHAM (population, 76).   Both churches are Early English, and both parishes—chiefly arable and meadow-land, comprising 1770 acres — are very scantily populated.   The two rectories are held by one incumbent, valued at £205, and in the gift of the Hon. R. Curzon.

On the bank of the Adur, and at the foot of a considerable range of hills, stands PULBOROUGH (population, 1825—*Inn :* The Swan)—*i. e.*, *pwl*, water, and *byrig*, ·an encampment—two words which aptly indicate its position.   The church is situated very near the point of intersection of the Horsham and Retworth, and Arundel and Dorking roads.   The great Roman via, from Regnum (Chichester) to Londinium, passed through this neighbourhood ; and possibly the Latin epicures appreciated, as highly as the gastronomes of a later day, the eels, pike, and trout which here disport themselves in the Adur.

At OLD PLACE there are some remains of a house built in the reign of Henry VI., and of a barn whose general style of architecture seems Edwardian.   The manor formerly belonged to the Apsleys.

Numerous Roman relics have been found, as might be expected, in this parish, and in the vicinity of the great Regnum highway.   Four pipes of lead—one of which is at Parham—were discovered here in 1824.   They were lettered—

" TCLTRPVTBREXAVG,"

which has been interpreted, with much ingenuity, as an abbreviation of Ti. Cl. Tr. Pvt. B. Rex. Avg., *i. e.*, " Tiberius Claudius, Tribunitiæ Potestatis, Britanniæ Rex, Augustus."—(*Gentleman's Magazine*).   At Mare-hill, in 1817, the remains of a Roman mausoleum were excavated.   On a circular mound, to the right of the village, remains a Roman arch, a portion of a Roman castellum commanding the Arun and the Rother.   Extensive traces of a Roman villa—the foundations 150 feet by 190 feet—may still be examined on the hill, at *Borough*, north-east of Pulborough street.

The CHURCH, dedicated to St. Mary, is partly Early English, and occupies a conspicuous position on a hill of sandstone.   The clerestory windows are worth examination.   The single-pillared font is Norman.   There are brasses for *Thomas Harling*, d. 1423, a canon of Chichester ; *Edmund Mille*, d. 1652, and *Matilda* his wife, and *Edmund Mille*, his son.   The Mille sepultuary-chapel is no longer in existence.   Colonel Wyndham is patron of the rectory, which is valued at not less than £1376 per annum.

☞ From this point the tourist may proceed to Billinghurst and into Surrey, or *by rail* to Horsham, or even through Chiltington to West Grinstead ; or descend, by way of Amberley, into Arundel.

The Adur valley will now be left behind, and at one and a quarter miles we shall cross the Rother.   Here, at the foot of a tolerably steep ascent, we come upon the pretty village of STOP-HAM (population, 161), and its quaint church, a building partly Norman and partly Decorated, and containing a series of brasses to members of the Bartelott family, hereditary stewards to the Earls of Arundel.   The stained glass in the chancel window was the work of one Roelandt, a Flemish glass-stainer, and removed from the hall of the old manor-house.   G. B. Bartelott, Esq., is the patron of the rectory, which is valued at £150.

One mile beyond, but on the left of the road, stands the church of FITTLEWORTH (population, 782), 8 miles from Arundel, 3 miles from Pulborough, and 3 miles from Petworth. It is partly Early English and partly Decorated, with a chancel, nave, and north aisle, but is void of interest.   The vicarage, valued at £371, is in the patronage of the Bishop of Chichester.

In a quiet valley, half a mile distant, lies EGDEAN (population, 105), with an antique manor-house, formerly the seat of the Dykes, and a small church, which need not delay the tourist. Colonel Wyndham is the patron of the rectory, valued at £110 per annum.

We now ascend the hill to PETWORTH (population, 3439—*Inns :* The Half-moon, the Swan), which looks down, from its breezy elevation, on a small stream of the Rother, winding its silver trail through pleasant meadows.   A modest and commodious market and court-house of stone, built by the Earl of Egremont, occupies a convenient position in the centre of the town. The market is generally well attended, and the fairs, for corn and cattle, draw hither a bustling throng of Sussex farmers. The Wyndham family are the principal landed proprietors.

PETWORTH CHURCH, a Perpendicular building, restored at an expense of £15,000 by the late Earl of Egremont—a liberal and judicious benefactor of the town and its neighbourhood—boasts a lofty spire, 180 feet in height, the work of the late Sir Charles Barry.   The chapel of St. Thomas contains several memorials of the Percies, the early lords of Petworth—a monument erected by the late Earl, in 1857, when he was eighty-six years old, representing religion leaning on a cross, at whose base a Bible lies open. The touching inscription is, " Mortuis Moriturus." Carew was the sculptor.

Among the notabilities interred at Petworth, are Dr. Price, a former rector, who, as chaplain to Monk, exercised considerable influence upon the transactions of the Restoration ; Henry, ninth Earl of Northumberland, who was implicated in the Gunpowder Plot, fined £20,000, and imprisoned for sixteen years in the Tower, d. 1632 ; Algernon, the tenth Earl, a parliamentary leader, d. 1668 ; and Josceline, the last Earl, d. 1670. Josceline de Louvaine, who received the manor of Petworth from Queen Adeliza, and Lucy Percy, Countess of Carlisle, the beautiful intriguante of Charles the First's court, whom Bishop Warburton called " the Erynnys of her time," and whose charms were celebrated by Voiture and Suckling, are also buried here. A fine sculpture by Baily commemorates the late Earl of Egremont.

The Wyndham family are the patrons of the living—a rectory valued at £856.

PETWORTH PARK (Lord Leconfield) is the great art-treasury of Sussex, and must on no account be neglected by the tourist. The glorious scenery of the grounds, and the unequalled interest of its picture-gallery, render it a shrine worthy of any pilgrim's devotion. The manor was granted by Adeliza, the dowager-queen of Henry I., to Josceline de Louvaine, her brother, who married Agnes, heiress of the Northumberland Percys. It remained with the Lords Percy and the Earls of Northumberland until the death of the last Earl in 1670, when his daughter, Lady Elizabeth Percy, brought it as her dower to her third husband, Charles Duke of Somerset (her second husband was Thynne of Longleat, murdered in 1682, by Count Königsmarck). By the marriage of their daughter Catherine with Sir William Wyndham, it passed into the hands of the present representative of the Wyndhams and Percys.

The ancient castellated edifice occupied the same site as the present mansion. It was " most famous for a stately stable, the best of any subject's in Christendom, as it afforded standing in state for threescore horses, with all necessary accommodation." Charles, Duke of Somerset, almost entirely rebuilt it, and the late Earl of Egremont effected considerable alterations. The frontage forms one unbroken range, 332 feet long, and 62 feet high, which is imposing from its size, but possesses no architectural recommendations. In the rear rises the spire of Petworth Church, with an effect which is not at all to be admired.

The PARK, which is about 14 miles in circumference, and open to all comers, is very beautiful. From the Prospect Tower on the higher ground a noble view may be enjoyed. The ancient stag park (between 700 and 800 acres), enclosed and cultivated by the late Earl of Egremont, spreads out its fertile expanse beneath. All around stretch exquisite turfy lawns, and shadowy dells, and bold abrupt knolls, crowned by magnificent oaks, and clumps of beech, and ash, and elm rear their dark green crests at every "place of vantage." A fine sheet of water dimples and sparkles in the hollow before the house, and herds of deer toss up their branching antlers in the cool and leafy coverts. In the distance rises the swelling line of the South Downs, light and shadow chasing each other across their verdurous slopes ; and Chanctonbury Ring, with its diadem of trees, towering sublime above the exalted range. Far away to the north-east, the dark leaf-masses and burnished plains of the Weald present a striking contrast, and when reddened in the rare splendours of the sunset, offer a landscape eloquent in beauty.

Let us now enter the HOUSE, which is thrown open to visitors with the utmost liberality, and glance at the precious works of art for which it is so deservedly famous. They are too numerous to be specified with much detail. We can but select the most noteworthy, and recommend the reader to the temperate criticism of Dr. Waagen in his "Art-Treasures of England," for fuller information.

[1. The GRAND STAIRCASE was painted by *Laguerre* (twin spirit with " sprawling Verrio "), for Charles " the proud " Duke of Somerset. Here Pandora and Prometheus figure in the most marvellous of attitudes, and the Duchess of Somerset rides in a car of triumph, attended by her daughters, while an allegory does justice to her singular fortunes. Her father, Earl Joscelin, died at Turin at the early age of twenty-six, leaving his daughter Elizabeth "heiress of all the immense estates of her family, and sole inheritrix of the hereditary glory of the Percys." It became her lot to be three times a wife, and twice a widow before she was sixteen. In her thirteenth year she married Harry Cavendish, Earl of Ogle, who survived the ceremony a few months only. In 1681, she married Thomas Thynne, of Longleat, separating from him at the altar, and pursuant to a previous arrangement, travelling on the Continent for a twelvemonth. Thynne, Monmouth's "wealthy western friend," and the "Issacher" of Dryden's satire, was assassinated by Count Königsmarck, February 12, 1682. The adventurer, however, did not obtain the wealthy prize he aimed at. In less than two months after the murder the heiress of the,

Percys was married to Charles Seymour, known as the proud Duke of Somerset, from his extraordinary arrogance. "He seemed little less in his conduct than if vested with regal honours. His servants obeyed by signs. The country roads were cleared that he might pass without obstruction or observation."—(*Burke's Romance of the Aristocracy*). The Duchess died in 1722, aged fifty-five ; the Duke in 1748, aged eighty-seven.

2. The SQUARE DINING-ROOM contains—By *Titian :*—Portrait of a Noble ; Catherine Coruaro, Queen of Cyprus ; his daughter Lavinia fondling a kitten. By *Vandyck :*—Earl of Strafford ; Henry Percy, 9th Earl of Northumberland (a masterpiece in colouring and expression) ; Prince William of Orange, father of the "Great Deliverer ;" Algernon, 10th Earl of Northumberland, his wife and child ; Lady Rich ; Anna Cavendish ; Sir Charles Percy ; Mrs. Porter, Henriette Maria's lady of the bedchamber ; Lord Percy of Alnwick ; Lord Goring and his Son. By Sir *Joshua Reynolds :* Woodward the Actor ; Virgin and Child.

Holy Family attended by Angels, *Andrea de Sarto ;* Allegory of Events in the Early part of Charles the First's reign, *Teniers ;* Jacob and Laban, with landscape, morning—one of the most important works of the master—*Claude Lorraine ;* Portrait of himself, *Tintoretto ;* Philip II. of Spain, Sir *Antonio More ;* Philip le Bel, father of the Emperor Clarles V., a pupil of *Van Eyck's ;* A portrait, *Geovanni Bellini ;* Queen Catherine Parr, *Holbein ;* Oliver Cromwell, *Walker ;* The Young Singer before the aged Connoisseur, *Hogarth ;* Joscelin, eleventh and last Earl of Northumberland, Sir *Peter Lely.*

3. DUKE OF SOMERSET'S ROOM :—Edward VI., when 10 years old (1547), *Holbein ;* Archduke Leopold, *Teniers,* and a priest, *Teniers ;* Thomson, author of "The Seasons," *Hudson ;* Henry ninth Earl of Northumberland, *Vansomer ;* Breughel the Painter, *Vandyck ;* Prince Regent, *Varelst.*

CARD PLAYERS, Matsys the younger ; A sea-shore landscape, *Claude ;* Two landscapes, *Hobbima ;* Landscape with a Man Angling, *Gasper Poussin ;* Landscape, *Van Goyen.*

4. The NORTH GALLERY.—By *Turner ;* Echo and Narcissus ; Jessica ("Merchant of Venice") ; An East Indiaman and a Man-of-War ; Cattle at a Pool, and Men Peeling Osiers ; Evening Landscape, with Willows Dipping into a Pond ; The Lake and Tower at Tabley, Cheshire ; The Thames near Windsor, at Evening ; The Thames from Eton College ; The Thames near Weybridge ; and the Thames and Windsor Castle. *Northcote :*—Richard III. receiving the Sons of Edward IV. in the Tower ; Murder of the Two Young Princes ; and Bridget Plantagenet, daughter of Edward IV., at the Nunnery of Dartford. *Gainsborough :* — Landscape, with Cattle ; landscape with Shepherd and Shepherdess. *Romney :* — Mrs. Charlotte Smith, the Novelist, as Melancholy, and Lady Emma Hamilton as Mirth ; Shakspeare watched by Tragedy and Comedy (the latter a portrait of Lady Hamilton). Sir *Joshua Reynolds :*—The Witch-scene in "Macbeth ;" and Death of Cardinal Beaufort, from Henry VI. ; Admiral Lord Viscount Rodney ; Mrs. Masters ; General Gardiner ; Lady Craven and her Son ; the Earl of Thanet's Children, with a dog. *Allston,* the American artist : — A figure of Contemplation ; and Jacob's Dream.

Children of Charles I., Sir *Peter Lely ;* Venus asleep, and Cupid attending her, *Hoppner ;* A sea-scape, with storm, Sir *Augustus Callcott ;* Still water, with rock and Castle, *Wilson ;* the Cognoscenti, *Patch ;* Windsor Park, *Howard,* R.A.; Musidora, *Opie ;* A copy of the Punch-drinkers, of *Hogarth ;* Rydal Water, *Copley Fielding ;* Invention of Music, *Barry ;* Rape of Europa, *Hilton ;* Alexander Pope, *Richardson ;* Sancho and the Duchess, *C. R. Leslie ;* Herodias, with John the Baptist's Head, *Fusch ;* Adam and Eve, expelled from Paradise, are abandoned by St.

Michael, *Phillips;* A Storm in the Alps, *Loutherbourg;* and Edwin, Beattie's *Minstrel*—" And yet poor Edwin was no vulgar boy, "—*Westall.*

SCULPTURE :—A Shepherd Boy ; and the Archangel Michael piercing Satan with his spear (from " Paradise Lost "), by *Flaxman.* A Bas-relief by Sir *Richard West-macott,* in illustration of the Horatian passage—

Non sine dies animosus infans.

5. RED ROOM.—By *Vandyck :*—Sir Robert Shirley, and his Caucasian bride Teresia (see p. 578) ; Frances Howard, Duchess of Richmond ; and Anne Bull, wife of Lionel Cranfield, Earl of Middlesex, "the citizen who came to be Lord Treasurer, and was very near coming to be hanged" (*Walpole*). By *Vansomer :*—Ludovic Stuart, Earl of Richmond ; Ralph, Lord Hopeton. Sir *Joshua Reynolds :*—Prince Boothby ; a Lady in a turban ; a Lady with letter. *Van der Meulen :*—Attack by Banditti upon a travelling-party ; Louis XIV. and the Dauphin at Lisle. Ador-ation of the Kings, *Albert Durer* (ascribed by Waagen, but, perhaps, on insufficient grounds, to *Hieronymus Bosch*) ; Scene near Nimeguen, with figures, *Albert Cuyp;* Battle of the Boyne, *Maas;* Storm at sea, *Vlieger;* Two Prelates kneel-ing, *Rubens;* A Lady, costumed in black, *Rembrandt;* Charles II. passing Whitehall in his carriage, *Theodore Stoop;* Countess of Egremont, *Gainsborough;* and Admiral Van Tromp, *Van der Helst.*

6. ANTE-ROOM.—Vandyck, *Dobson;* Sir Isaac Newton, *Kneller;* Colonel Wyndham (Lord Leconfield), his wife and sons, *Grant;* Marquis of Granby, *Rey-nolds;* Sir Edward Coke, *Jansen;* A nobleman at prayers, *Van Eyck;* Study for " the preaching of Knox" in Sir Robert Peel's Collection, *Wilkie.*

7. CARVED DINING-ROOM.—Remark here the exquisite carvings in wood of dead game, wreaths of blossoms, and foliage by *Grinling Gibbons.* They enrich the walls and cornices of this noble chamber (60 feet long, 24 feet wide, and 20 feet high), with almost priceless ornamentation. " Appendant to one is a vase with a bas-relief of the purest taste, and worthy the Grecian age of Cameos. Selden, one of his disciples and assistants—for what one hand could execute such plenty of laborious productions—lost his life in saving this carving when the house was on fire "—(*Horace Walpole*). The decorations were completed by Jonathan Ritson, a Cumberland artist, who was employed for the purpose by the late Earl of Egre-mont and the present Lord Leconfield.

The pictures are inserted in deep, red-coloured panels, which seem to require some relief. Observe the following—By *Turner :*—Petworth Park, a sunset land-scape of extraordinary beauty ; The Lake in the Park ; a sea-view of Brighton ; Chichester Canal, at sunset. By *Clint :*—Portraits of Ritson, and Grinling Gibbons. *Kneller :*—The proud Duke of Somerset, and thrice-married heiress of the Percys. By *Jansen :*—Lord and Lady Seymour of Trowbridge. By *Holbein :*—Henry VIII. (painted about 1541).

8. The LIBRARY.—Newmarket Heath, in 1724, introducing the Duke of Somer-set, who is addressing the Duke of Cumberland, *Wootton;* Visit of the Allied Sove-reigns to Petworth in 1814, *Phillips;* Charles III. Emperor of Germany, who visited the house in 1703, and Ferdinand d'Adda, Papal Nuncio to James II., both by *Kneller;* Giving Bread to the Hungry, a sketch, *David Teniers;* The Primitive Christians engaged in teaching, *Pasqualino;* and Virgin, Infant Jesus, and Joseph, *Correggio.*

9. The WHITE and GOLD ROOM.—By *Vandyck :*—Lady Dorothy Sidney, Countess of Sunderland, Wallis's " Saccharissa ;" Lady Lucy Percy, Countess of Carlisle, " undoubtedly the most enchanting woman at the Court of Charles I. "— (*Jesse*)—" flattered in French by Voiture, and in her native tongue by almost all the

contemporary wits and poets, and more especially by Waller in verse, and in prose by that singular and mysterious person Sir Toby Matthew"—(*Miss Aikin*); Lady Dorothy Percy, Countess of Leicester, sister of the aforesaid beauty, and mother of Algernon Sidney ; Lady Elizabeth Cecil, Countess of Devonshire ; and Lady Anne Carr, Countess of Bedford, daughter of Carr, Earl of Somerset, James the First's infamous minion. By *C. R. Leslie* :*—Lady Lucy Percy, Countess of Carlisle, brings his pardon to her father, the 9th Earl of Northumberland, imprisoned in the Tower for his share in the Gunpowder Plot. Raleigh, and those famous mathematicians, Harriot, Hughes, and Warner, " the Earl of Northumberland's Three Magi," are also introduced.

10. The BEAUTY ROOM contains the following panelled portraits :—By *Dahl* :— The Countess of Portland ; Duchess of Ormond ; Duchess of Devonshire ; Countess of Carlisle ; Lady Howe ; Countess of Pembroke ; Lady Longueville. The portraits of Louis XIV. in this chamber are by *Van der Meulen.*

11. The MARBLE HALL :—Portraits of unknown personages, *Holbein ;* Peg Woffington, *Hogarth ;* Macpherson (" Ossian), Lord North, and Lady Thomond, *Reynolds ;* The Ferry-boat, with sailors, and figures on the shore, *Cuyp ;* A Youth, *Bronzino :* Leo X., *Titian ;* His own portrait, *Vandyck ;* Cervantes, *Velasquez :* Marshal Turenne, *Frank Hals ;* Guidobaldi, Duke d'Urbino, *Raffaelle ;* and Rembrandt and his wife, *Rembrandt.*]

Among the royal visitors to Petworth have been Edward VI. in 1551, the emperor Charles VI. in 1703, Prince George of Denmark ; and the Prince Regent, Alexander of Russia, the King of Prussia, the Prince of Wirtemburg, and the Grand Duchess of Oldenburg, in 1814.

The CHAPEL attached to the ancient mansion is in excellent preservation. Both walls and windows are radiant with the emblazoned escutcheons of the lords of Petworth.

The Petworth marble, dark-coloured and interlaced with purple veins, resembles that which is found in the quarries of Bethersden in Kent.

* The late Lord Egmont was a munificent patron of Leslie's, and Leslie spent many of his happiest hours and painted some of his best pictures at Petworth. Those broad Venetian mirrors, tapestried chairs, China jars and monsters, brocade and damask hangings, and recherché vases which he has introduced upon his canvas with an accuracy so minute, he saw at Petworth. You may see there the screen and chairs which he has painted in the " Rape of the Lock ;" the old globe introduced in the " Lady Carlisle;" the carved mirror and jewelled casket of the Duchess's toilet-table ; Sophia Western's china jars and console ; the window, with its look-out on the swelling slopes of the park, where sweet Lady Jane Grey sits absorbed in *Plato,* while the hounds and horns are making merry music in the sunshine without. Poor Haydon was another of the Petworth artists, and warmly appreciated the munificence of the noble owner. " The very flies," he writes, " seem to know there is room for their existence—that the windows are theirs. Dogs, horses, cows, deer, and pigs ; peasantry and servants, guests and family, children and parents, all share alike his bounty, and opulence, and luxuries." For interesting details relative to Petworth and Lord Egremont, see the " Autobiographical Recollections of Leslie," edited by Mr. Tom Taylor.

☞ North of Petworth, and about one mile west of the Guildford road, lies LURGASHALL (population, 744), with an uninteresting church dating from about 1730. " On the south side of the nave is a kind of cloister, of timber frame, furnished with benches for the accommodation of the parishioners at *Sunday dinner.*" Lord Leconfield is the patron of the rectory, which is valued at £235 per annum.

NORTH CHAPEL (population, 864), is situated on the Guildford road, 5 miles west of Petworth. The CHURCH is dedicated to St. Michael, and the rectory, valued at £284, is in Lord Leconfield's patronage.

Two miles north of this quiet hamlet we cross the boundaries of Surrey.

MAIN ROUTE RESUMED—SHOREHAM TO ARUNDEL.

The rail, after passing through Shoreham, crosses the Adur, and, following pretty nearly the coast line, soon reaches LANCING (population, 828), which derives its name from Wlencing, son of King Ælla, and skirts an ample stretch of pleasant turf, terminating in a shingle-bank, some few feet above the sea-level. The *Inns* here are The Farmers' and the Sussex Pad. Lodgings are moderately dear, the air is wholesome, the bathing is good, and society is anything but—lively. Philanthropic monarchists will remember, that here Queen Caroline embarked in 1822 ; the lover of poetry, that Coleridge favoured its seclusion and marine scenery. On the hill above the village, and conspicuous from the railway station, stands St. NICHOLAS' COLLEGE, established in connection with an upper-class school at Shoreham, board and education £40 per annum, and a farmer's school at Hurstpierpoint, yearly cost £23. At Lancing the sons of small tradesmen are boarded and educated for £14 per annum. The three schools are under Episcopal supervision, and were established by what are called " High Church" clergymen. Lancing church is partly Norman, partly Early English, and partly Decorated.

Two and a half miles further and we arrive at the popular watering-place of WORTHING (population, 5000—*Inns :* The Sea-Horse, Nelson, Steyne), 52 miles south of London. From a poor fishing village it rose into sudden importance when George IV.'s patronage of Brighton attracted the attention of the fashionable world to the pleasures of sea-bathing and the beauties of the south coast. For their convenience an agreeable sea-walk or esplanade has been constructed, three-quarters of a mile in length. The sands extend their firm and pleasant surface for quite ten miles. The temperature is well adapted to invalids, the sea-scapes are beautiful, and the town is, in all respects, identical with other popular sea-side resorts. There are — a theatre, first opened in 1807 ; a Sea-house Hotel, where Queen Adelaide resided in 1850 ; a CHAPEL OF EASE, built in 1812, and CHRIST CHURCH, erected in 1843. The Downs rear their green crests in the rear of the town, at the distance from the sea of upwards of a mile.

EXCURSIONS FROM WORTHING.

[DISTANCES OF PLACES.—Bramber, 7 m. ; Broadwater, ¼ m. ; Cissbury Hill, 2½ m. ; Clapham, 6 m. ; Findon, 4¾ m. ; Highdown Hill, 4 m. ; Michelgrove, 3½ m. ; Muntham, 7 m. ; Offington, 2 m. ; Salvington, 1½ m. ; Sompting, 2½ m. ; Steyning, 6¼ m. ; Warminghurst, 5¼ m. ; West Tarring, 1 m.]

DESCRIPTIVE NOTES.—BROADWATER (population, 5970, including Worthing), is situated in a country of " thick hedgerows and hedgerow elms." The parish, formerly included in the possessions of the knightly family of Camoys, could number but 300 inhabitants in 1724. In 1801 it boasted of 1018, in 1831 of 4576. The CHURCH, Transitional Norman, should certainly be visited. It is cruciform in plan, with a low square central tower. Remark the groined roof of the chancel, and the rich four-lighted east window. The cross (in flutes), on the north wall. The palm leaves on the capitals of the columns indicate that the founder was a crusader. Early English arches separate the nave from the aisles. The tower arch is enriched with a zig-zag moulding. Observe the canopied monument, in Caen stone, to *Thomas Lord Delawarr*, d. 1526 ; a rich memorial, in the same style, for *Thomas*, 3d *Lord Delawarr*, d. 1554 ; and a brass to *John Mapleton*, rector, chancellor to Catharine, wife of Henry V., died 1432. The Rev. E. K. Elliot is patron of the rectory, which is valued at £600 per annum.

CISSBURY HILL (*i. e.*, Cissa's byrig—from Cissa, one of the sons of Ælla, king of the South Saxons) rears its stately head above the plains at about 2½ miles north of Worthing, from which point it is easily reached. A single FOSSE, from 8 to 12 feet in depth, and a broad and lofty VALLUM, enclose an oval camp, about 60 acres in extent. Roman coins and pottery have been discovered here, and traces of the foundation of a prætorium ; so that it is probable the Roman legionaries kept " watch and ward " upon this solitary height long before Ælla and his sea rovers hunted the Britons out of their woodland villages. Some circular pits on the west side appear to be of British origin, and resemble those at Rowborough in the Isle of Wight. Celt, Roman, and Saxon, may therefore in turn have had their stronghold here. Southey, in February 1837, ascended this noble hill, and was delighted with the landscape which it commands—a landscape embracing the whole coast from Beachy Head to the Selsea Bill. " Worthing," he says, " appeared like a ruined city, such as Baalbec or Palmyra, in the distance, on the edge of what we knew to be sea, but what as well might have been a desert, for it was so variegated with streaks of sunshine and of shade, that no one ignorant of the place could have determined whether it was sea or sky that lay before us."

CLAPHAM (population, 252), is very picturesquely situated in the heart of green sloping downs and richly wooded dells. The village, one long irregular street, winds up a gentle ascent, at about 6 miles from Worthing. The CHURCH consists of a chancel, nave, north and south aisles, and low tower surmounted by a shingled spire. It is principally Transition Norman. Among the memorials observe — a monument of Caen stone, with effigies, for Sir *William Shelley*, Justice of the Common Pleas, and his wife *Alice ;* a brass for *John Shelley*, *temp.* fifteenth century ; and figures of an armed knight and his wife, Sir *John Shelley*, d. 1550, and his wife *Alice.* The patron of the rectory (£157 per annum) is the Duke of Norfolk.

FINDON (population, 559), as its name indicates, is situated on the chalk-hills, on the road from Worthing to Horsham. The beautiful seat of MUNTHAM (Marchioness of Bath), with its wooded slopes, is but a short distance north of the church ; and FINDON PLACE (M. W. Richardson, Esq.), is close at hand. The Early English CHURCH is dedicated to St. John the Baptist, and consists of a chancel, nave, north aisle, and manorial chapel. A shingled spire surmounts its low, square, western tower. The patronage of the vicarage is vested in Magdalene College, Oxon. Its yearly value is computed at £500.

HIGHDOWN HILL rises like a tower out of the green Clapham woods, and looks out upon pleasant Clapham Common. " On crossing the hill," says Pennant, " we saw a curious monument, protected by rails, with a funereal yew at each corner, and a shrubbery adjacent, built by a miller still living, for his place of interment ; the monument is strewed with many a pious text out of the burial-service, and some poetical inscriptions—the effusions of his own muse. He is said to have his coffin ready ; it runs on castors, and is wheeled every night under his bed. I was told that he is a stout, active, cheerful man ; and, besides his proper trade, carries on a very considerable one in smuggled goods." This eccentric miller was named John Olliver, and died in 1793. His coffin, at his funeral, was borne round the meadow by persons dressed in white, and was preceded and followed by some young women attired in white muslin. A funeral sermon was read over his grave by one of these white-stoled virgins. The tomb, a flat stone slab supported by some brick work, stands almost in the centre of an irregular earthwork, which encloses an area of 300 feet by 180. The view from this point is good, but not extensive.

The hill is situated in the maritime parish of FERRING (population, 312),—*i. e.,* the horse-pastures. The manor-house contains some remains of an ancient building where St. Richard of Chichester fed 3000 persons with bread only sufficient for 90— not so difficult a miracle as his monkish biographers would have us believe !

MICHELGROVE (Duke of Norfolk) was the seat of an ancient family of the same name, and afterwards of the Shelleys. The house was pulled down by the Duke of Norfolk about thirty years ago, but this spot is still to be visited for the sake of its exquisite bits of paint-like scenery. Hill and vale here succeed each other in agreeable alternation.

OFFINGTON—*i. e.*, a settlement of the Offingas—is a manor included in the parish of Broadwater. The ancient seat of the Delawarrs is now the residence of J. F.

Daubenny, Esq. It liés about half a mile west of Broadwater, in a small park which has long been colonized by " a family" of rooks.

SOMPTING (population, 559)—*i. e.*, a settlement of the Somptingas—has an in-teresting church, picturesquely situated on the slope of a hill, embosomed amid venerable elms. A portion of the manor formerly belonged to the Norman Peverels, and another to the Abbey of Fécamp ; hence the names, retained to the present day, of Sompting Peverel and Sompting Abbots. The church is cruciform in plan, with a nave, chancel, and transept, and a western tower terminating in a pointed gable, out of which rises a shingled spire. The tower and east end of the chancel are said to be Saxon; the remainder of the edifice seems Transition Norman, unless we ascribe a pure Norman origin to the chancel. Perpendicular windows have replaced the original circular-headed lights. Early English arches, springing from circular pillars, divide the north transept into two aisles. Both north and south transepts open into the nave with lofty circular arches. Remark the triangular piscina on the south side of the chancel,—a Perpendicular altar-tomb without name or date,— and the double aumbry over the altar. A rude sculpture (Early English) of a bishop in the act of benediction is placed in the south transept, and in the north, a similar figure of the Saviour with an open book, surrounded by the Evangelist symbols.

The lower outer wall of the tower is evidently Saxon. Remark its courses and bands of stone. The upper portion has Norman enrichments. The church may therefore be regarded as a Norman enlargement of a small building erected towards the close of Edward the Confessor's reign.

E. Beuker, Esq. is the patron of the vicarage, which is valued at £160 per annum.

WARMINGHURST (population, 116), nestles among the trees, 1 mile north of Ashington, and 1¼ mile west of the Worthing and Horsham road. A long but plea-sant day's excursion may be made from Worthing to this pretty village, by way of Sompting, Findon, and Washington ; returning through Sullington, across the downs to Clapham, and home by way of Durrington (where some remains of an ancient chapel may be noticed), Salvington, and West Tarring.

The view from the hill on which Warminghurst is perched embraces a consider-able portion of the east of Sussex. From the site of the ancient manor-house the prospect eastward extends to the windmill at Cross-in-hand, and the monument to the memory of " the hero of Gibraltar," at Heathfield.

The church is Early English, with a large pointed east window, *temp.* Edward III. A brass, with figures of a man and woman, their seven sons and three daughters, commemorates *Edward Shelley*, d. 1554, Master of the Household to Henry VIII., Edward VI., and Queen Mary, and his wife *Joan*, d. 1553.

The Duke of Norfolk is lord of the manor, and patron of the perpetual curacy.]

We resume our westward route. On our right lies WEST TARRING (population, 573)—a settlement of the Terringas—at about 1½ mile north-west of Worthing. The tourist will not fail to notice the abundant fig-orchards for which this parish is re-markable. It was planted in 1745 from some old stocks in the parent garden, which are traditionally reputed to have been brought from Italy by Thomas à Becket. The compiler of the *Acta Sanctorum*, however, ascribes them to the horticultural tastes of St. Richard of Chichester (Bishop Richard de la Wych).   There are now about 120 trees, which annually produce upwards of 2000 dozen.*

Tarring was given by King Athelstane to the see of Canterbury, and the Archbishops long had a palace here, of which some portions are embodied in the National School-House.   The south part is Early English, but has undergone considerable modification.   The tracery of the windows is Perpendicular, and was inserted long after the windows were completed.   The hall, on the west side of the building, is Edwardian.

"A range of buildings adjoining the premises of the rector, and still called the Parsonage Row, affords good specimens of domestic architecture in the reign of Henry VI."   The vicarage is inhabited by the vicar and rector, the Rev. J. W. Warter, B.D., son-in-law of the poet Southey, who visited Tarring in 1837.

The Early English CHURCH, dedicated to St. Andrew, has a lofty shingled spire, a chancel with a fine five-light window, a nave with clerestory windows, and north and south aisles.   The tower-window was placed by Mrs. Warter, the eldest daughter of Southey, as a memorial of the poet.   The vicarage, valued at £474, is in the patronage of the Archbishop of Canterbury.

Crossing the churchyard, and following the meadow-path for about half a mile, the tourist will reach SALVINGTON, a small hamlet in the manor of Tarring.   A small house called LACIES, at the entrance to the village, was the birth-place of John Selden, the illustrious author of "De Jure Maritima," History of Tythes," and "Titles of Honour" (born December 16, 1584, died November 30, 1654).   His father was, it is said, an itinerant musician, and Selden received his early education at the Free School of Chichester.   When only ten years old he carved on the lintel of the cottage-door a Latin distich, singularly illustrative of his character,—

"Gratus, honeste, mihi, non claudar, inito, sedebis,
  Fur abeas, non sum facta soluta tibi."

From Tarring we may easily regain the high road at GORING (population, 569), a distance of 1½ mile.   There is here a station on the Brighton and Portsmouth Railway, and we may therefore

* A bird which visits no other part of Sussex, migrates every year in the fig-season to Sompting and Tarring, and remains nearly two months. Can it be the Italian *beccafico*?

abandon pedestrianism, and once more call to our aid the loco motive.

To the north rises CASTLE GORING (Sir G. T. Petchell Bart.), out of an environment of trees. The mansion is imposing in appearance, but in its combination of Gothic and Grecian is somewhat *bizarre*.

GORING CHURCH, dedicated to St. Mary, is partly Norman, partly Early English. The chancel, however, dates from the fourteenth century. An inlaid brass commemorates *John Cooke*, " and Emma Lys, his wife." The vicarage, valued at £146, is in the patronage of David Lyon, Esq.

We next arrive (2½ miles) at ANGMERING (population, 1012), whence we may proceed north to ANGMERING PARK (Duke of Norfolk), a richly wooded demesne of great beauty. A colony of herons migrated here from Penshurst, when some venerable trees were felled in that extensive chase, and, on some trees being again cut down at Angmering, again departed, and settled themselves at Parham, where they still abide.

New Place was the seat of the Palmers, of whom Sir Edward Palmer married Alice Clement, of the Moat, at Ightham, and by her had three sons, born on three Sundays successively,—Whitsunday, Trinity, and the first Sunday after Trinity,—who were all three knighted for their valour by Henry VIII.

There were churches both at East and West Angmering, but of the former there are no remains. The latter, dedicated to St. Peter, dates from the fifteenth century. The escocheon of the nunnery of Sion is carved over the entrance-door, with the date —*Anno Dom. Milesimo Quingesimo Septimo*—from which it would appear that the tower was built in that year, and at the expense of the nuns of Sion. Sir G. B. Pechell, Bart., is patron of the vicarage, valued at £258.

PATCHING (population, 271) is situated on the left of a lane which diverges from the Arundel road, about 2 miles from the Angmering station. PATCHAM PLACE (Col. Payne) is, indeed, visible from the line. The land here is divided between cornfields and cattle-pastures ; and Patching butter has more than a local reputation. The angler may try his skill with, possibly, satisfactory results in PATCHING POND, a large piece of water, stored with trout, eels, pike, tench, and carp ; the architectural student may occupy himself in studying the details of the Early English CHURCH, a small but well-ordered edifice. The Archbishop of Canterbury is the patron of the rectory, whose yearly value is £200.

The gastronome should be told that in the beech-woods here, truffles (*Lycoperdon tuber*) are very abundant.

At 2½ miles from Angmering, and 18 miles from Brighton, we reach the ARUNDEL and LITTLEHAMPTON STATION— the former lies about 2 miles north, the latter, on the coast, 3 miles south. Conveyances are always in waiting for either place. But we must first take note of POLING (population, 192), a settlement of the Polingas, and LEOMINSTER (population, 794), both of which lie to the right of the line, between Goring and Arundel.

POLING has a large decoy for wild fowl, supplied by a tributary of the Arun ; a modern dwelling-house " converted" out of the chapel, formerly attached to a Commandery of the Knights Hospitallers ; and a fifteenth century CHURCH, containing some fragments of stained glass, and a brass for *Walter Davys*, vicar. The Archbishop of Chichester is the patron of the vicarage (£158).

LEOMINSTER has a picturesque Church, partly Transition-Norman in its style, and partly Early English. It is dedicated to St. Mary Magdalene. The font, standing on five pillars, is Norman. The Bishop of London is patron of the vicarage, which is valued at £350.

" Near the church is a pond, about 60 feet in diameter, and 20 feet deep, supplied from a never-failing spring at the bottom. It is the most copious spring on the south side of the Downs, and is called the Knucker-Hole"—(*Horsfield*).

ARUNDEL (*i.e.*, THE VALLEY OF THE ARUN, or *fr.* ARUNDO, A REED).

[Population, 2748. *Inn:* The Norfolk. 60 m. from London by rail; 61 m. by road; 10 m. by road, and 11 m. by rail, from Chichester; 19 m. from Brighton, by road; 6½ m. from Bognor; 11 m. from Petworth.]

" Descending a steep hill," says Pennant, " we crossed a narrow tract of rich meadows ; opposite to us was a range of lofty banks clothed with wood, diversified every now and then with a contrast of chalk which bursts out in the face of the cliffs. Arundel Castle filled one space, and impended nobly over the river Arun and the subjacent meads. We crossed the bridge, and immediately entered the town of Arundel, which consists chiefly of one handsome broad street running straight up the steep slope of the hill, with the castle on the summit on one side, and the church on the other." A brief but graphic description of the position of the most picturesque town in southern England, but since Pennant's time an uninteresting suburb has sprung up on the left bank of the river.

Crossing the neat stone bridge of three arches which here spans the " wild Arun " of the poet, we breast a steep and abrupt hill, crowned by the towers of Arundel Castle, winding through a street which, happily, still rejoices in many an " old gable-fronted, half-timber house." Here at the NORFOLK ARMS we may obtain excellent accommodation, while we glance at the annals of the ancient town.

How did it obtain its name ? Was it from *arundo*, a reed, because the neighbouring marshes abound in reedy growth ? Or from the river Arun, which sparkles through the leafy dell overlooked by the castle-crowned steep ? Or from *hirondelle*, a swallow, the device of the corporation seal ? Or, finally, from *Hirondelle*, the famous horse of the notable giant Bevis, the mythic warder of the Castle, whose bones, with those of his steed's, were interred, as everybody knows, in the shadowy hollow of Pughdean ? The reader may even choose for himself.

Arundel has returned members to Parliament from the reign of Edward the First, but the Reform Act of 1832 deprived it of one of its representatives. It was incorporated by Queen Elizabeth, and is duly governed by a mayor and six aldermen. Its port has been held in some estimation from a period anterior to the Conquest, and its trade now-a-days, in timber, coal, and corn, is not inconsiderable. During the Civil Wars it suffered severely from the outrages of Waller's soldiers, when the Roundhead leader besieged the castle (December 1643), and his artillery terribly shattered the beautiful Church. The townsmen are reasonably proud of their river, which affords them a water communication with the inland agricultural districts, and is connected with the Wey, thus bringing Guildford, Weybridge, and the Thames into correspondence with them. Honour to the Arun ! It not only

encourages trade, but ministers to the wants of the ichthyopha-
gist. The *Arundel mullets* (mugit cephalus) have had a long
lease of fame, and are as welcome to the epicure as to their persevering foe, the mullet-hawk or osprey. Let it be added that
the scenery of the Arun is of the richest and goodliest character.

But the most notable " show-place" in Arundel (next to the
Castle) is ST. NICHOLAS' CHURCH, a Perpendicular building, partly
of flint and stone, which is still interesting and still beautiful,
despite of Roundhead iconoclasts and eighteenth century church-
wardens. Waller's soldiers were quartered here in 1643, and
found ample scope for the exercise of their religious zeal. In
1782 the carved roof was taken down, and its timbers, according
to Mr. Tierney, " were suffered to fall at random on whatever
might be beneath." So, thanks to Puritans and carpenters, the
Arundel monuments have suffered grievous devastation.

Roger de Montgomery established here in 1094 a Benedictine
Priory, which he bestowed upon the Abbey of Seez, in Normandy.
In 1830, this Priory was converted, by Richard Fitzalan, Earl of
Arundel, into a College, dedicated to the Holy Trinity, for a
master and twelve secular canons. He then began building the
present CHURCH, with the view of connecting it with his new
foundation. The College Chapel (82 feet by 28 feet) still exists,
at the east end, beyond the chancel. It is " large and lofty," and
contains five of the Arundel tombs. The Church is a cruciform
building, " spacious and handsome," with a nave, north and south
aisles, transept, and low square tower, surmounted by a leaden
spire. The nave measures 82½ feet by 50½ feet, and is ceiled
with Irish oak. Two frescoes on the north wall of the nave
represent the Seven Deadly Sins and Seven Works of Mercy.
The clerestory windows enclose quatrefoils. The vicarial pew
seems to have been the ancient stone pillar. In the south aisle
stands the original high altar, the only one in England, it is said,
which escaped destruction or removal at the Reformation. The
College Chapel opens through three pointed arches into the Lady
Chapel, 54 feet by 20 feet, containing brasses for a knight and
his wife, date 1418 ; and "Sir" *Ewan Ertham*, first master of
the College, d. 1432.

The Arundel tombs are as follow :—

1. *Thomas, fifteenth Earl of Arundel*, Lord Treasurer, and
his wife *Beatrice*, daughter of John, King of Portugal. The
former, " a beardless figure in white marble, recumbent, in robes

and coronet, with a horse at his feet ;" the latter, " dressed in her robes, lies on an altar-tomb, surrounded by twenty monkish figures, under a rich canopy of Gothic work." Died, 1215.

2. *John*, sixteenth Earl, who defended Southampton against the French, and d. 1422 ; and *Alianore* or *Eleanor*, daughter of Sir John Berkeley. The brasses have been despoiled. Their tomb is in the centre of the Lady Chapel.

3. *John*, seventeenth Earl, in plate armour, with a close sur-coat and collar of SS. " Beneath, in the hollow of the tomb, he again appears in his shroud, emaciated by death, well cut in white marble—too well to afford any but humiliating reflections"— (*Pennant.*) He died in 1434.

4. *William*, eighteenth Earl, d. 1488, and his Countess *Joan.* Their effigies are recumbent upon the altar-tombs of *Thomas*, twentieth Earl, d. 1524, and *William*, twenty-first Earl, d. 1544. Their own tomb, without its figures, stands under a canopy of exquisite lightness, supported by four richly carved pillars. Remark the lady Joan's peculiar oblong head-dress. She was the sister of Richard Neville, the king-making Earl of Warwick.

5. *Thomas*, twentieth Earl, d. 1524. His tomb stands on the north side of the altar, and bears, by a curious misappropria-tion, the effigy of Earl William. He was the patron of Caxton the printer. In the same tomb lies the dust of

6. *William*, twenty-first Earl, d. 1544.

7. *Henry*, twenty-second Earl, d. 1579, last of the Fitzalans of Arundel, is commemorated by a tablet over the tomb last described. He was imprisoned in the Tower by Elizabeth for his share in the Duke of Norfolk's—his brother-in-law—con-spiracy in favour of Mary, Queen of Scots. He introduced the use of coaches into England.

There are no monuments to the Howards, though many of them are here interred, and among them *Thomas*, twenty-fourth Earl of Arundel, d. 1646, the collector of the Arundelian marbles and the friend of John Evelyn.

The Earl of Albemarle is the patron of the vicarage of Arundel, which is valued at £199 per annum.

Some remains of the collegiate buildings, especially the entrance gateway, adjoin the churchyard. The master's house occupied the south-east angle ; the refectory stood on the east ; the cells of the brethren ranged along the south and west sides of the quadrangle. This College possessed the privilege of sanctuary, and the Constable of the Castle having on one occasion violated it by seizing a certain John Mot, who had grasped in due form the ring on the outer door, Rede (bishop of Chichester) ordered him to be soundly cudgelled, and to perform a severe penance.

A Hospice, dedicated to the Holy Trinity, and named the *Maison Dieu*, was founded, about 1380, by Earl Robert. It provided for twenty poor men. The building formed a small quadrangle, with a chapel and refectory, and was destroyed by Waller's soldiers in 1643. The present bridge was built out of the ruins in 1742.

The TOWN HALL, an ambitious castellated building, was erected by Bernard, Duke of Norfolk, about thirty years ago, at a cost of £9000. The principal room is 50 feet by 30, and 23 feet high.

Such are the notabilities of Arundel. We reserve the Castle for a separate article (see EXCURSION, ARUNDEL AND ITS LORDS),* and now proceed to notice the surrounding country.

[HINTS FOR RAMBLES.—1. Through Leominster and Poling to Angmering. Thence southward to East Preston, and through Rustington and Littlehampton return to Leominster, and into Arundel. 2. Cross Arundel Park to Bury Thence to Bignor; return to Madehurst. Thence to Slindon, and through the Arundel Coverts into Arundel. 3. To Ford and Climpton. Thence to Yapton. Cross to Wallerton, and return by way of Binsted. 4. By rail to Woodgate. Walk from thence to Bognor, and return by way of Felpham, Middleton, Yapton, and Ford. 5. By rail to Angmering. Visit Patching, Cissbury Hill, and Clapham. Cross, by way of Michelgrove, to Burpham, and return to Arundel.]

Within an easy distance of Arundel lie Littlehampton, Preston, Rustington, and Climping.

LITTLEHAMPTON (population, 2436), 4 miles south of Arundel, takes its name, traditionally, from Ham the assassin, slain by Arviragus when Gwydyr repulsed the Romans under Claudius. Its *true* etymology will be easily understood by the tourist. It forms one long street on the bank of the Arun—from whose mouth, the ancient haven of Arundel, it is three quarters of a mile distant—intersected by another at right angles. Here the Empress Matilda landed in 1139. The piers which protect the river mouth were constructed in 1797. The canal between Littlehampton, and Arundel and Portsmouth, was formed in 1820-3, at a cost of £160,000. A floating-bridge, as at Portsmouth, ferries from shore to shore (370 feet), and vessels of 150 tons

* Black's Guide to Hampshire and the Isle of Wight.

burthen can ascend the river as high as the bridge at Arundel, while barges can sail up into the Wey. Pleasant lodgings may be obtained on the marine promenade, known as Beach Terrace.

The CHURCH, 100 feet by 50, was erected in 1826 at a cost of £3000. It embodies some remains of the ancient building— The vicarage, valued at £150, is in the patronage of the Bishop of Chichester.

RUSTINGTON (population, 342) is situated on the coast, about 1 mile east of Littlehampton. The CHURCH is partly Transition Norman. The chancel and north aisle are of later date. The Bishop of Chichester is patron of the vicarage, valued at £159.

PRESTON (population, 310) is a small tract (570 acres) of rich arable land, with a few houses in its centre, half a mile from the shore, and a CHURCH, some distance from them, which dates from the fifteenth century. The north door however, is Norman. The vicarage, as well as the rectory of Kingston (population, 40), is attached to the vicarage of Ferring (valued at £250), in the gift of the Bishop of Chichester.

CLIMPING (population, 273)—a settlement of the Saxon Clepingas—is situated on the western bank of the Arun in a peculiarly sequestered position. " It includes all that remains of the parish of Cudlawe or Cudlowe, of which little more than 100 acres have escaped the devastations of the sea "—(*Horsfield*). The CHURCH is an Early English cruciform building of singular design, and supposed to have been founded by John de Clymping, bishop of Chichester, in 1253, although the chevron enrichment of the tower certainly points to an earlier date. The roof is remarkably high-pitched, and the western windows enclose double quatrefoils. The Lord Chancellor has the patronage of this vicarial living, valued at £226 yearly.

BRANCH ROUTE—ARUNDEL TO RUDGWICK.

Our road conducts us through the pleasurable glades of Arundel Park, where majestic trees, sunny avenues, and leafy dells, dotted with herds of deer, and hills which afford prospects of astonishing extent and richness, combine to produce a succes-

sion of changeful and attractive pictures. To the east of the
park, and beyond the Arun, lies BURPHAM (population, 267),
where there is a church of some antiquity but no particular
interest. Near the churchyard a considerable entrenchment of
uncertain origin may be examined. The soil here is chiefly
chalk, and layers are frequently found composed of an aggregate
of ".detached ossiculæ of star-fishes." If we followed the course
of the river, we should come to SOUTH STOKE (population,
106), with its Early Norman church, and 1 mile further to
NORTH STOKE (population, 80)—both of them seated in a
neighbourhood which abounds with relics of our Celtic ancestors.
At North Stoke, in 1834, a British canoe was dug up on the
river-bank.

[The vicarage of BURPHAM, value £145, is in the patronage of the Dean and Chapter of Chichester ; the rectory of SOUTH STOKE, value £233, has for its patron the Earl
of Albemarle ; the patronage of NORTH STOKE, perpetual curacy, belongs to Lord
Leconfield].

About 1 mile from the north boundary of the park the road
passes to the left of HOUGHTON (population, 193). Its ancient
chapel contains a brass, inserted in a slab of Petworth marble,
for *Thomas Cheyne*, d. 1486. The forest of Houghton formerly
supplied deer for the Bishop of Chichester's table.

About $5\frac{1}{4}$ miles from Arundel we reach AMBERLEY (population, 671), one of those picturesque old-world villages which
may still be found beyond the influence of the railway navvy.
Its aspect, however, would seem to vary with the seasons, for the
local adage runs—in winter, it is " Where do you belong ?" "To
Amberley—God help us !" but in summer, " To Amberley—
where *would* you live ?" The cottages here are unprofaned by
civilizing innovations ; there is an old ruin ; the farms are quaint
and comfortable ; the trout have not wholly deserted the Arun ;
cranberries may be gathered in the WILD BROOK (" brook " a pro-
vincialism for " marsh") ; and the ancient CHURCH, half Norman,
half Early English, with its traces of mediæval frescoes—its red
consecration crosses—its pulpit hour-glass, a memento for long-
winded ecclesiastics—and brass for *John Wanlett*, d. 1424, is of
the highest interest. But the ruins of the palace of the Bishops
of Chichester, the CASTLE, built by Bishop Rede, *temp.* Richard
II. (1369-79), must be regarded as the best of the many good
things of Amberley. They occupy a low rock of sandstone, over-

looking the Wild Brook, and its fringe of cranberry bushes. The original plan was nearly that of a parallelogram. At each corner a square tower rises above the walls, which were 40 feet high; the massive and imposing gateway was flanked by two round towers (compare that of Lewes Castle) ; and the south side was defended by a fosse. The present dwelling-house in the Green Court was built by Bishop Sherbourne, in 1508.

The best view is obtained from the bridge which spans the fosse. Over these ruins, the handiwork of Waller's Roundhead troopers in 1643, the eternal ivy has thrown its rank luxuriance and unwholesome beauty.

The patron of the vicarage of Amberley is the Bishop of Chichester ; its yearly value, £166.

Beyond the sixth milestone, our road diverges to the right, and passes through COLDWALTHAM (population, 120), *i. e.*, the village in the bleak woodland—and HARDHAM (population, 98), to PULBOROUGH. At HARDHAM there is a small Early English church, and the river Arun flows through a tunnel, 400 yards long, bored in the hill of sandstone on which the village is situated.

We cross the downs at PULBOROUGH (see p. 586), and proceed over North Heath, and through a wild romantic countryside, to BILLINGHURST (population, 1458), one of the settlements of the Saxon tribe of the Belingas, situated on the main road in a richly-wooded and well-watered district. It is 14 miles N.E. by N. of Arundel. The Roman STANE STREET, from Regnum (Chichester) to London, crossed this parish, and terminated at BILLINGSGATE. The CHURCH, dedicated to St. Mary, has a spire which rises to the height of 120 feet, a landmark for the peasants in the depths of the surrounding Weald. It contains a brass for *Thomas Bartlett*, d. 1489, and *Elizabeth* his wife. Sir C. Goring is the patron of the vicarage, valued at £139.

Five miles further, and our road joins the highway which connects the Dorking and Guildford roads. Turning to the right, we may reach Rusper, Ifield, and Crawley ; turning to the left, we shall arrive at RUDGWICK (population, 1031). The village is seated on a hill, commanding some fair prospects of Sussex and Surrey. The CHURCH, dedicated to the Holy Trinity, consists of

a chancel, nave, north aisle, and western tower.   There are three
stone sedilia, under an arched canopy, in the chancel.   Patron of
the vicarage, Bishop of Chichester ; yearly income, £260.

Having conducted the tourist to the borders of Surrey, we
again return to our Chichester route.

MAIN ROUTE RESUMED —ARUNDEL to CHICHESTER.

The FORD STATION (2¼ miles) affords the advantages of railway
communication to the villages of FORD (population, 106),—a
ferry across the Arun, and TORTINGTON (population, 104), where
a house of Black Canons was founded by Hawse de Corbet, *temp.*
Richard I.   The CHURCH was probably built about the same time.
Its font is enriched with Lombardic ornaments, and the chancel-
arch with a moulding of grotesque heads of birds and beasts.

YAPTON (population, 609) is situated on the turnpike-road.
Its CHURCH, except the chancel, is Early English.   The font is
very curious, and either Saxon or Early Norman.   It is composed
of black granite ; is large, circular, and rests on a square base.
A cross patie fitchy is sculptured in each of the six semicircular
niches which enrich the sides.

Yapton vicarage is attached to that of Walberton, valued at
£460, and in the patronage of the Bishop of Chichester.   WAL-
BERTON (population, 578) lies one mile north of the Yapton
station.   WALBERTON HOUSE (R. Prime, Esq.) is a stately mansion
set at the head of an ample lawn.   It was built in 1817, from
the designs of Smirke.   The CHURCH, dedicated to St. Mary, is
partly Early English.

We run through a country of little interest, catching pleasant
glimpses of the sea on the one hand, and of the undulating crest
of the Downs on the other, until, at 5 miles from Arundel, we
reach the WOODGATE STATION, where the Bognor Conveyance
Company's omnibuses are in attendance for visitors to BOGNOR
(4 miles south).

BOGNOR (population, 1913.   *Inns :* York, Norfolk)—*i. e.*,
the rocky coast — is Worthing's twin-sister, a quiet, healthy
watering-place, seated on a level, in face of the ever restless
channel.   A reef of rocks, about 2 miles in length, juts out from
the shore, and forms a natural but insufficient breakwater.   The

geologist will find here septaria, turritella, rostellarieæ, and nautili.*

About 1786, Sir Robert Hotham, a wealthy Southwark hatter, determined upon acquiring the glory of a sea-side Romulus, and set to work to erect a town of first class villas in this pleasant spot, with a view of creating a truly *recherché* watering-place, to be known to posterity as "Hotham town." He spent £60,000, erected and furnished some commodious villas, but did not succeed in giving his name to his own creation, and died broken hearted in 1799. Fashion, however, after some slight delay, patronized the new English bath, and Bognor grew by degrees into its present prosperity.

The best streets are the Crescent, Hotham Place, and the Steyne. The CHURCH, dedicated to St. John, was built in 1793.

The PARISH CHURCH is at SOUTH BERSTED (population, 781), dedicated to St. Mary Magdalene, and built in 1405. The Archbishop of Canterbury is patron of the vicarage, which is valued at £214.

One mile east of Bognor, at a short distance from the shore, and, perhaps, in a situation which is even pleasanter than that of Sir Richard Hotham's "salubrious" but not very "lively" watering-place, is FELPHAM (population, 596). Here, in a delightful villa—standing almost in the centre of the hamlet— lived and died *William Hayley*, the author of the "Triumphs of Temper," but certainly better known to the readers of to-day as the friend and biographer of the poet Cowper. His death took place on the 12th of November 1820. Only forty years ago, and yet who reads a line of the poems of the man whom Mrs. Opie panegyrized, whom Cowper and Romney esteemed, whom his contemporaries regarded as "a gifted minstrel ?"

FELPHAM CHURCH, dedicated to St. Mary, is mainly Perpendicular. The font is large and ancient. Remark the monument to Hayley, with an epitaph, long and verbose, by Mrs. Opie.

In the churchyard lies interred Dr. *Cyril Jackson,* d. 1819,

* "The sandstone rocks of Bognor are the ruins of a deposit once very extensive ; the lowermost part is a dark grey limestone, the upper part is silicious. The Barn rocks, between Selsea and Bognor, the Houndgate and Sheet rocks on the west, and Mixen rocks on the south of Selsea, are portions of the same bed"—(*Dr. Mantell*).

Dean of Christ Church, Oxon, and tutor to George IV. He spent the last years of his life at Felpham, and was visited here on his deathbed by his royal pupil.

The following lines, on the tombstone of one William Steele, a blacksmith, were written by Hayley :—

> " My sledge and hammer lie reclin'd ;
> My bellows, too, have lost their wind ;—
> My fire's extinct,—my forge decay'd,
> And in the dust my vice is laid ;—
> My coal is spent,—my iron gone,—
> The nails are driven,—my work is done."

Felpham is a sinecure rectory, worth £20, in the gift of the Dean and Chapter of Chichester, and a vicarage, valued at £166, in the patronage of the rector.

[A pleasant excursion may be made either from Bognor, the Woodgate, or Drayton Stations to PAGHAM (population, 1022), a fishing village situated upon an inlet of the sea, named Pagham Harbour, which dates from the fourteenth century. It is a tidal harbour, with two islands before its narrow mouth. In a place called the PARK,* outside the entrance, anchorage may be obtained in 4½ fathoms of water.

The " curiosity" of Pagham is its HUSHING WELL. The air is forced by the sea from some submarine gully or cavern in the Pagham Bank, through the shingle, so as to fret and disturb the whole surface of the water in an area of 130 feet by 30 feet, and produces a peculiar hissing noise which may be heard at a considerable distance. The " edible" of Pagham is the Selsey cockle, found off this part of the coast in great quantities, and to be classed by Fuller with the Amberley trout, the Arundel mullet, and the wheat-ear of the Downs, among the " good things " of Sussex. There is excellent sport in this vicinity for the disciples of Bishop and Joe Manton. In every little creek, on every solitary spur of sand, the wild fowl congregate like a cloud of wings,—osprey, and tern, and the shrieking gull,—dusky sandpipers, whirling ring-dotterels, choughs, puffins, and guillemots.

The Early English CHURCH of Pagham, spite of repairs, is interesting. It is dedicated to Thomas à Becket, and was therefore built after his canonization. The manor belonged to the see of Canterbury, and the Archbishop had a palace here, of which there are no remains. The vicarage is still in their patronage, and valued at £300 per annum.

From Pagham the pedestrian may keep along the sands, when the tide is out, for some miles, and visit Selsea (Seal's Island), and the bold promontory of SELSEA BILL. The whole peninsula was at one time green, with an extensive forest,—the Forest of Manwood, whose name may be traced in that of the Hundred (Manhood) wherein the peninsula is now included. It is now a low flat plain, of London clay, with occasional deep marshes; and is given up without remorse to the grazier. Nothing of the romantic, nothing of the beautiful relieves its dreary uniformity. The sea itself seems to have surrendered its ancient grandeur, and instead of rolling in thunder against a precipitous wall of chalk, steals craftily and silently over the muddy shore.

---

* The PARK, as late as the reign of Henry VIII., was a chase for deer. Bishop Rede excommunicated certain unfortunates who had presumed to " rouse the hart " in this episcopal preserve.

Its power as a Destroyer, however, has been asserted here for centuries, and the coast-line yearly recedes before its insidious advance.

Selsea Isle is famous in Ecclesiastical History. Here Wilfred of York was wrecked about 680, and hospitably received by Edilwalch, King of the South Saxons, who with his Queen had previously been converted to Christianity, but reigned over a Pagan people. " Bishop Wilfred," says Bede, " by preaching to them, not only rescued them from the torment of eternal perdition, but also from the sufferings of temporal death, for no rain had fallen in that country side for three weary years, and a terrible famine had arisen, and cruelly struck down the people. Indeed, it is said, that groups of 40 or 50 men, worn out with want, would rush together to some steep rock, or down to the sea-shore, and perish by the headlong fall, or be devoured by the waters. But on the very day whereon the people accepted the baptism of faith, there fell from Heaven a soft and plenteous rain : once more the earth grew glad, the verdure again sprang up in the meadows, and a pleasant and abundant harvest followed"—(*Eccl. History*, v. iv. c. 13). The good bishop, however, was wise enough not to trust himself wholly to miraculous interposition. " He taught the people to get their food by fishing, for their seas and rivers abounded in fish, but they had no skill to catch any fish but eels. So the bishop's men, having borrowed eel-nets everywhere cast them into the waters, and by God's blessing they caught 300 fish of various kinds; and dividing these into three portions, bestowed a hundred upon the poor, a hundred upon those from whom they had hired the nets, and a hundred they reserved for their own use." A practical reading of the monkish homily, " Laborare est orare"—Work is Prayer—which we commend to the reader's admiration.

Here Wilfred founded a monastery, and he placed in it those of his disciples who had been banished from Northumbria. Its site, it is said, was about 1 mile east of Selsea Church, but the waters long ago overwhelmed its foundations, and neither of the old Saxon abbey, nor of the cathedral of the Episcopate of Selsey, can a stone be found by the most industrious archæologist.

SELSEY CHURCH was built, it is supposed, by Bishop Rede of Chichester, about 1369-1385. It stands about 2 miles inland. The roof is of recent date. The tower has never been completed. Here are several grave-stones of Sussex marble, inscribed with a cross, memorials probably of the old Saxon priests, removed from the ruins of the ancient cathedral. Effigies of a man and woman, with figures of St. George and St. Agatha, their patron-saints, commemorate *John Lews*, and *Agatha* his wife, d. 1537. A grave-stone in the churchyard, to the memory of two young men drowned while rendering assistance to a wrecked vessel, bears an epitaph by Hayley.

The fosse and vallum of the British encampment adjoin the churchyard.

Population of Selsey parish, 934 ; value of the vicarage, £759 ; patron, the Bishop of Chichester.

☞ There is little to interest the tourist in the numerous villages which stud the Selsey peninsula. For his convenience, however, we append a few notes in a tabular form :—

BIRDHAM (population, 531), 4 miles from Chichester. CHURCH dedicated to St. Leonard. Rectory valued at £396, is in the patronage of the Dean and Chapter of Chichester.

EARNLEY (population, 137), 6½ miles from Chichester. Rectory valued at £440, in the patronage of the Bishop of Chichester, and, every third presentation, the Duke of Norfolk.

ITCHEVOR, WEST (population, 254), 6½ miles south-west of Chichester. Small Early English CHURCH, dedicated to St. Nicholas. Rectory, valued at £151, in the patronage of the Lord Chancellor.

SIDLESHAM (population, 941), retains the name of its Saxon proprietor, whose "ham" or "home" is now situated at the head of a deep creek of the channel, and on the road from Chichester (6½ miles) to Pagham Harbour.　There is an extensive tide-mill on the bank of the estuary already spoken of, "occasioned several centuries ago by a sudden irruption of the sea at Pagham, by which 2700 acres were devastated."　The CHURCH, an Early English building, dedicated to St. Mary, is worth a visit.　It contains an Edwardian font (*Dallaway*).　Its embattled tower is probably Perpendicular.　There is here an oaken chest, finely carved, and near the chancel is placed a mural monument, with effigies for *Rebecca Taylor*, d. 1631.

The vicarage, valued at £182, is in the patronage of the Bishop of Chichester.

EAST WITTERING (population, 233), 1 mile from the sea, and 7 miles southwest of Chichester.　"From the mouth of Chichester Harbour to the extremity of Chichester Hill, a distance of about 8 miles, the sea has encroached so as to have absorbed a considerable portion of the prebendal manor of Bracklesham"—(*Horsfield*).　The bay thus formed has excellent sands, affording at low water a capital promenade, and its occasional "patches of soft clay" are full of fossil shells.　The most interesting spot is immediately in the neighbourhood of Bracklesham Barn, "especially at about a furlong to the east, where there is a small break or chine in the low clay cliff.　Here there is a stratum of light green marly sand, abounding in venericardii planicosta" (*Bowerbank*), myliobates, turritella, lucina serrata, cerithium giganteum, and other fossils.

EAST WITTERING CHURCH is partly Early Norman.　The Bishop of London is the patron of the rectory, which is valued at £190.

Between East and West Wittering lies the hamlet of CAKEHAM.　The Bishops of Chichester had a marine residence here, and Bishop Sherbourne, inspired by the noble sea-view which this position commands, erected a lofty prospect-tower of brick, hexagonal in construction, which is still in existence.　We take our hats off, as we pass it, in honour of a prelate of such excellent taste.

. WITTERING, WEST (population, 609), is 7½ miles south-west of Chichester.　The district is low and level, but nevertheless it affords "marine views" of uncommon extent, variety, and magnificence.　The CHURCH dates from the thirteenth century. Three oaken stalls are preserved in the chancel, and a canopied tomb of Caen stone, sculptured with bas-reliefs of the Annunciation and Resurrection, commemorates *William Ernley*, d. 1545.　The vicarage, valued at £165, is in the patronage of the Bishop of Chichester.]

During this long digression we must fain suppose that "the gentle·reader" has sped through a rich but level country, past the WOODGATE STATION [OVING (population, 876),—*i. e.*, the sheepfold—lies to the right], and arrived at the cathedral city of

CHICHESTER—*i. e.*, CISSA'S CEASTER, OR CISSA'S CAMP.

[Population, 8331. *Inns:* The Dolphin, the Globe.　60 m. from London, by road; 79 m. by rail; 28 m. from Brighton, by rail; 13 m. from Petworth; 10 m. from Arundel; 16 m. from Portsmouth; 3½ m. from Boxgrove; 6 m. from Bognor; and 10 m. from Midhurst.

☞ Omnibuses run between the city and the station.　Coaches run daily to and from Godalming, three times a week to Petworth, and daily to Midhurst.

CHICHESTER, the ancient REGNUM, presents, in its main streets, running in straight lines east and west, and north and south, and its lesser streets diverging at right angles from them—an exact reproduction of the old Roman plan. Its walls, 1½ mile in circuit, stand on the foundations of the ancient walls, and are fashioned out of their materials. A portion of the old wall, on the west side of the city, now forms a pleasant public walk. Coins, urns, bits of tesselated pavement, and other relics, remind us, at almost every step, of its Roman masters—of the city where Cogidubnus, King of the Regni, and the viceroy of the Emperor Claudius, held his royal state. It stood at the point where the Stane Street, which connected Regnum with Londinium, crossed the great *via* to Portus Magnus (Porchester); at the head of the east branch of the creek now known as Chichester Harbour, and in the shelter and shadow of the lofty Southern Downs. When Ella landed on the Sussex coast, his forces pushed forward from their point of disembarkation (at CYMEN'S ORA, now Keynor, 7 miles south, so named from one of Ella's sons) across the level marshes into Regnum, which they devastated with fire and sword, and out of its ruins built up a Saxon settlement, called, in honour of their chief leader, CISSA'S CEASTER. We hear but little of it during the Anglo-Saxon supremacy. After the Conquest it was absorbed among the possessions of Robert de Montgomery, who built a small castle in its north-east quarter, destroyed in the first year of Henry the First. Three mints were established here, *temp.* King John. Its walls, strengthened by 16 semicircular towers, were frequently repaired, but could not resist the assault of Sir William Waller's troops, who surprised here Lord Hopton and the royalists in 1642. The siege was of the briefest. " They within the town were easily reduced to straights they could not contend with ; for besides the enemy without, against which the walls and the weather seemed of equal power, and the small stock of provisions, which in so short a time they were able to draw hither, they had cause to apprehend their friends would be weary before their enemies, and that the citizens would not prove a trusty part of the garrison ; and their number of common men was so small that the constant duty was performed by the officers and gentlemen of quality, who were absolutely tired out ; so that, after a week or ten days' siege, they were compelled, upon no better articles than quarter, to deliver the city "—(*Clarendon*).

The victorious Roundheads immediately began their icono-

clastic labours. They demolished the cathedral organ, " crying
in scoff, ' Hark ! how the organs goe !'" defaced its ornaments,
destroyed its tombs, and despoiled them of their brasses; battered
down the churches of St. Pancras and St. Bartholomew ; and
pillaged the houses of all who were suspected of' being " malig-
nants."   Sir William Waller fixed his head-quarters at the Grey
Friary House, and " billeted " his soldiers in the Cathedral.

It may be added that Algernon Sidney was governor of
Chichester in 1645.

The poet Collins was born in this quiet cathedral city on
Christmas day, 1720, and died here, in a house in the cloister,
in 1756. Another of its worthies was Bishop Juxon, born August
24, 1591.   Hayley was also a Chichester celebrity — " a star of
the sixth magnitude," which hid " its diminished head" after the
uprising of greater minds. A good portrait of Cowper's friend
and biographer, by Romney, is preserved in the house of Mr.
Mason, and other *souvenirs* of general interest. This gentleman
also possesses some' specimens of the art-labours of George Smith
and John Smith, " whose genius in the art of landscape painting obtained for them a merited distinction in their native
city."

The first object in Chichester to which the tourist's attention
will naturally be directed, is its CATHEDRAL, established here
temp. William I., on the removal of the episcopate from Selsey
to the ancient Regnum.   It was erected on the site of a Saxon
monastery, dedicated to St. Peter, and had but a brief existence.
It was destroyed by fire in 1114. Bishop Ralph immediately
commenced another building, and so energetically pushed forward
its works, that it was nearly completed in 1123. Of this venerable structure much remains. The additions it has received will
best be understood from the following chronological statement :—

STYLE.	ADDITIONS.	DATE.
Norman.	The Nave, North and South Aisles, and Tri-forium, are Bishop Ralph's	1115-23
Early English.	The higher stones of the South-west Tower, and the Clerestory of the Nave, the West and South Porches, were added by Bishop Seffrid, who lengthened the Choir and vaulted the Roof	1188

STYLE.	ADDITIONS.	DATE.
Early English.	The Marble Shafts, chiefly of Petworth marble, were erected by Bishop Fitzrobert	1204-10
,,	The Spire and Chapter House, by Bishop Neville	1222-24
,,	The two Exterior Aisles, North and South, Bishop de la Wych . . .	1245-53
,,	The Lady Chapel (now the Library), Bishop de St. Lespard	1288-1304
Decorated.	The Presbytery, Sacristy, South Transept, and Bell Tower, by Bishop John de Langton,	1305-38
,,	The Rendos and Carved Stalls and Decorations of the South Transept, by Bishop Sherbourne.	
Perpendicular.	The Oratory, now the Organ Screen, by Bishop Arundel	1447
,,	The Organ, built by Harris, 1678, improved by Gray and Davison, 1844, and Hill	1851
,,	The Throne, by Bishop Mawson . .	1749

Entering the Cathedral by its WESTERN PORCH (Early English, and built by Bishop Seffrid II.), we first remark the five divisions of the NAVE—a characteristic which distinguishes it from all other English Cathedrals, but which is not altogether to be admired. Much picturesqueness of effect, however, is produced by their constantly shifting lights and shadows. The clerestory, and the Purbeck marble of the piers are to be ascribed to Bishop Seffrid. Bishop Richard de la Wych (1245-1253), was the builder of the additional aisles, designed for chantries or side chapels. The piscinas and aumbries in the walls indicate the positions of the different altars. Observe that the side-shafts are triple, the bearing shafts " clustered in threes," with three triple vaulting-ribs above, symbolic of the Holy Trinity, to whom Bishop Seffrid dedicated this part of the Cathedral.

The stained glass in the two western windows is by Wailes. The larger one is a memorial to the late Dean Chandler, erected by the parishioners of All Souls, St. Marylebone, where he was rector for many years. The memorial window, in the north aisle, to Sir Thomas Reynell, is by O'Connor, that to F. E. Freeland, by Willement.

The ARUNDEL CHANTRY is in the north aisle. It contains the tomb of Caen stone—restored in 1843 by Richardson,—for

CHICHESTER CATHEDRAL.

The Discovery of the Remains of the Daughter of Canute at Bosham.

Some discussion next took place among the members respecting the interesting discovery of the remains of the daughter of Canute at Bosham. We gave an account of this in our columns two or three weeks ago, and the paragraph was copied into most of the London and local newspapers. Mr. Durrant Cooper expressed a hope that the Lord Bishop would intimate to the incumbent of Bosham a desire that he would not permit those remains to be removed, or even touched. If the coffin was removed under any pretence, doubts would be thrown on the subject of the discovery. The Bishop strongly concurred in the opinion that the coffin should not be touched under the pretence of searching out anything, or for sketching or other purposes; and the Rev. H. Mitchell, the rector, gave a pledge to the meeting not to allow the remains to be in any way disturbed. The rev. gentleman then handed round some photographic copies of the contents of the coffin. These had been taken from a drawing, and showed the remains of the child, who was about eight years old. Mr. Mitchell said there was a tradition at Bosham that Canute's daughter was buried in Bosham Church, and there was a piscina on the south side of the chancel near an altar before which it was alleged masses were said for her soul; and, knowing this, and having the opportunity, they dug on the spot where the remains were said to be. There were three other persons present besides the masons engaged in the work; and, to their great delight, they were able to confirm the truth of the tradition in every respect. The child lay in a very rude coffin, one of the earliest stone coffins, quite plain, with a very rude covering, seven inches thick. It was evidently a coffin of early date, because there was no place for the head, as was the case with coffins of a later date. He believed there were no stone coffins of a later date than the 13th century, and those coffins had always a place cut for the head to rest in. But the coffin in question was quite plain, a clear indication of a much earlier date.—The Bishop remarked that the circumstance gave an additional interest to Bosham, which had an historical reputation as being the port from which Harold set sail when he went, willingly or unwillingly, to the coast of Normandy, where he was made a detenu by William Duke of Normandy, a circumstance fraught with consequences which affected this Kingdom of England up to the present day, namely, that he conquered her and obtained possession, as we all knew.—Mr. Mitchell mentioned that a Bazaar was to be held next Thursday (this day) and Friday, in the grounds of Admiral Berkeley, of Old Park, Bosham, in aid of the funds for the restoration of the very old and very interesting Church of Bosham, and he hoped that as many members of the Archæological Society as could make it convenient would attend.

Richard Fitzalan, Earl of Arundel, beheaded for high treason in 1397. This tomb was opened by order of Richard II. shortly after the earl's interment, because the common people believed that a miracle had been wrought, and that his head had grown to his body again.

A CHANTRY, dedicated to ST. JOHN THE BAPTIST, occupies the end of the aisle. Here there is a stately Decorated tomb, with effigy, of a nameless lady, supposed by some authorities to be Maud, countess of Arundel, and pronounced by Flaxman the finest in England.

MEMORIALS IN THE NAVE.—The Hon. *William Huskisson,* d. 1830, the statue by Carew ; *Collins,* the poet, d. 1756, the medallion by Flaxman. The poet is pictured as studying the Scriptures. " I have but one book," he said to Dr. Johnson shortly before his death, " and that is the best." At his feet lies a volume of " The Passions." Two female figures, Love and Religion, are placed upon the pediment, and underneath is lettered an epitaph by Hayley and Sargent,—

" Ye who the merits of the dead revere,
Who hold misfortune's sacred genius dear,
Regard this tomb ; where Collins' hapless name
Solicits kindness with a double claim.
Strangers to him, enamour'd of his lays,
This fond memorial to his talents raise.
For this the ashes of the bard require,
Who touch'd the tenderest notes of Pity's Lyre."

The monuments (in the south aisle) of *Jane Smith* and *Agnes Cromwell,* are also Flaxman's handiwork. The memorial window, representing the martyrdom of St. Stephen, is by Wailes.

The CHOIR, and the east aisles behind it, were built by Bishop Seffrid. The latter are Transition Norman in style, and exhibit the gradual change from the circular to the pointed arch. Observe the grotesque bones in which the vaulting ribs terminate. It is difficult to imagine what object the sculptor could have had in view when he carved those monstrous human faces. Was it satirical ? Did any of his contemporaries trace a likeness to certain living notabilities in those exaggerated lineaments ? Behind the altar-screen stand the monuments of Bishop *Stone,* d. 1503 ; Bishop *Henry King* (1641-69), poet and prelate ; Bishop *Grove,* d. 1596 ; and Bishop *Carlton,* d. 1705. A purbeck slab, in the pavement, is figured with two hands holding up a heart, and inscribed " Ici git le cœur de Maud." The rest is illegible. The tomb of Bishop *Day*, d. 1556, is on the right.

The SCREEN which separates choir and nave was erected by Bishop *Arundel* (1458-78), and is known as his " Oratory." A nicked arcade surmounts these arches, which are enriched with quatrefoils in their spandrils. The stalls in the choir, the altar-screen, and the decorations of the south transept, were the gift of Bishop Sherbourne, and justify old Fuller's quaint eulogy :— " Now though ˙Seffride bestowed the cloth and making on the church, Bishop Sherbourne gave the trimming and best lace thereto."

The NORTH TRANSEPT forms the parish church of St. Peter the Great, more commonly called the Sub-Deanery. The SOUTH TRANSEPT was lengthened, and its beautiful window inserted, by Bishop Langton (1305-38), but the Roundhead troopers destroyed the stained glass. The Bishop's tomb, considerably defaced, stands beneath it, and close at hand, the memorial of *John Smith*, Esq. of Dale Park. The tomb near the choir is considered to be that of Bishop *Richard de la Wych*, d. 1253, the last Englishman who received " the honour " of canonization. In the ACTA SANCTORUM may be read, in considerable detail, the miracles wrought by St. Richard of Chichester. The tomb was restored by Richardson in 1847, and the small figures in the arches are entirely his handiwork. Hither the devout pilgrims of Kent, Sussex, and Hampshire were wont to repair, and lay their offerings, and branches plucked on the road, on the shrine of the Sussex saint.

The figures of the Bishops of Selsey and Chichester which enrich the walls were Bishop Sherbourne's donation to his Cathedral. From the " family-likeness " between them, one would imagine that they respresent a succession of great grand-fathers, fathers, and sons, all of the same remarkable race. The English sovereigns are presented on the opposite wall, and above them a picture, in two panels, represents Cadwalla bestowing Selsey upon St. Wilfrid, and Henry VIII. confirming the grant to Bishop Sherbourne. Cadwalla is a portrait of Henry VII., and all the kings, nobles, and ecclesiastics introduced are costumed in the Tudor style. A Flemish artist, Theodore Bernardi, and his sons were the artists employed by Bishop Sherbourne.

The railed-off portion of the transept is now made use of as **an** ecclesiastical court. The old consistory (Perpendicular in style) was a room over the porch, to which access was obtained by a spiral staircase in the nave. It opened upon the Lollards' Prison through a sliding panel.

A very curious oaken chest, 8 feet long, preserved in the SACRISTY ; and two carved slabs (discovered in 1829) which represent the Raising of Lazarus, and Martha and Mary meeting the Saviour, are supposed to have been removed from Selsey. Near these sculptures stands the tomb of Bishop *Sherbourne*, d. 1536, restored at the expense of New College, Oxon, to which foundation the prelate had intrusted its custody.

At the extreme east end of the Cathedral is the LADY CHAPEL, built by Bishop de St. Lespard (1288-1305), at an expense of 1250 marks. It is now little better than a mortuary chapel for the Duke of Richmond's family. A slab is inscribed " DOMUS ULTIMA, 1750,"—an inscription which suggested to Dr. Clarke, one of the residentiaries, the following bitter epigram :—

> " Did he who thus inscribed this wall,
> Not read, or not believe, St. Paul,
> Who says there is, where'er it stands,
> *Another house*, not built with hands ?
> Or may we gather from these words
> That house is not a house—for Lords ? "

Under two arches in the passage which leads to the Lady Chapel, is placed the black marble slab inscribed to Bishop *Ralph*, d. 1325.

The large canopied tomb in the north aisle is that of Bishop *Moleynes*, a faithful adherent of the Lancasterian party, murdered at Portsmouth in 1449.

The CHAPTER LIBRARY, with its rare MSS., printed books, and relics, is preserved in the Lady Chapel. Among the relics are a silver chalice and paten, an agate thumb-ring (or Basilidian gem) inscribed with a Gnostic talisman, two other rings, and a leaden cross, discovered in 1829 in the stone coffins of two prelates, who are supposed to have been *Godfrey*, the second bishop of Chichester, d. 1091, and Bishop *Seffrid II.*, d. 1205.

From the south aisle we pass into the quiet CLOISTERS (Perpendicular), which afford some fine views of the general characteristics of the Cathedral. The space they enclose is called "Paradise." The SPIRE* (dating from 1337) was 270 feet from the

---

* This beautiful structure has lately fallen into ruins, and a fund is being raised to provide for its restoration—(May 1861).

ground, and so resembled that of Salisbury that the local saying ran,—"The master-mason built Salisbury, and his man built Chichester." Mr. Truman, in an able paper on the architecture of the Cathedral, to which the tourist may with advantage refer (*Sus. Arch. Coll.*, vol. i.), points out that in these Cathedrals alone there is "a visible centre and axis to the whole building, viz., the summit of the spire, and a line let fall from it to the ground. Salisbury was so constructed at first. Chichester was made exactly central, to an inch, by the additions of the Lady Chapel and west porch. Michael Angelo's most perfect outline, the pyramidal, is thus gained. The eye is carried upward to the spire point from the chapels clustering at the base, along the roof of pinnacles." Detached from the building, on the north side, rises the campanile or bell-tower, 120 feet high. It has four turrets at its summit, exactly similar to those at the base of the spire, whence it has been conjectured that it was built (at the same period) to receive the bells from the old tower. The stone made use of was quarried near Ventnor, in the Isle of Wight.

DIMENSIONS OF THE CATHEDRAL.

	Length in feet.	Breadth in feet.	Height in feet.
Nave	156	91·9	62·3
Choir	105	59	60
Presbytery	52·2	...	...
Lady Chapel	62·9	20·7	22
Spire	...	...	271
South-west tower	...	...	95
Transept	131	24·3	...
Campanile	...	...	120

Total length 380 feet.

The Cathedral establishment includes a dean, four canons, five minor canons, seven lay vicars, ten choristers, and four Wykehamical prebends. The average yearly income is £5,100.

Among the more notable bishops may be named—Ralph de Neville, Lord Chancellor, 1222-45 ; Richard de la Wych, or St. Richard, 1245-53 ; Adam Moleynes, Henry VI.'s councillor, 1445-9 ; Lancelot Andrewes, the sycophantic favourite of James I., 1605-9 ; Brian Duppa, 1638-41 ; and Francis Hare, the adversary of Hoadley, in the famous Bangorian controversy, 1731-40.

The EPISCOPAL PALACE is situated to the west of the cathedral, and consists of a spacious mansion whose two wings are connected by an open corridor. The CHAPEL is of the age of Henry III., with windows of a later date. Remark the timber ceiling of Bishop Sherbourne's REFECTORY, painted in compartments with scrolls and armorial bearings by the Bernardis.

The MARKET CROSS, at the point of junction of the four great Cistercian thoroughfares, was built by Bishop Storey about 1480, and considerably defaced by Waller's troopers. The dial was given, in 1724, by Dame Elizabeth Farrington. "Its vaulted roof is supported by a thick central pillar, and by a series of arches octagonal in form, and highly ornamented with coats of arms and other ornaments." It is altogether an interesting and a picturesque structure, which the townsmen keep in excellent repair.

The TOWN HALL, situated in the priory park, near the end of North Street, was formerly a chapel belonging to a monastery of Grey Friars. Behind the magistrates' seats may be seen the ancient Early English sedilia. A circular mound in the garden was, perhaps, the Calvary of the ancient priory.

A rapid visit to the Parochial Churches of the city must now be undertaken.

ST. PETER THE GREAT is now converted into the north transept of the cathedral. Attached to it on the east is a chancel, with a low roof formed upon intersecting ribs, which have Norman mouldings. Within the precincts of this parish, and in the cathedral cloisters, lies *William Chillingworth*, d. 1644, the famous author of "The Religion of Protestants a safe way to Salvation." When his funeral procession arrived at the grave, it was met by his impetuous opponent, the Presbyterian Cheynell, who flung Chillingworth's immortal work upon his coffin "to rot," he said, "with its author, and see corruption!"

ALL SAINTS', IN THE PALLANT, is of great antiquity. Some portions may be Early Norman. Hayley, the poet, was baptized here, November 25, 1745.

The church of ST. ANDREW, in East Street, was built *temp.* Henry VII. At a depth of 4 feet beneath it lies a Roman tessellated pavement. Collins was buried here in 1756.

ST. MARTIN'S, in St. Martin's Lane, was rebuilt about forty years ago, in a style which may be denominated Modern Gothic. The east window, with its stained glass, is good.

ST. OLAVE'S, in North Street, recently restored, occupies the site of a Roman building, and is, perhaps, the oldest Christian church in England. Roman bricks were employed in its construction, and the small door on the south side may even be of Roman work.

ST. PANCRAS' CHURCH stands at a small distance beyond the East Gate. It was nearly demolished during Waller's siege of the city in 1642, and not rebuilt until 1750. ST. BARTHOLOMEW'S was destroyed at the same time. There is nothing of interest in the present building.

The CHAPEL, dedicated to St. John, stands on the site of the Black Friars', near the East Gate. It was built in 1813 from the designs of James Elmes.

[The patrons and annual incomes of these benefices are as follows :—All Saints, R., £45, Archbishop of Canterbury ; St. Andrew, R., £80, Dean and Chapter of Chichester ; St. Martin, R., £67, the same patrons ; St. Olave, R., £56, the same ; St. Pancras, R., £95, Simeon's Trustees ; St. Peter the Great, V., £110, Dean and Chapter ; St. Peter the Less, R., £56, the Dean ; St. Bartholomew, P. C., £65, the Dean ; St. Paul's, P. C., the Dean and Chapter ; St. John's, Trustees.]

ST. MARY'S HOSPITAL is a picturesque Decorated pile, which the tourist must not fail to visit. It was founded in 1229, and replaced a nunnery originally established in 1173. The revenues are apportioned among a *custos* or warden, six women, and two men, whose rooms are constructed in the side walls of the Refectory or Long Hall. The CHAPEL, which contains some excellent carved work, is divided from this hall by an open oaken screen. The arched roof and its huge timbers, resting on low stone walls, deserves examination.

Some houses in the upper part of South Street were built, it is said, by Wren. The Philosophical Society have their Museum of Local Antiquities and Natural History in this street, which communicates with the Cathedral Close by the CANONS' GATE, built by Bishop Sherbourne, whose arms are sculptured above the entrance.

The OTTER MEMORIAL COLLEGE (for training schoolmasters), founded by Bishop Otter, and erected in 1849-50, from Butler's designs ; and the entrenchment on the Goodwood road, known as the BROYLE (from *bruillum*, a coppice), have each a special interest for different classes of tourists.

[HINTS FOR RAMBLES.—1. To Tangmere and Boxgrove Church. Visit Halnaker House ; cross to Goodwood and return by East Lavant.—2. Through Appledram, Donnington, and Sidlesham, to Selsey. Return by way of Pagham and North Mundham.—3. By the Portsmouth road to Bosham. Keep northwards to Funtington. Thence to West Stoke and Mid Lavant.—4. Keep across the hills to Cocking, and thence by way of Heyshot and Graffham into the Guildford road. Return through Boxgrove.—5. By road to Arundel. Visit Arundel Castle and Leominster. Return from Arundel Station by rail.—By rail to Woodgate Station. Visit Bognor and South Bersted. Cross the country to Oving and Tangmere (north), and return by the Brighton road.]

BRANCH ROUTE—CHICHETSER to PULBOROUGH.

If we leave Chichester by the Guildford road we shall reach, at 2 miles from the cathedral city, the highway which diverges to Brighton. TANGMERE (population, 221) lies at some small distance beyond us. Its Early English Church, dedicated to St. Andrew, consists of a nave and chancel. Part of the paving of the latter is a curious combination of bricks, stones, plain and ornamented aisles. The Duke of Richmond is patron of the rectory, which is valued at £282.

A cross road leads us from this little village through BOX-GROVE (population, 755), into the Guildford road, 4 miles from Chichester.

BOXGROVE CHURCH is not one of the least interesting in the country. It embodies portions of Boxgrove Priory, founded in 1117 by Robert de Haiâ, Lord of Halmacro, for three Benedictine monks, and dedicated to the Virgin and St. Blaise. Roger St. John, who married the Lord of Halmacro's heiress, added three more, and his sons increased the number to fifteen. When suppressed by King Henry VIII. there were but nine monks, and their annual revenues were estimated at £189, 19s.

The present parish church is supposed to have been the original choir. Some portions of the ancient nave (apparently of a still earlier date) may be traced in the broken arches west of the church. The Chapter House is attached externally to the north transept. Its Norman doorway probably led to a cloister which extended to the Refectory and the habitations of the monks. A gap, generally inhabited by browsing sheep, now separates the Refectory from the Church. Marks of a piscina may just be discerned.

The CHURCH consists of a low tower, nave, and chancel, side aisles, and north and south transept, and a space westward of the tower which has been characterized as the most ancient part of the whole building. Its length is 124 feet ; width of the nave, 24 feet ; of each of the aisles, 13 feet 6 inches. The east window is Early English, of three large lights, and very fine.

The interior contains six tombs of great antiquity, but which it is almost impossible to identify with any degree of satisfaction. Two of the three placed against the south wall of the south aisle probably contain the dust of Olive and Agatha, daughters of William de Albini, Earl of Arundel, and Queen Alice the Fair. Other two tombs *may* enshrine the remains of *Thomas de Poynings*, d. 1429, and his wife *Philippa*, Countess of Arundel. The Delawarr SACELLUM, or SHRINE, dated 1532, is very curious and beautiful. Its length is 14 feet, its height 12 feet, and it bears the inscription—" Of y^r charite pray for ye souls of Thomas La Ware and Elyzabeth hys Wyf." It is richly carved in stone, and profusely ornamented.

The pulpit is of carved oak. The font is ancient. The Duke of Richmond is patron of the vicarage, which is valued at £687.

About half a mile to the left lie the scanty remains of HAL-NACRE or HALNAKER HOUSE, built by Sir Thomas West, Lord Delawarr, who also fashioned for himself " a poor chapell" at Boxgrove Church. The walls were castellated. The gateway, furnished with a portcullis, was furnished with small octangular towers, leading into a square court. The surrounding Park is enriched with noble groups of Spanish chesnut, in whose shadow a large herd of deer disport.

We cross from this point westward into GOODWOOD PARK (Duke of Richmond), to which the tourist has at all times ready access. The mansion can only be seen during the family's absence. Of the luxuriantly wooded park (1214 acres) much might be said and written in commendation ; with respect to the house it is otherwise. The architects were Sir William Chambers (who built the south wing) and Wyatt. The centre is 160 feet long, and ornamented with a double colonnade ; each of the two receding wings is flanked by towers, and 106 feet in length.

[The COLLECTION of PICTURES is large, but contains few *chefs d'œuvres*. The HALL is adorned by some fine Vandykes—Charles I., Henrietta Maria in all her fatal beauty, and their five children ; Charles II. by Sir *Peter Lely ;* Louise de Querouailles, Duchess of Portsmouth, *Kneller ;* her son, Charles, first Duke of Richmond, and his wife Anne, *Kneller ;* Sir William Waller, by *Lely ;* and the Duchess of Richmond, Sir *Thomas Lawrence.*

The DRAWING-ROOM, 35 feet by 23, is hung with Gobelin tapestry (the gift of Louis XV. to Duke Charles), representing the adventures of Don Quixote. The chimney-piece, sculptured by Bacon with the story of Venus and Adonis, cost £150. Here are preserved in a cabinet " a worked shirt of Charles I., and some silver articles used during the infancy of Charles II."

The DINING-ROOM, 45 feet by 23 feet, where the allied Sovereigns were banqueted on their visit to England in 1814, contains a bust of Wellington, by *Turnelli;* and Nollekens' busts of William Pitt and the Marquis of Rockingham. The MUSIC ROOM contains a fine picture of a ruined sea-port by *Salvator Rosa ;* portraits of the Marquis of Montrose, Henry Carew the song writer, and witty Pettigrew, by *Vandyck ;* the Duke of Monmouth, *Kneller ;* and specimens of Lely and others. In the ANTE-ROOM may be noticed four portraits by *Sir Joshua*, and a William Pitt, by *Gainsborough.*

The LIBRARY presents to our notice the third Duke of Richmond, by *Romney ;* and the fourth Duke, by *Jackson.* The BILLIARD ROOM, Lord Anson, by *Romney ;* and some tolerable landscapes by the two Smiths of Chichester. Here, too, is hung the highly curious " Cenotaph of Lord Darnley," removed from the Chateau D'Aubigny, where it was accidentally discovered. In the right hand corner an inscription indicates the subject of the picture :—" Tragica et lamentabilis internecio serenissimi Henrici Scotorum Regis." Other inscriptions record that the picture was begun in October 1567 (seven months after the murder), and completed in the following January. It has been ascribed to Levinus Venetianus. Small designs representing the scene of the murder, the murdered man's body beneath a tree in the orchard, the battle of Carberry Hill, and the city of Edinburgh, surround a large oval composition in which King James, the Earl and Countess of Lennox (Darnley's parents), and others are pictured kneeling before Darnley's corpse, which is deposited at the base of an altar.

The walls of the STONE STAIRCASE are enriched with *Hogarth's* picture of " The Lady's Last Stake ; " the Judgment of Paris, *Guido ;* Marriage at Cana, *Paolo Veronese ;* the Madonna, *Parmegiano ;* Antiochus and Stratonice, *Barry ;* Duke of Monmouth, *Lely ;* and specimens of the Smiths of Chichester, Hudson, and Romney. The LONG HALL contains two views of London from the terrace and gardens of Richmond House, Whitehall, by *Canaletti.*

The PARK is finely ordered in its alternations of the artistic and the natural ; from the ascent in the rear of the house some good prospects may be enjoyed. About 150 cedars of Lebanon remain out of 1000 planted by the third Duke of Richmond in 1761. There is a noble avenue of chesnuts, and some glorious cypresses in the High Woods, near the house, where, also, is preserved the remarkable Brito-Roman slab discovered at Chichester in 1731 (together with the remains of the stone wall of a temple), when the foundations for the Council Chamber were excavated. It is a slab of grey Purbeck marble, and was thus inscribed. [The letters in italics indicate those which have been conjecturally supplied.]

> " *N*eptuni et Minervæ temptum
> *Pro* salute *d*omus divinæ
> *Ex* anchoritate *Ti*beriis Claudii
> *Co*gidubin r. leg. aug. in Brit.
> *Co*lle*g*ium fabror. et qui in eo
> *A sacris* sunt d. s. d. donante aream
> *Pude*nte pudentini fil."

*** In explanation of this inscription it may be added that the " collegium fabrorum " was probably a company of smiths or shipwrights of Chichester, who would naturally regard Neptune and Minerva as their patrons. Cogidubnus was highly rewarded for his fidelity to the Roman alliance, and, according to the Ròman fashion, assumed the name of his patron, the Emperor Tiberius Claudius. The site of the temple, whose foundation stone was laid by Cogidubnus, was given by Pudens, son of Pudentinus, who is supposed to be the British Christian, a disciple of St. Paul's, referred to in conjunction with Claudius in the second epistle to Timothy, c. iv., v. 21, and also named by Martial.]

The GOODWOOD RACE COURSE, on the high ground, 1 mile north-east of the house, commands a magnificent landscape. The *Goodwood races*, a well-known aristocratic gathering, were established in 1802. Other points of different degrees of interest, either in the Park or its immediate vicinity, are *Cairney Seat*, so named from an old retainer of the Richmonds ; the *Pheasantry*, in a leafy hollow of the chalk ; the *Stables*, which are complete in every detail ; the great *Lebanon Cedar*, 25 feet in girth ; the pleasant rustic villa at *Molecomb* ; the circular camp of the *Trundle*, enclosing 5 acres, which crowns the summit of St. Roche's Hill (locally Rock's Hill), 702 feet above the sea-level.

Goodwood, or Godinwood, derived its name from its Saxon owner, Godwinus. It was purchased from the Comptons, in 1720, by the first Duke of Richmond, the son of Madam Carwell (Louise de Querouailles) and Charles II.

About 2 miles from Boxgrove, to the right of the main road, and at some short distance from it, lies EARTHAM (population, 103). Hayley resided here until 1800, when he disposed of his estate to Huskisson, the statesman, whose life was the first sacrifice to " the railway giant." He enlarged the house, and made considerable improvements in the vicinity. The Early English CHURCH consists of a chancel, nave, and north aisle. The chancel arch is Norman, and very fine. A beautiful sculpture by Flaxman commemorates *Thomas Hayley*, d. 1800, the poet's only child. There is a tablet in the north aisle to Huskisson's memory, but the unfortunate statesman was buried at Liverpool.

The vicarage, valued at £186, is in the patronage of the prebendary of Chichester.

We next reach UP WALTHAM (population, 67)—where there is an Early English CHURCH, with an apsidal chancel—and turning to the right, ascend the slopes of Sutton Hill. From its crest we command a panorama of wood, and dale, and glen, and village, which we treasure up as one of " things of beauty," which are " joys for ever." Passing through SUTTON (population,

389. *Inn :* The White Horse) we wind through a pleasant blooming lane to BIGNOR (population, 203), on an excursion into
Roman England. For it is neither BIGNOR PARK nor BIGNOR
CHURCH that draws us hither into the depths of the Weald, but
the remains of a Roman villa, of more than ordinary interest,
first excavated in 1811. Bignor is the " Ad decimam " of the
itinerary of Richard of Cirencester, that is, a station at the *tenth*
milestone from Regnum,—" a halting-place which was 'probably
established at this point of the Roman road on account of the
vicinity of the great villa ; just as a modern railway ' lord' procures
a station in the neighbourhood of his own residence."

The remains are now protected from the weather by some
wooden huts. The fields where they are situated have been long
known as the Berry field, and the Town field ; " the former no
doubt because it had been the site of a principal mass of buildings (from the Anglo-Saxon *beorh*), and the other because it was
an old tradition among the inhabitants of the parish that the
town of ' Bignor' once stood there."

In July 1811, a ploughman, at work in the Berry field, struck
his share against what proved to be part of a beautiful Roman
pavement, which had evidently belonged to a large and handsome room. A series of careful excavations, under the superintendence of Lysons, the antiquary, brought to light the pavements
and foundations of a Roman villa of considerable magnitude.
They were traced in fact to an extent of about 600 feet in length,
and nearly 350 feet in breadth. The principal household buildings formed about half that length. They stood round an inner
court, which was nearly a rectangular parallelogram, about 150
feet by 100 feet. Its aspect was, in its length, nearly north-
west and south-east. Round this court ran a beautiful *crypto-
porticus,* or covered gallery, 10 feet wide, with a fine tessellated
pavement. At the north angle there was a small square room,
with an " extremely elegant tessellated pavement." On the north-
east side were placed the chief apartments. The first apartment
was here discovered in 1811, and presented two divisions (as in a
London front and back drawing-room), which may probably have
been separated by movable hangings. In each division may
be noticed a circular compartment, one 16 feet in diameter,
the other 17 feet 6 inches ; the larger pictorially illustrated with
dancing nymphs,—the smaller with the rape of Ganymede. " This
pavement so completely resembles one at Avenches in Switzer-

land, executed about the reign of Titus, that this Sussex villa has been assigned to the same period"—(*Murray*).   There is a stone cistern or fountain in the centre of the larger room, 4 feet·in diameter, and 1 foot 7¾ inches in depth, which appears to have been filled by a jet d'eau.   "To judge by the remains, the walls had been beautifully painted in fresco, fragments of which were lying about, the colours perfectly fresh.   A fragment or two of small Doric columns were found among the rubbish of this apartment"—(*Wright*, Wanderings of an Antiquary).

The next room exhibits another handsome pavement, which had been adorned at the angles with figures symbolical of the Four Seasons.   That of Winter remains : a woman's head shrouded in drapery, a leafless branch at her side : colour and expression of no ordinary degree of merit.   A third room boasts of a yet more fanciful decoration ; the pavement, divided into two apartments, is ornamented with Cupids, dressed as gladiators—*retiarii*, with their short swords and entangling nets ; *secutores*, helmeted and greaved ; and *rudiarii*, the veteran "masters of the ceremonies."   Here you see the athletes making ready for the coming fight ; there, the struggle has commenced.   Here, the rudiarius comes to the succour of the wounded retiarius ; there, he lies disarmed, "butchered to make a Roman holiday."   A semicircular division in the north angle of the pavement presents a charming female head, adorned with a wreath of blossoms, and enriched by a light azure halo.   There are some remains of small Doric columns.

Another room, 14½ feet by 17 feet, contains a *caminus*, or *focus*—an open fire place—instead of the hot-air-hypocaust.

The Bath-room is at the south-west corner of the Crypto-porticus, and contains extensive portions of the bath.   Adjoining it are large rooms with hypocausts for heating the sudatorium. "Other large rooms adjoin the south corner at the extremity of the south-east end of the inner court, in the middle of which end was the grand entrance into this inner court from a much larger outer court.   This outer court seems to have been surrounded with bare walls, although tracings of buildings were found in various parts of the interior.   The walls of this outer court seem to have been continued so as to surround the whole edifice, which perhaps, externally, presented merely the appearance of a great irregular square-walled enclosure.   It must have been a princely residence, and it is evident that the luxurious comforts of the interior were no less studied than the beauty of the scenery around"—(*Wright*).

A few fragments of pottery are preserved at the villa ; and at Bignor Park there is shewn a gold-ring, set with an exquisite intaglio, which depicts a warrior holding his shield before him.

☞ The Bignor remains are exhibited to the tourist on payment of a small fee. Application must be made to Mr. Tupper at the neighbouring farm. It is understood that their owner would be glad to dispose of the site and its relics, and suggestions have been made for the removal of the latter to the British Museum. Let us hope that they will be suffered to remain *here*, on the land which of old they occupied as portions of the royal villa of some haughty proprietor or august legate ; and that so the tourist's imagination may be inspired to people the surrounding hills with the stalwart soldier-colonists sent forth by imperial Rome,—to hear the soft voice of Lydia or Aglaia repeating the graceful love-songs of Tibullus,— to see the social life of Roman England seething, and toiling, and whirling all around him, where now in the grassy valley only murmurs the music of the winds !

We return now to Bignor ($\frac{1}{2}$ mile west), and visit the uninteresting CHURCH, small in itself, but "a world too large" for the congregation which ordinarily assembles there. The churchyard boasts of two noble yews. Lord Leconfield is the patron of the rectory, which is valued at £143.

BIGNOR PARK (S. H. Hawkins, Esq.) was originally " an appendage to the Castle of Arundel, and used for fatting deer driven in from the forest"—(*Horsfield*). The present house, commanding rich and extensive views of the lofty sweep of the South Downs and the brown leaf masses of the Weald, was begun in 1826, and occupies the site of an old Tudor mansion. Charlotte Smith, the author of " The Old Manor House," died 1806, and Mrs. Dorset, author of the " Peacock at Home," were the daughters of Nicholas Turner, Esq., who long enjoyed this picturesque estate, and they resided here for many years. In her " Sonnets," Charlotte Smith has duly celebrated the charms of this neighbourhood and of the valley of the Arun.

[From Bignor the tourist may diverge south-east to BURY HILL, where there is a large tumulus, and whence a fine prospect may be obtained ; or he may keep away southward to DALE PARK (G. Fletcher, Esq.), which commands some exquisite views of the surrounding country. SLINDON PARK (Countess of Newburgh) lies to the south-west of Dale Park, from which it is separated by the village of SLINDON (population, 599). It was erected by Sir Garret Kempe, *temp.* Elizabeth, on the site of a mansion originally built—as early as the thirteenth century—by an archbishop of Canterbury, and reported to be the scene of the death of the great Stephen Langton. SLINDON CHURCH, Early English, contains the effigy of a knight under a niche in the chancel.]

Returning through SUTTON and BARLAVINGTON (population, 128), into the Guildford road, we speedily reach, at 2½ miles south of Petworth, the small parish of BURTON (population, 28), chiefly included within the ring-fence and palings of BURTON PARK (S. Biddulph, Esq.), formerly the seat of the Gorings. The present building retains some portions of " a new, spacious, and splendid structure," designed by Giacomo Leoni, which was nearly destroyed by fire in 1826. The park includes 210 acres. It is abundantly wooded and well watered. The ponds are stored with carp, trout, and pike, and haunted by wild fowl. An oak, near the house, is 25 feet in girth.

BURTON CHURCH contains some memorials, in Sussex marble, for members of the Goring family. Divine service is now performed in the parish church at COATES (population, 63), and the united benefices are in the patronage of G. Wyndham, Esq., and valued at £113.

[At DANETON (population, 272), on the northern slope of the chalk hills, the remains of a Roman hypocaust were discovered in 1815, about 140 yards north-east of the church. It probably belonged to a Roman public military bath.]

Keeping north from Burton we pass on our right the terminus (2 miles from Petworth, of the Petworth and Horsham branch of the London and South Coast Railway ; cross the Rother, and soon see before us the grassy glades and waving demesne of Petworth Park.

BRANCH ROUTE—CHICHESTER, *via* MIDHURST, TO HASELMERE.

We leave the cathedral city by the direct Guildford road, which runs through a country of singularly romantic character. After passing the Broyle, to our right lies WEST HAMPNETT (population, 637), or Hamplonette, whose workhouse or " Union" exhibits considerable remains of the ancient Elizabethan Place-

House, built by Richard Sackville. The ceiling of the Great Staircase is covered with an allegory of St. Cecilia. To the aforesaid *Richard Sackville*, and *Elizabeth* his wife, there is a curious mural monument in the chancel of St. Peter's church, with " one of the worst representations of the Trinity that can possibly be conceived." The Duke of Richmond is the patron of the vicarage, which is valued at £40.

At 2 miles from Chichester we pass MID LAVANT (population, 284), and beyond it, EAST LAVANT (population, 421). Pennant derives the word "Lavant" from the Celtic TELEVAN, and says it indicates "a place alternately covered with water, or left dry at the recess of the tides." Hence he infers that "the harbour of Chichester formerly flowed higher up the country, and washed even the walls of the city." The Lavant is now a small rivulet, which empties itself into Chichester Harbour. It rises in Charlton Forest.

MID LAVANT CHURCH is as commonplace in character as most of the churches built after the Restoration generally prove. It contains a marble effigy of Dame *Mary May*, d. 1681. The Duke of Richmond is patron of the curacy, valued at £52.

EAST LAVANT CHURCH consists of a nave and chancel, and contains a brass for *Thomas Cawse*, and a slab of Sussex marble, inscribed in Longobardic characters,—" *Priez çi passez par ici. Pour l'alme Luci de Mildebi.*"

The rectory, valued at £410, is in the patronage of Lord De Broke.

At Mid Lavant a road branches off across the downs, over-looking in its course the rich masses of Goodwood Park, while another keeps to the left along the base of the hill, and passes WEST DEAN (population, 669). WEST DEAN PARK (Rev. L. V. Harcourt) is a luxuriantly wooded demesne, sheltered by an environment of pleasant hills. The mansion has a front-age of 300 feet, in a quasi-Gothic style, and was built by Lord Selsey in 1804. Near Chilgrove, in this parish, Roman sepul-chral urns have been occasionally found.

WEST DEAN CHURCH, dedicated to St. Andrew, is partly Early English, and consists of a nave, chancel, transept, and west tower. A stately monument on the right side, with a full-length figure recumbent, and two effigies in a devotional attitude, commemorates three of the Lewknor family—uncle, son, and nephew. Dates of decease, 1616, 1602, —. There are some other noteworthy memorials of the Selseys, Peacheys, and Lewknors. The Dean and Chapter of Chichester present to this vicarage.

Either at West Dean or East Dean (*dene*, a valley), some authorities place the first interview between King Alfred and the learned Asser.

At SINGLETON (population, 603) both roads unite, and the highway winds through a richly-wooded valley, until, climbing the northern range of the South Downs, it reaches the village of COCKING (population, 482), situated in a narrow gap, from which, on either side, the green slopes of the hills ascend with, so to speak, a billowy swell. The Early English CHURCH here has a nave, chancel, and south aisle. The Bishop of Oxford is patron of the vicarage, which is valued at £250.

[A pleasant excursion may be made from this point through HEYSHOT (population, 432), GRAFFHAM, and LAVINGTON (population, 170), to Burton, and thence northward to Petworth. The road runs along the crest of the Downs, and commands, as may be imagined, a landscape of peculiar charm and beauty. Hills, shrouded in leafy woods, rise before us as we ascend, and beneath us sweeps the long valley of the Rother from Pulborough, where it breaks through the chalk-range to the very borders of Hampshire. Beyond, rises the elevated ridge of the lower greensand, and far away, against the misty skies, swells the undulating outline of the Surrey hills. Everywhere, a quiet village, an ancient grange, a gray old church-tower, a gabled manor-house, recalls some interesting association or picturesque tradition. HEYSHOT CHURCH is an uninteresting Perpendicular building. GRAFFHAM CHURCH, partly Early English and partly decorated, is dedicated to St. Giles.]

At 2 miles north of Cocking, and in a country whose characteristics are sufficiently indicated by its name, lies MIDHURST (population, 1481. *Inns* : Angel, New Inn, Eagle), on an ascent rising gently from the bank of the Rother, which is navigable from hence to Pulborough, where it meets the Arun. It is a quiet, old-world town, with little trade, but in the centre of some delightful scenery. On ST. ANNE'S HILL, across the river, remain the ruined foundations of the old castle of the Bohuns. A strong CHALYBEATE SPRING wells out unheeded from the turfy depths of a pleasant little dell, near Coster's Mill. At GREAT TODHAM are traces of an old Jacobean manor-house. The MIDHURST GRAMMAR SCHOOL (on the Petworth road), founded by Gilbert Hannam in 1672, bears a good reputation, and is con-

nected with Winchester College.   Here Sir Charles Lyall, the
geologist, was educated.   MIDHURST CHURCH, Perpendicular in
style, is dedicated to St. Dennis, and consists of a nave, chancel,
south aisle, and low embattled tower.   The Montague sepulchral
chapel, south of the chancel, has recently been deprived of its
most remarkable monument (see EASEBOURNE).   The Earl of
Egmont is patron of the benefice, a perpetual curacy, valued at
£170.

FROM MIDHURST TO PETWORTH—EAST.

[COWDRAY PARK (800 acres) lies to the east of Midhurst.   The Petworth road
runs quite through it.   Its wooded knolls and ferny hollows, its grassy glades and
broad stretches of crisp green turf, are the very luxuries of beauty.   An avenue of
Spanish chesnuts is especially grand in its full and vigorous leafiness ; and there
are everywhere nooks of greenery and shadowy dells, which boon to poet and artist
will offer a fresh and genial inspiration.

The ruins of Cowdray, the great house of the great Montagues, are not extensive,
but they are interesting.   The arms of Sir Anthony Browne, Henry VIII.'s favourite,
and the standard-bearer of England, adorn the entrance-gateway.   Traces of the
paintings which enriched the walls are visible ; the windows of the hall and chapel
are almost entire ; within the quadrangle lie, half-consumed, the bucks carved in
wood which formerly ornamented "the Buck Hall."   We may stand here amid the
ivy-shrouded ruins, and reproduce in imagination the stately mansion which, raised
by Sir William Fitzwilliam, Earl of Southampton,—stepson of Sir Anthony Browne
—about 1530, was embellished with Roberti's paintings and Groupe's statues ; with
the genius of Holbein, and the fancy of Pellegrini ; with curious antique fittings and
furniture ; a noble quadrangle, a richly decorated chapel—all consumed or scathed
by fire on the night of Tuesday, September 24, 1793.   Its owner, George, eighth
and last Viscount Montague, was at the time on the continent, and before the news
of the destruction of his ancestral mansion reached him, was drowned in a rash attempt to pass the falls of Schaffhausen in Switzerland.

Cowdray now devolved upon his sister, who had married W. S. Poyntz, Esq.
This gentleman built a cottage ornée about 1 mile from the ruins, which he named
COWDRAY LODGE, and which, with the demesne, was sold in 1843 to the Earl of
Egmont.

Queen Elizabeth passed five days at Cowdray in 1591, on a visit to Lord Montague, who had attended her at West Tilbury with 200 horsemen.   The "Close Walk,"
where she exhibited her regal magnificence to the dazzled eyes of her courtiers, and
where she brought down with a cross-bow three or four deer which were driven past
her covert, still flourishes in leafy luxuriance.

Beyond the park gate, and on the right of the road to Petworth, stands EASE-
BOURNE CHURCH, a Perpendicular building, dedicated to St. Margaret.   The south
aisle was a nun's chapel, attached to a nunnery founded by John de Bohun, *temp.*
Henry III., of which some remains are extant.   An ancient monument in the
chancel, with the effigy of a knight carved in oak, commemorates Sir *David Owen*,
son of Owen Tudor, d. 1541-2.   The stately tomb of the Montagues will not fail to
attract the visitor's attention.   Upon an altar-tomb adorned with two female figures
in robes of state, rises another tomb, where recumbent lies the effigy of Sir *Anthony
Browne, Lord Montague*, d. 1592, in armour and ruff.   The female figures represent
his two wives, Lady Jane and Lady Magdalen.

The perpetual curacy of Easebourne, valued at £130, is in the patronage of the Earl of Egmont. Population of the parish, 1076.

LODSWORTH (population, 661) lies about 2 miles north-east of Easebourne, on the left of the road to Petworth. Its ancient church *may* be interesting. It is said that on the right side stands "an open cloister of timber-work." At TILLINGTON (population, 982), we reach the borders of Petworth Park. A family of the true Saxon name of Aylings have held land here upwards of 300 years. The small church is mainly Decorated, and consists of a nave, chancel, south aisle, and "a light and lofty tower, constructed, in 1807, at the sole expense of the Earl of Egmont." There is a brass for *William Spencer*, d. 1593, "a gentleman of great wisdome, pietie, and discretion," and his wife, d. 1592. Another tablet commemorates *William Cox*, D.D., precentor of Chichester Cathedral, *temp*. Charles I., and his wife, who expressed a wish to be buried here, in the hope of a better consort hereafter—"hic, ope melioris consortii, recondi voluit."

Lord Leconfield is the patron of the rectory, which is valued at £740.

The road from Midhurst to Petworth is one of great variety, and unusual beauty. It keeps in a broad open valley, whose north boundary is a ridge of the greensward, its south, the western range of the South Downs. The river Rother winds through meadow and coppice on the right, at some points approaching closely to the main road.]

From MIDHURST to PETERSFIELD—EAST.

[The road to Petersfield passes through the villages of Stedham, Trotton, Tirivick, and Rogate, before it crosses the boundaries of Hampshire. STEDHAM CHURCH, dedicated to St. James, dates from the reign of Edward I. The font is Norman. The tower was built in 1677. Population, 533. TROTTON (population, 484), is situated on the banks of the river Rother. It was originally a portion of the possessions of the Camoys family, and Thomas, Lord Camoys, early in the fifteenth century, built the bridge over the Rother, and the CHURCH, which he dedicated to St. George. There are two good brasses in the chancel, for *Marguerite de Camoys*, d. 1310, and on a large altar-tomb for *Thomas, Lord Camoys*, d. 1419, and his wife, *Elizabeth*, the widow of Hotspur, and the witty lady Kate, so vividly presented by Shakspeare in the second part of Henry IV.

Otway, the dramatist, was born at Trotton, March 3, 1651. His father was curate of the parish, and it was here that the author of "Venice Preserved" passed his boyish years,—

> "Wild Arun, too, has heard thy strains,
>   And echo, midst my native plains,
>   Been sooth'd by pity's tale"—*(Collins)*.

At TERWICK (population, 97) there is nothing to delay the tourist. ROGATE (population, 1117) has a small Norman Church, dedicated to St. Bartholomew. DURFOLD ABBEY, in this parish, was founded for Premonstratensian canons in 1169, by Henry Hoese or Hussey, Lord of Harling. A portion of the monastic edifice is embodied in the modern house. About ½ mile south of the village is HABEN BRIDGE, and near it, on a knoll above the Rother, are the remains of a moated castle, which may have been erected by one of the Camoys family.

In this neighbourhood is DUNFORD HOUSE, the estate presented by his friends and admirers to Richard Cobden, whose "plain unadorned eloquence" contributed largely to the repeal of the Corn Laws, and whose exertions in concluding the recent Commercial Treaty with France have received so large a meed of public approval.]

We now resume our route to Haselmere. WOOLBEDING (population, 320) lies about ½ mile on our left. Its situation on the north bank of the Rother is very delectable. The manorial mansion is " an elegant modern residence," in pleasant grounds. The marble fountain was removed from Cowdray. The CHURCH is ancient, contains a Norman font, and some coloured glass in the chancel from Mottisfont Priory. The Hon. Mrs. Ponsonby presents to its rectory, which is valued at £250.

After crossing the greensward ridge we reach, at 4 miles from Midhurst, the pleasant village of FARNHURST (population, 768), the centre of much changeful and certainly romantic scenery. Its Early English CHURCH has a small nave, chancel, and shingled spire. The perpetual curacy, valued at £111, is in the patronage of the Earl of Egmont.

Deep in the oak groves of VERDLEY (east of the village) are the ruins of an old hunting castle, appendant to the lordship of Midhurst. It was a quadrangular building, nearly twice as long as broad—that is, 60 feet by 33. It was reduced to its present condition some 30 years ago, when the roads were repaired with its materials ! The spot, however, should be visited for its solitary beauty.

Nearly 3 miles north-west, on the slope of the hill which here overlooks the boundaries of Surrey and Sussex, stands LINCHMERE (population, 339). The CHURCH is utterly uninteresting, but at no considerable distance from it lie the remains of SHULBREDE PRIORY, founded by Sir Ralph de Ardenne, early in the thirteenth century, for five Augustinian canons, and suppressed by the Bishop of Chichester in 1525. The " prior's chamber " is still in tolerable preservation, and its walls are covered with rude but characteristic frescoes. One of these mediæval pictures represents the nativity of the Saviour, and introduces certain animals bearing testimony to that event in Latin phrases, which have a certain resemblance of sound to their natural cries. Thus the cock crows " Christus natus est," the duck quacks " Quando, quando ?" The raven croaks a reply, " In hâc nocte," a crow bellows " Ubi, ubi ?" and the lamb bleats out " Bethlem." The whole is surmounted by the inscription " Ecce virgo concipiet, et pariet filium, et vocabitur nomen ejus Emmanuel."

☞ The road now winds along the hills for about 2 miles (from Farnhurst), and crosses the Sussex boundary into Surrey, whence it proceeds to GUILDFORD ; but for a description of the country through which it passes, the tourist must be referred to our " Guide to the History, Antiquities, and Topography of Surrey." Our exploration of Sussex is nearly ended, and that portion of the road from CHICHESTER (whither we now return) to PORTSMOUTH, which lies within this pleasant county, we shall describe, for obvious reasons, under the head of " Hampshire."

INDEX.

SUSSEX.

Thos. Miller's Tomb Heytabury Hill near Worthing.

Reeve & Co London 1st Sep 3.

20 Nov 1893

BREADS'S

NEW

GUIDE AND HAND-BOOK

TO

WORTHING

AND ITS VICINITY.

WITH ILLUSTRATIONS.

LONDON:

HAMILTON, ADAMS, AND CO.
LONGMAN, AND CO., PATERNOSTER ROW.
WORTHING:
BREADS, LIBRARY, 31, WARWICK STREET.

1859.

THE TOWN.

I.—Origin—Situation—Climate—Mortality.

The rise of the Watering Places of the South Coast dates from the last quarter of the past century. The disturbed condition of continental Europe at that period, shut out wealthy English families from most of their usual places of Summer resort, and threw them upon the resources of their own country for that periodical change of scene and air which is as essential to health as it is conducive to enjoyment. Different situations invited different tastes. The sanitary advantages of the sea-side were urged by the Faculty on such as sought of it a remedy for the exhaustion of business, or the enervation of pleasure. The contrast was greater than that afforded by one inland station with another; the change more complete, and, generally, the hygienic effects of the air more decided. Fashion, content for once to march in the van of reason, gave the word; and her obedient votaries swarmed towards the coast wherever a fishing hamlet, or a solitary farm-stead gave promise of accommodation even of the rudest kind. Perhaps the unwonted shifts which luxury had to endure in these first rude quarters added piquancy to the enjoyment. It is certain that the example thus set, rapidly spread through the upper and middle classes; for whose yearly increasing numbers, hamlets grew into towns, and spots on which the shepherd's hut, or the fisher's cabin had been the only human habitation, were covered by speculative men with buildings combining the elegance and comfort of refined life.

From such causes, and by such a process, the transformation of WORTHING towards the close of the last and beginning of the present centuries was effected. Its pretensions to any more remote historic existence, are of a very slight and uncertain nature. Its name, compounded of the Anglo-saxon word for *Village*, and the diminutive, *ing*, would favor the idea that it existed as a *little village* at the period when that language furnished the nomenclature of the country. At the busy epoch of the Roman occupation it probably formed one of their settlements, or at least, temporary stations. Pottery, and coins of Diocletian and Constantine, were found in 1826-8, when digging the foundations for Park Crescent; and Funereal Vessels of elegant design were disinterred in making the shallow cuttings for the railway a little to the west of Ham-bridge. By the fourteenth century it must have attained to some importance, since a charter for holding a market was granted by Edward III.; and in the beginning of the succeeding century there is record of a license for the performance of service in a Chapel, of which no trace remains. But whatever picture of ancient Worthing the imagination may construct out of these materials, it admits of no dispute, that, just before the close of the last century, it was but a scanty hamlet to the village of Broadwater, inhabited by fishermen and smugglers. The first recorded visitor came down from London for sea-bathing in 1759, and had to lodge and board at a farm house; but he would seem to have been the solitary swallow that does *not* make a summer, as the next authentic glimpse we get of Worthing, fourteen years later, shews no advance. It occurs in a letter written by the notorious *John Wilkes* in 1773, and indicates the relation the fishing hamlet bore to the mother-village at that date. He writes from Littlehampton.—"Next Sunday I intend after Church to go to Broadwater, and to lie there in order to be ready for the great fishery the next morning at Worthing, only one mile distant."

Royalty may be said to have assisted at its birth, since, at its very earliest stage of emergence from the chrysalis into the butterfly state, in 1797, the Princess Amelia came hither at the recommendation of her physicians; and her visit was quickly followed by that of many other of the high leaders of fashion. The period of twelve or fifteen years following upon that date, was one of rapid growth, and high prosperity to the town. The company, though less in positive numbers than more recent seasons have presented, was larger in comparison with the amount of house and trade accommodation the town then afforded. Prices were proportionate to the briskness of the market; it was Worthing's golden age. A period less favourable to the interests of the town succeeded; partly from the caprice of public favor, and partly, perhaps, from deeper-seated causes, presently to be referred to. These causes have been removed; and it is believed, a more substantial, and therefore more abiding hold upon popular opinion is established. An era of healthier prosperity has set in, (as the last few seasons give ample proof), under which the town trusts to no factitious circumstances for maintaining its position; but relies upon conditions that court the investigation of science, and appeal to practical common-sense.

The site of Worthing, probably at no very remote period, partook of the character of a peninsula. The sea flowed up the lowlands a mile and a half eastward, towards Lancing, and three miles westward at Ferring, as the presence of shingle and marine shells in those localities testifies. Not only tradition, but actual vestiges occasionally uncovered by storms, shew that the land at Worthing ran out to what is now low water mark, and probably far beyond. The materials which the sea carried away from this point silted up the creeks that existed on either side; and so the configuration of the coast line gradually became a gentle curve. This encroaching power of the sea is still going on under the eyes of the present generation, where not checked by groyns, which serve to retain the rolling shingle. It may be seen in destructive operation a mile to the eastward of the town. Worthing stands upon a ridge, probably the heaping up of an old beach which is found from 10 to 20 feet below the surface mould; the geological era of which is not determined, as no shells are found in it. The crest of this ridge is at least 30 feet higher than the land at the foot of the Downs.

The natural situation of the town produces a combination of advantages such as no other place of similar character can excel, and few even rival. Its position is on the coast line, which sweeping inwards, forms a bay, having Beachy Head on the east and Selsea Bill on the west for headlands. By these it is protected from the effects of storms that sweep down the channel, which visit it only with oblique and abated force. The background of the South Downs, a mile and a half to the north, effectually screens it from the keen north and north-east winds. The prevailing winds are the south and south-west, which, from a well-known property of the sea they traverse to maintain a higher temperature than the earth in winter and a lower

in summer, arrive here laden with a modifying influence
for each extreme. The climate resulting from these
circumstances is mild and genial in autumn and winter ;
and through all seasons preserves an equability which
medical art prescribes as the prime condition of a
Sanitarium. A resident member of the British Meteor-
ological Society, DR. W. G. BARKER, who has for a
number of years carried on a series of observations which
have been published by the Society, and also by the
Registrar General in his Quarterly Reports, and who has
devoted special attention to the subject of climate and its
influence upon the cure and alleviation of disease, has
favoured us with the following results of his observations :—

"The climate of Worthing may justly be compared
with the most favored localities in England or even abroad,
its ranges of temperature being remarkably slight, agreeing
closely in this respect with those of Torquay, Ventnor and
Guernsey, which, with Worthing, are, as a rule, the least in
the Kingdom, and afford a striking contrast with more northerly and inland situations; and in proportion as the winters
are cold or the summers hot, so does this appear the more
evident, the temperature in some winters having been as
much as 17 degrees higher than in less favored places ;
and in summer the contrast is equally great, there being
a difference occasionally of 18 degrees between the temperature at Worthing, and the interior. To the robust these
conditions are by no means unimportant, but when persons are in delicate health or suffering from disease, especially of the lungs, they exercise a most important influence, and contribute materially to their alleviation and
cure. The climate may also be confidently recommended
to the aged, to those enfeebled by a long residence in hot
climates, and to the rheumatic and dyspeptic. For it is the

extremes of temperature which excite disease and swell the bills of mortality.

" The subject of *Ozone* has of late attracted much attention from Medico-Meteorologists. There is still a doubt as to what this principle is, but it would appear to be a purifying agent, for during the prevalence of the Epidemic Cholera in London, no ozone was detected at any station near the river Thames, and our complete immunity hitherto from that disease, would seem to support the opinion; for here, as at other sea-side places where the sanitary laws are efficient, there is a large amount of ozone. From observations I have been able to make upon this mysterious subject, I infer that it also produces a gently stimulating influence upon the lungs and air tubes during the process of respiration, and is *one* of the agents at the sea-side, where it exists to a far greater extent than inland, which exert such a beneficial influence in Pulmonary complaints."

Further evidence of the genial character of the climate in the surrounding vegetation must strike the least observant, and convince the most sceptical. Not only is it luxuriant, but the most delicate plants flourish in open situations. The myrtle, verbena, fuchsia, hydrangia and magnolia, are unbiassed witnesses to the mildness of the winters ; and surely indicate to "the tenderest plant of human mould" a spot where *it* may hope to pass that trying season unharmed and in comfort, among a company so choice in the selection of its habitat. As a *winter residence* the claims of this locality are year by year gaining a wider appreciation.

A natural result of these climatic conditions is, that the rate of mortality is among the lowest in the kingdom; which the reports of the Registrar-General fully confirm.*

* See Appendix A.

II.—General aspect—Extent—Buildings— Population.

In its general aspect the town is eminently neat and clean ; the streets are open, airy and well kept, and free from offence to the sense of sight or smell. The sea front, consisting mainly of Lodging-Houses, extends three quarters of a mile from east to west. Along its entire extent, runs a broad and well-kept Esplanade, which, from the materials of its construction, may be used for promenading immediately after a shower. Throughout three-fourths of its length, there is an outer walk on the crown of the beach ; with a narrow lawn running between the two promenades. These form a principal resort of the company, both morning and evening. The out-look over the sea comprehends a range of forty miles, from Beachy-head to the Isle of Wight, and presents some ever-varying object of interest. Its own changing aspects, which the state of the tide, the position of the sun, a passing cloud, a veering breeze, will vary :—the motions of the small craft that ride near at hand ; and the appearance in the distance of those grander objects that make the Channel their highway to all quarters of the globe, looming and vanishing afar like stately phantasmata, will keep the mind alive to external impressions occupied with pleasing ideas. On the outermost line—that "marriage of the sea and sky," magnificent atmospheric phenomena may often be observed in the evening, especially towards the end of summer. The line of coast which the eye follows takes in Lancing, Shoreham, Kingston, Brighton, and the cliffs that mark the position of Rottingdean and Newhaven, on the east ; Littlehampton,

Bognor, and in very clear weather the Isle of Wight, on the west. The employments attending the preparations for fishing and boating which are carried on upon the beach through all hours of the day, are not without the interest of novelty to the dweller inland.

The Beach is smooth and easy of descent, by which unimpeded access to the sands is afforded, and all care for the safety of children left to roam at freedom is removed. The sands are dry and firm, and from their extent well adapted for driving or riding. They stretch for an uninterrupted space of fourteen miles between the mouths of the Arun and the Adur ; and have a breadth of nearly half-a-mile at low water. The configuration of the beach, and the firmness of the sands conduce to make bathing both secure and comfortable.

The general character of the architecture on the sea-front is light and agreeable ; and variety must be allowed to be among its merits, since it nowhere presents half-a-dozen houses of the same design and elevation. The town extends about half-a-mile inland, not reckoning its more scattered outskirts. This space is filled by terrace-rows looking upon gardens ; by detached villas surrounded by their own grounds, and by business streets.* The number of houses is 1200, of which about one third are let furnished as lodging-houses, or accommodate visitors in apartments. A profuse intermixture of foliage gives the place a half-rural aspect, which cannot fail of being grateful to those who come to refresh their spirits and senses with a taste of nature and quiet.

Among the public buildings may be noticed the TOWN HALL at the north end of South street, erected in 1835. It has a neat and unpretending exterior. Within it is

* For List of Streets, &c., see Appendix B.

fitted for the County Court, which is held once a month, and the Petty Sessions, every fortnight. It is also used by the Local Board for its meetings ; and the Savings' Bank business is transacted there. The Surveyor to the town has an office there ; as also the collector of town rates. On the walls of the hall hangs a landscape by *Hobbima*, whose works, says *Pilkington* the Art-historian, are very scarce. There is also another painting by a less eminent hand—both the gift of the late Earl of Egremont; whose bust in marble is placed beside them.

During the summer of 1855, this Hall was for seven weeks the scene of an EXHIBITION OF WORKS OF ART, which was admitted by numerous strangers who were drawn hither to inspect it, to be alike creditable to the locality, and worthy of the imitation of larger towns. The nobility and gentry of the neighbourhood, headed by His Grace the Duke of Richmond, freely and liberally contributed from the treasures in their possession. From these sources was gathered a collection of works of the first masters, ancient and modern, of undoubted authenticity, many of them priceless heirlooms ; plate curious for its workmanship ; articles interesting from association with famous personages of past ages ; rare and curious books ; and a multiplicity of objects illustrative of ancient art and modern ingenuity. During the continuance of the Exhibition, numerous strangers of note came from considerable distances to visit it. The Sussex Archæological Society also visited it in a body.

The CHAPEL OF EASE, situated in Chapel Road, opposite Union Place, is a proprietary building erected under an Act of Parliament obtained in 1809, and was consecrated in 1812. The exterior has no architectural pretension, except a doric portico at the east end. The interior bears an aspect of simplicity and neatness. There is pew accommodation for 700 persons, and free sittings for 150 more, besides 250 school children. It possesses an organ of considerable power. Within the communion rails is a handsome tablet of white Sicilian marble, to the first chaplain. The career of that lamented gentleman is so intimately connected with the growth of the town, and of many of its best institutions, as to warrant the insertion here of the inscription by which a grateful community attests his worth.

To the REVEREND WILLIAM DAVISON, M.A., Chaplain of this Chapel for nearly 40 years, this Tablet, with the Altar-Piece, is erected by Public Subscription, as a Memorial of the undeviating principle, unaffected piety, and untiring zeal with which he fulfilled his duties, whether as Minister, Counsellor, or Friend. To him the National Schools of this Town are indebted for their foundation and success, and to them he may be said to have devoted himself even unto Death. Actively benevolent, with unsparing hand, yet with excellent discretion and sound judgment, he widely dispensed his Charities, so that when the Ear heard him it blessed him, and when the Eye saw him it bare witness to him, because he delivered the poor that cried, and the fatherless, and him that had none to help him; and he caused the Widow's heart to sing for joy. An accomplished Scholar, and Gentleman, he was ever ready to encourage and promote the advancement of Learning and Science. He greatly contributed to the establishment of the Worthing Institution, (of which he was President) and its Members desire to commemorate their lasting gratitude for his valuable services, by joining in this tribute to his memory, He was born at Morpeth, 13th June, 1779; Died 26th April, 1852. and is buried in the Parish Church of Broadwater.

Divine service is performed on Sundays at 11 *a.m.*, 3 *p.m.* and half-past 6 *p.m.* Pews and sittings may be engaged by visitors between the hours of 2 and 4 on Saturday afternoon, at the Chapel. It is a perpetual curacy in the gift of the Rector of Broadwater. The present incumbent is the REV. W. READ, M.A., who was appointed in 1852. Residence, *Church Cottage.*

A feeling of the want of church accommodation for the poor led to the erection by private subscription of CHRIST CHURCH, at the west end of Ambrose Place, which was opened in 1845. It is an unpretending building, consisting of nave, chancel and transepts : with a tower at the west end. The exterior is faced with split flints, with white brick dressings ; the interior has Caen stone pillars and dressings to the arches. It is fitted with the low open seats now usually adopted, and comprises 850 pew sittings; 463 free to the poor ; and 200 for the schools. A handsome painted memorial window adorns the east end. There is a small organ for leading the choir. In 1855, a portion of the town was constituted a District Chapelry, and attached to this church, the Rector endowing the incumbency with a yearly charge upon the commuted tithes, a small portion of glebe, the fees and pew rents. There is also a residence attached ; but upon which there yet remains a considerable debt. It is a perpetual curacy ; the presentation lays with the Rector of Broadwater, and the present holder is the REV. P. B. POWER, M.A., *Christ Church Parsonage*. Divine service commences at 11 *a.m.* and half-past 6 *p.m.* on Sundays, and 11 *a.m.* on Wednesdays. An officer is in attendance at the Church on Saturdays, from 2 till 4 *p.m.*, when visitors may secure sittings. Baptisms, marriages and burials are solemnized here.

The INDEPENDENT CHAPEL in Montague street, is the oldest place of worship in the town, but has been much altered and improved from its original plan. It now accommodates about 650 persons. The minister is the REV. W. BEAN, *Westbrook Villas*. There is service on Sunday at 11 *a.m.* and half-past 6 *p.m.* ; and on Monday and Friday evenings at 7.

The WESLEYAN CHAPEL, in Bedford Row, is of more recent erection ; it is adapted for a congregation of 500. Service on Sunday at a quarter to 11 *a.m.* and half-past 6 *p.m.* ; and on Tuesday evening at 7.

It is at once a gratifying evidence of the general character of the population, and a testimony to the excellence of the ministrations at these several places of worship, that they are well and fully attended.

Scarcely second in importance to any of the public buildings are the WATER TOWER and works adjacent, which should not be omitted to be viewed by the visitor. The tower is an elegant structure, after the design of an Italian campanile. It is built on a square of forty feet, and rises to the height of 110 feet. A tank and belvedere crown the whole. From the latter is obtained a charming prospect on all sides ; access to it being by a skilfully contrived spiral stair through the centre of the shaft and tank. These works were erected in 1855-6, being a part of the important sanitary improvements effected at that time. A portion of the grounds around have been recently planted with shrubs ; and may be transformed into a highly ornamental feature of the town.

The DISPENSARY, a building in the Elizabethan style, to the north of the Town Hall, was erected by subscription in 1846.

The DAVISON INFANTINE SCHOOL at the north end of Chapel Road, is one of several testimonials to the eminent usefulness of the great and good man whose name it bears. *This* memorial has a peculiar appropriateness, inasmuch as he to whom it is erected was one of the earliest, as well as most energetic, labourers in the field of infant education in this country.*

* See Section V.—*Schools.*

The BOYS' NATIONAL SCHOOL in Richmond Place, near the Chapel of Ease, is a plain building but well adapted for its purpose; and comprises within it a residence for the master. The Girls' school, and another Infant school, have at present very inadequate and mean accommodation. A scheme is being zealously propounded to provide more seemly edifices for these important objects.

HUMPHRYS' ALMSHOUSES, close to Christ Church, are six connected and uniform habitations of handsome exterior, recently erected; and do honour to the liberality of the founder and the taste of the architect, Mr. Hide.

The POLICE STATION, near the Town Hall, is a plain building, well arranged within for its purpose. A resident officer may always be found on the premises.

MONTAGUE HALL, originally a Chapel, is now let for concerts, lectures, &c.; is well suited for the purpose, and is capable of accommodating over 300 persons.

The necessity for a MARKET was among the earliest of the town's wants, and an Act was obtained in 1809 for the present building; but its use has long been superseded by resident purveyors. The change in the channel of supply is to the advantage of visitors, since it is more regular, certain and continuous.

Of what was once the THEATRE nothing now remains but the walls and the name. Its uses are changed; its glories are dimmed. It was built in 1807, and had a highly successful course for many years. The foremost exponents of the drama through the first half of this century, fretted their little hour upon its stage. It is now dismantled; a store for soap, cheese and bacon! *Sic transit !*

The stationary population of the town is 5000. To this, through the season, there is a shifting addition of between 2000 and 3000 more.

III.—Sanitary Provisions.

Sanitary science may be said to be wholly the growth of the present century—and the second quarter of it too. If past generations made great progress in the *curative* art, it was reserved for this to discover the *preventive* art. So the refuse of large communities was hidden from sight, its viewless dangers were unsuspected, or disregarded. It demanded some extraordinary visitation of epidemic disease to awaken attention to the less severe, but continuous, ravages which were going on from *preventible* causes. This warning came in the Cholera years, 1847-9. Happily, though upwards of six hundred towns are recorded to have suffered from it in that latter year, and among them towns on this coast, Worthing yielded not a single victim to the destroyer. But fortunately it accepted the warning, without having paid the penalty. The townsfolk opened their eyes to the actual condition of their own defences in case the enemy should sweep down upon them ; and the review was not satisfactory. A necessity for a radical alteration in the system of drainage had been growing with the growth of the town. The system which had sufficed for a community of 2000 persons, was inadequate when that number became more than doubled. Besides substantial evils that required abatement, there existed prejudices still stronger that needed dissipating.

For a considerable number of years complaints had arisen of foul air from imperfect drainage penetrating the houses, of a want of wholesome water, and above all, of an intolerable effluvium on the marine promenade during certain positions of the wind. That there was exaggeration in all this—

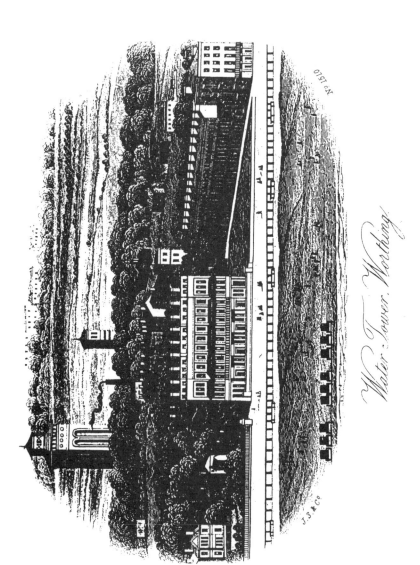

Water Tower, Worthing.

No. 1510

J. S. & Co

proved by the co-existing healthiness of the inhabitants, did not the less make the effects of these complaints felt in declining seasons ; but had much to do with that change for the worse, which came upon Worthing after the first flush of her prosperity was past.

A movement was set afoot by a few persons for applying a thorough but costly remedy to all this. The work to be done was to construct an entirely new system of drainage, to abolish cesspools, to carry the outfall of the sewage to a distance, which had hitherto been discharged upon the sands on the front of the town ; and to lay on to each house a supply of water by which these sewers should be flushed and kept free, and also to supply, where the want existed, a constant service of wholesome water for domestic uses. The acts of Parliament under which the affairs of the town had been administered since 1803, not giving authority for such extensive operations, it was determined, though not without considerable opposition and delay, to ask Parliament to apply the Health of Towns' Act to the place. The Bill passed in the session of 1853; and the Local board established under its provisions, proceeded with their appointed task as rapidly as its extent, and the difficulties of the new course permitted.

An epitome of the works carried out may satisfy the stranger of the thoroughness of the measures taken for securing a pure atmosphere and healthy population. The works were designed by Mr. Ranger, an eminent Civil Engineer, but whose subsequent engagements compelled him to relinquish their superintendence. This was undertaken by Mr. R. Rawlinson another distinguished member of the profession. This gentleman continued to be the Consulting Engineer to the completion of the works. In pursuance of the plans, a main brick sewer, or culvert, of an egg shape, measuring 3 feet 2 inches by 2 feet 3 inches, has been carried through the main streets, at a depth in some parts of over 20 feet. Branch drains of stone ware cylinders, varying in diameter from 15 to 6 inches, diverge into the side streets, and so conduct the sewage of every house towards the central culvert. This latter terminates in a soilpit 6 feet 2 inches by 2 feet 10 inches, and a well 30 feet deep, with a diameter of 10 feet at the top, reduced to 6 feet at bottom. This well is situated on the north east of the town. A sewage pump consisting of three 15 inch barrels connected with the steam machinery in the water tower by a shaft and driving gear lifts the sewage to the level of the outfall sewer, which thence runs nearly two miles to the east and discharges into the sea. By this means the beach and sands in front of the town are freed from pollution by the sewage, and noisome smells no longer exist there.

But the cleansing process would have been imperfect without provision for driving the refuse of each house quickly and effectually from its neighbourhood, and into and through the main sewers. For this purpose it was necessary to lay a water service on to every house. To ensure an unfailing supply, a well was dug, 70 feet deep, and lined with iron cylinders to exclude the surface water. Below this depth, a bore was driven into the chalk 295 feet; from which gushes an abundant supply of the purest water, very free from organic matter, and resembling in composition the better class of spring waters.* Besides this, a water tower was raised with a total elevation, as has been already stated, of 110 feet. The tank on the top is of cast iron; the plates, of from three-eights to half-an-inch in thickness, are screwed together. It is 40 feet

*See Appendix C.

square, and 13 feet deep, and holds 110,000 gallons. The engine for raising the water is a high pressure one, of 16-horse power; and was made by Headley and Manning of Cambridge.

The result is that cesspools have everywhere been filled up; and water closets substituted to every house. The pure element, uncontaminated by the soakage which often makes town well water unwholesome in a high degree for drinking, is obtainable by all. The supply is unlimited, and the service constant.

The perfect success of the experiment is matter for high congratulation. Its cost to the town has been large —exceeding £30,000; but large as the sum is, it is felt that it is well spent in purchasing such a high position as Worthing now takes, and under the blessing of Providence must continue to occupy, among the cleanest, purest, and most salubrious places of summer resort in this country.

———o———

IV.—GOVERNMENT.

The public affairs of the town are regulated by the LOCAL BOARD OF HEALTH, consisting of nine members, elected for three years; a third of the body going out in rotation every year. To this body pertains the construction and supervision of all public works, sewers, groyns; paving, lighting and cleansing the streets, licensing hackney coaches, &c.; raising and disbursing the rates; and, generally, such duties as are transacted by a Town Council in corporate towns.

The MAGISTRATES sit fortnightly to take cognizance of all infractions of the peace; and have the assistance of a body of the COUNTY POLICE, permanently established here.　Happily crime is both infrequent and light in character, a circumstance which may probably be traced to the excellent provision for the education of the poorer classes.

In PAROCHIAL matters, the administration of relief to the poor is in the hands of local officers, and not by a Relieving Officer under the Poor Law Board.　The parish of *Broadwater* (of which Worthing forms a part) in conjunction with many surrounding parishes, is incorporated under *Gilbert's Act*, which saved them at the passing of the New Poor Law from being included in the new system. Many efforts have subsequently been made to do this, but they have been effectually withstood.　And as the mode of conducting parochial affairs here, has more than once extorted the commendation of Inspectors sent purposely to spy out its defects for Parliamentary ends, it may be permitted to congratulate the community upon having warded off from their poorer brethren that rigid rule which is drawn on such inexorably straight lines as to preclude any deviation into sympathy for poverty.*

———o———

V.—SCHOOLS—CHARITABLE INSTITUTIONS.

The SCHOOLS of Worthing have been a permanent source of interest to the more reflecting and benevolent of the Visitors for the past forty years.　Their history is that of the early struggles of the educational movement, before it grew popular, and when a doubt of the necessity and even safety, of putting the poor in possession of the elements of knowledge betokened a respectable conservatism of principle.　Worthing was early in laying aside

*For list of Local Officers,&c., see Appendix D.

this prejudice:—upon one point it claims to be *the earliest*. A tablet exhibited in its schools challenges refutation in these unequivocal terms :—

"Worthing and Broadwater Infantine Schools were established in 1817; and were the first established in England.

"Westminster Infantine School was established in 1819; and the Spitalfields School in 1820. (See Wilderspin on Infantine Schools, pages 23 and 30, Second Edition.)

"Lord Brougham and the Bishop of London have frequently, both in Parliament and elsewhere, complimented each other as the originators of these Institutions. If there be any merit in such a matter, let it be given to whom it is due; namely to the inhabitants of Worthing and Broadwater.

"Render to all their dues."

It need only be added, that the authority for the above statement was the prime instrument in founding that School of 1817.

A NATIONAL SCHOOL FOR BOYS was established in 1812, and has entered 2225 scholars on its books up to this time. The present number exceeds 150. One for GIRLS was opened in 1815; since which date 1606 have passed through the school. The present number is 130. It has always been an object with the managers of this school to place out such girls as have passed creditably through it, in respectable situations; an object which is kept steadily in view in the mode of training adopted. The general course of instruction in both schools, besides the primary object of the inculcation of Christian principles, comprises a sound knowledge of reading, writing and arithmetic; with a more cursory acquaintance with the outlines of history and a few of the more popular sciences, and a plentiful sprinkling of "Common things." The girls, in addition, are taught that important part of female economy, the use of the needle. Both schools are supported by weekly payments of two-pence by each scholar—aided by subscriptions, and sermons preached on their behalf twice during the season. The amount of idleness and mischief these establishments may be assumed to have corrected and prevented (to ascribe to them no higher utility) is enough to move the philanthropist in their favor. But when, as every visitor is at liberty, and indeed invited, to do, the general proficiency of the children attending them in the elements of useful knowledge, and their cleanly appearance and orderly behaviour are witnessed, it will be confessed, that a more agreeable reminiscence of Worthing can scarcely be carried away, than that of a visit to her schools.

The two INFANT SCHOOLS, one in Chapel Road, the other in Chapel Street, are also supported by voluntary contributions in aid of a small weekly payment from each child. The combined number attending the two schools is at present 470.

There are SUNDAY SCHOOLS attached to Christ Church and to the Chapel of Ease; as also to the Independent and Wesleyan Chapels, in all of which the instruction is carried on by volunteer teachers of both sexes.

The WORKMAN'S READING ROOM, in Montague Street, is opened during the winter months, with the laudable object of offering a counter attraction to the beer shop and skittle-alley. Fire, light, coffee, books and papers are provided, and smoking is permitted. These, with an admixture of entertaining lectures, music, and other innocent recreations, are happily found to attract the class they are addressed to. The place is supported by voluntary contributions in money, books, &c., which are received by the *Rev. P. B. Power, Christ Church Parsonage.*

Among the charitable institutions of the town must be ranked THE WORTHING MESSENGER AND WORKMAN'S

FRIEND, a monthly periodical, edited by the *Rev. P. B. Power, Incumbent of Christ Church*, and circulated, for the chief part gratuitously, among the poor, to whose comprehension the matter and style are especially addressed. As it relies mainly upon charitable subscriptions for its support, the circulation is restricted to 1000 copies.

That highly useful and important institution a SAVINGS' BANK was established in 1817, and has up to the present time been the depositary of small savings to the amount of £143,976. Of this sum, there was at the last yearly balance £27,366 (inclusive of interest) standing to the credit of 1166 depositors. The great majority of these are Workmen, Labourers, Domestic Servants, and Children.

The DISPENSARY is an institution for affording medical aid to persons of the town and neighbourhood not in a position to pay for it, yet above the class that has recourse to the Parish Surgeon. It was founded in 1829, and is supported by subscriptions and the proverbial liberality of the Profession; three resident members of which—W. Harris, Esq., Dr. Collet, and Dr. W. G. Barker, attend each two days in the week, from 10 till 11 o'clock, to prescribe gratis. The institution provides medicines. This charity is made extensively available; the last yearly report shews 662 patients within the twelve-months. Since its establishment, 17,133 have been admitted to participation in its benefits. Every subscriber of One Guinea is entitled to nominate six patients. *W. H. Dennett, Esq,, Bedford Row*, is the Honorary Secretary.

HUMPHRYS' ALMSHOUSES.—The origin and design of this charity is set forth in the inscription on the front of the building, as follows :—

These Almshouses for Six Aged Poor Men and their Wives, Members of the Church of England, were Erected and Endowed to perpetuate the Pious Memory of Harry Humphrys, Esq., by his sorrowing Parents, 1858. His body rests in a Tomb nearly opposite. Blessed are the poor in spirit, for their's is the Kingdom of God.

These Almshouses are endowed with, a sum of One Thousand Pounds, Bank Annuities, for the maintenance of the buildings, and expenses of management; and a yearly rent-charge of £78 upon property situate in Lambeth, to provide an allowance of five shillings weekly to each couple of the inmates, or the survivor. The persons eligible are married couples of good reputation, who shall have resided five years in the parish, and whose ages shall neither of them be under 55 or above 70 at the time of election. They must also be members of the Church of England. Failing a sufficient number of applicants of the foregoing class, widows or single women, within the above conditions, may be presented. This grateful haven for indigent age originated in the dying wish of the Mr. Harry Humphrys whose memory is alluded to in the inscription; a gentleman of no ordinary attainments, but whose usefulness was restricted by oft recurring and acute fits of bodily suffering. His parents have liberally carried out his benevolent conception, at a total cost of Five Thousand Pounds. The endowment is vested in a body of Trustees, of whom the Rector of the Parish, and the Perpetual Curate of the Chapel of Ease are members. The Lay Trustees at present are Mr. Robert Humphrys (the founder), Dr. Collet, Messrs. H. Smart, C. Roberts, and W. F. Tribe.

The PAROCHIAL CHARITIES, of which a succinct yearly report is published by the Rector, comprise a Dorcas Society; a Permanent Society for the assistance of lying-in women, and District Visiting Societies ; besides branch associations for the following missionary objects :—The Propagation of the Gospel in Foreign Parts ; Church Pastoral Aid ; Irish Church Missions ; London City Missions ; Christian Knowledge, Bible, and Jews' Societies ; Church Missionary, Curates' Aid, Moravian Church Missionary, Soldiers' Scripture Readers', and Colonial School and Church Societies.

———o———

VI.—SOCIAL CONVENIENCES, &c.

The facility for rapid communication between different places is universally recognized as one of the greatest social conveniences of modern times. To a watering place it is of prime necessity. The heads of many families leave the metropolis only for short periods ; returning thither weekly, or oftener, to attend to their affairs. Worthing possesses this facility in the *South Coast Line of Rail*; by which it is distant from London sixty-one miles. In the summer season about ten trains run both up and down daily. The transit is made in an hour and three-quarters ; gentlemen can thus go up in the morning, and return to dine with their families—which many do. The railway further gives facility for visiting numerous places of interest along the coast, from Portsmouth to Hastings, and on to Dover. For the times and fares, which are often altered, it will be necessary to consult the Company's tables. There is Omnibus and Fly conveyance between the station and town on the arrival and departure of every train.

The railway's auxiliary and rival, the ELECTRIC TELEGRAPH, gives direct communication with the following

B

places, and at the prices affixed for a message of twenty words, viz :—Brighton 1s., Shoreham 1s., Arundel 1s., Woodgate (for Bognor) 1s., Chichester, 1s., Havant 1s. 6d., Portsmouth 1s. 6d. London Bridge 2s. The office is at the entrance to the Railway Station.

VEHICLES of nearly every description of build and taste are readily obtainable at all hours—Clarences, Barouches, Stanhopes, and Pony Basket Carriages, on terms ranging from 2s. 6d. to 1s. 6d. per hour. They will be found standing for hire along the Esplanade and in South street ; or may be sought of the job-masters at their respective stables.

A good stud of RIDING HORSES is kept in the season for the convenience of equestrians ; to which class the beauty of the neighbouring downs is especially enticing. The ordinary rate of hire is 2s. 6d. per hour.

The patient long-eared quadruped, whose services are so valued by timid females and tender juveniles, is procurable at 1s. an hour with attendant.

PLEASURE BOATS, from the little Dingie that needs only one pair of hands to scull it, to the Yacht that demands a crew to manage her, and will carry twenty-five or thirty passengers, are here in every variety. Boating is naturally a much followed amusement of the occasional visitors to the sea-side. To such whose condition makes it desirable that their system should imbibe as much as possible of the sanitive elements of a marine atmosphere, an hour or two spent daily upon a calm summer sea is eminently beneficial. The craft is for the most part trustworthy, and the boatmen will be found obliging and skilful.

Next to boating, BATHING takes rank as a peculiar sea-side amusement, and acknowledged restorative of enfeebled muscles. Medical men recommend the earlier half of the day as the most desirable time ; and the construction of this coast makes high water, or from an hour before to an hour after, the most convenient period.* The machines for ladies, and those for gentlemen, are placed at distinct portions of the beach. The former are attended by bands of ancient females—Duennas of the ocean—whose weird costume must be presumed to be adopted to scare profane eyes from their lovely charges, or perhaps, to make emerging Venuses more amiable by contrast with such odd attendant Graces.

For those whom health or inclination does not permit exposure to the open wave and wandering breeze, the ROYAL BATHS offer every luxury of Cold, Hot, Douche, Shower, and other varieties in which the limpid element is made conducive to personal gratification.

The principal LIBRARY, which was established in 1812, is situated in Warwick street, and contains a collection of 10,000 volumes. The London morning and evening papers, reviews, magazines, and all the local journals, may be seen there. An extensive stock of piano-fortes of the newest construction are to be had on hire. The present proprietor, Mr. Owen Breads, succeeded the late Miss Carter, well known to visitors for upwards of forty years.

PARKER'S LIBRARY AND MUSIC WAREHOUSE is also in Warwick street, where instruments with all the newest improvements may be had.

TINSON'S LIBRARY, in Montague street, contains a small collection of books for general reading.

The MECHANICS' INSTITUTION was founded in 1838 ; and is designed for the intellectual advancement of the working classes, more especially the young. It possesses

* To find the time of High Water, see Appendix E.

a library of more than 2,000 volumes. Courses of lectures formed part of the intention of the founders; and were carried on with much spirit through a number of years, but of late have languished and almost ceased. The average number of members is about 180. It is at present established in Warwick street.

There are several SCHOOLS for both sexes, of high character, and well attended; the importance of a pure atmosphere to the intellectual and moral, as well as physical, developement of youth, being recognized by many parents, numerous pupils are sent from a distance to profit by the rare sanitary advantages of this place.

The HOTEL accommodation is good; comfort and economy being the aim of the proprietors. Their success in these aims is evidenced by the fact that families often prefer a residence in their establishments for months in succession to a private house. The chief hotels are the Royal Sea House, which was honoured in 1849 with a fortnight's residence of the late QUEEN ADELAIDE and suite; the Royal Steyne Hotel, and the Marine Hotel; all on the sea-front of the town.

The several NURSERY GARDENS offer a means for the gratification of a taste for flowers. At *The Rosery, in Park Crescent; Baker's Grounds in Crescent Road; Bushby's in Anchor Lane;* and *Purser's in High street,* will be found choice specimens of the rarest plants. Superb hot-house grapes may be obtained at all these places; and every variety of table fruit at the two last named.

The CRICKET CLUB affords entertainment during the season to all who find pleasure in participating in, or witnessing, this national game. Matches are played weekly or fortnightly on a capital ground at Broadwater; and the general character of the play fully sustains the reputation which Sussex men have long borne. Admission to the Club may be obtained by applying to *Mr. Gray, Secretary, Warwick street.*

There are two BANKS ; Messrs, E. & G. Henty's, whose London correspondents are Sir J. W. Lubbock, *Bart.*, & Co., is in Warwick street, and opens daily from 10 to 4 o'clock. A Branch of the London and County Joint Stock Bank in South street, is open on Wednesday and Friday from 10 to 4.

The POST OFFICE receives mails twice a day ; in the morning, and at 1 *p.m.* Letter carriers commence the delivery at 7 *a.m.* and half-past 1 *p.m.* Letters are despatched at noon, and 8-15 *p.m.*

Weekly during the season, a VISITORS' LIST is published by Messrs. Wilkins & Patching, Printers, and sent round *gratuitously* to the lodging houses. Copies may also be had free on Wednesday mornings, at the office of publication, 5, Warwick street.

THE NEIGHBOURHOOD.

I.--GEOLOGY—BOTANY—ENTOMOLOGY—ORNITHOLOGY.

The influence of pleasant scenery upon the spirits is scarcely inferior to that of pure air upon the vital forces. Health and length of days are the reward of a cheerful habit; and of purely external influences, few bear upon this habit more directly than the circumstance of *place*. Hence the scenic character of the surrounding country is only second in importance to the qualities of air and climate in determining the merits of a watering-place. The neighbourhood of Worthing puts in its claim, as a favourable example of cheerful English landscape. An alternation of open down and wooded tract, of green lanes and cultivated fields, of village centres and scattered farmsteads, prevents monotony, which, even if it be of beauty, soon palls upon the sense. The elevation of the downs adds the element of grandeur, in the extent of sea and land views it opens on every side. Those who climb to the summits will find not only their system invigorated by the sober cordial of sweet air, but their mind expanded in contemplation of the rich variety of Nature's good gifts that lie spread around.

Before enumerating the points of scenic or historic interest that will fall under the stranger's notice in his walks or rides, a few cursory remarks on the NATURAL HISTORY of the locality may not be deemed out of place. Though they be but bare hints, they will be suggestive to some minds, which may derive both amusement and instruction in following the subjects out to further issues.

First on the GEOLOGICAL character of the district.

This is known to belong, generally, to the extensive field of upper Cretaceous rocks, which covers large areas in Europe, Asia and America. But, without ascending to a period anterior to the deposition of the chalk, and its solidification and upheaval, the footprints of subsequent local change lead us back to a time when the sea washed the foot of the downs. In its waters a deposition took place of broken chalk and argillaceous matter, the former subsiding to the bottom and constituting a stratum of marl; the latter settling down upon this, in a layer of clay. These beds thin out as they approach the downs. The steps of the sea's recession are marked by a beach where the village of Broadwater now stands, twelve feet below the present surface ; and a more recent one under the site of the town. The existing beach does not denote the limit of the sea's retreat southward, as both tradition and other evidence prove that *it* has for centuries been again falling back upon the land. This alternate recession and advance of the coast line indicate that this tract has at a (comparatively) recent period been subjected to repeated elevation and subsidence.

But the prime interest the district excites, centres in the Chalk ; the long swelling line of Downs standing up as it were from a submerged world, to tell of a condition of things over which the waters of the past have closed for ages. In the uninstructed, these vast mounds of friable rock awaken little interest beyond that which attaches to their surface and outlines ; but the eye of science regards them as mighty *barrows*, embedding myriads of beings, minute as individuals, but incalculable in multitude.

The hills of this locality form part of that chain of South Downs which commences at the bold bluff of Beachy Head, and skirts the coast till it joins the Hampshire hills. It is a succession of rounded elevations—of which one of the highest points, exceeding 800 feet, is at Chanctonbury in this neighbourhood; and has an average breadth of from five to seven miles. The upper soft white chalk prevails here; but examples of the lower gray chalk occur not far distant—as at Washington. Though to the naked eye it appears quite destitute of any organic character, the microscope shews it to be chiefly composed of fragments of corals and sponges, the shells of forminiferæ, and minute infusoria. The larger organisms embedded in it are numerous both in species and individuals. The often recurring quarries worked for building or agricultural purposes, facilitate the labours of the collector. In these 'pits' as they are called, are found bones of saurians, birds, fishes; fossils of asteridæ, echinoderms, testacea, belemnites, encrinites, &c.—contemporaries in some oceanic convulsion, and sealed up in the particles of triturated shell and coral which the turbid waters deposited over them.

Another feature peculiar to the upper chalk, and suggestive of much speculation, is the layers of flints which most of the pits of this neighbourhood exhibit, horizontally disposed at intervals of from two to eight feet. The formation and situation of these nodules have been alike the subjects of scientific perplexity. The most of them enclose an animal organism, generally a sponge; but many, teeth or scales of fish; and infusoria not unfrequently constitute the nucleus. Dr. Buckland's opinion is generally received, that these bodies were lodged in the matter of the rock while it was in a pulpy unconsolidated state; and before the separation of the siliceous and calcareous ingredients was effected. The silex is assumed to have had a tendency to attach itself to these organic remains, and solidify round them ; and their weight then sunk them to the bottom of the chalk-fluid layer in which they formed. It will be perceived that this view necessitates the supposition that each layer of nodules denotes a distinct deposit upon a previously consolidated bed. Very beautiful calcedonies are found in some of the pits. The only metal which this formation yields is iron, which may be commonly met with in the form of pyrites. On breaking these, a small shell is often found to be the nucleus of crystallization.

The BOTANY of the district has few special features, though rich in the number of indigenous species.

Of forest trees, the oak, ash and elm are most common ; the latter attaining to great height and girt. In the neighbourhood of Sompting, especially, we could indicate specimens to excite the admiration of the artist.

The long slopes of the Downs are gay with plants of smaller growth. Large patches of furze (*U. europæus*), common Ling (*E. vulgaris*) ; a more general diffusion of wild thyme, harebell, bird's-foot trefoil, and the ever-present, ever-welcome daisy ; with many species more sparsely scattered, among them not to be overlooked the rest-harrow (*O. spinosa*), yellow mullein (*V. thrapsus*) form a garden which, common as its ornaments may be, will certainly not be contemned by such as think it no derogation to " consider the lilies of the field."

In the hedge-rows, copses and fields, will be found the sheep rose, honeysuckle and wild clematis ; eye-bright, crane's bill, lychnis, pimpernel, especially the rarer blue variety ; and occasionally, spotted orchis, fox-glove and forget-me-not. The wild strawberry, wood anemone and bee orchis though not common, are to be met with. The more delicate species of ferns, which rejoice in a sandstone district, are absent; but fine specimens of the commoner sorts are readily obtainable. The navel-wort *(cotyledon umbilicus)* whose habitat Withering assigns almost exclusively to Devonshire, Cornwall and South Wales, and the Malvern hills, is found flourishing in great vigor on old walls at Broadwater, Sompting and West Tarring. It may interest the *gourmand* not less than the naturalist, to know that the morel *(phallus esculentus)* is found in Clapham woods; and the truffle *(lycoperdon tuber)* is not unknown there.

But the hills and the woods are not the only haunts that invite attention to their productions. The sea has its meadows and parterres, of which its waves are continually casting specimens at the feet of man to challenge his admiration.

As Marine Botany is a subject hardly yet popularised, and differs so greatly from the terrene branch in outline, one or two general remarks on the subject may not be superfluous.

The *Algæ* derive no nourishment through the roots, which serve merely for grapnels or clasps to retain them in position. They do not penetrate the bed of the sea, but lay hold of stones, wood, or any protuberant substance. They have no part analogous to flowers; but the fructification consists of wart-like excrescences, called capsules, or spots on the surface of the fronds, called granules. In some sorts fructification takes place in both these shapes.

A modern classification of Algæ is by colour, viz :—I. *Melanospermeæ*, olive-green series; II. *Rhodospermeæ*, red series; III. *Chlorospermeæ*, grass-green series.

The plants of the first division grow to a large size, and are more perfect in structure than those of the other two. They are most frequent about half-tide level. Of the following, beautiful specimens are to be met with here,— *cystoseira fibrosa, fucus serratus,* several varieties of the *laminariæ,* and the little miniature palm-like *sphacelaria scoparia.* Of the *Rhodospermeæ* it is in deep water only that the richest tints of pink, rose-red and purple are developed ; in shallow water they degenerate to a greenish or yellowish white. But the sea casts up specimens of numerous species in perfect colour ; including *delesseria sanguinea, porphyra laciniata, plocamium coccineum, ptilota plumosa, griffithsia corallina, callithamnion tetragonum, &c.* Of *Chlorospermeæ* we will instance only *ulva lactuca,* for its delicate green colour.

It is not unusual for visitors, on first making acquaintance with these delicate marine plants, to desire to carry specimens away with them, not less for their intrinsic beauty, than as agreeable mementoes of the sea-side. The art of preserving them is easily attained ; and practised without any great amount of trouble. But two or three plain hints may not be unacceptable to those who are new to the employment.

Care should be taken to procure specimens as soon as practicable after the water has left them. They should then be placed in an oilskin lined basket, or bag of that material, as exposure to the sun and air spoils their colour. Wash the plant in fresh water ; then place a sheet of paper in a plate, put the plant on it and fill up with water. If it be one of the finer sorts, a camel-hair pencil should be used to spread the plant out. Then gently raise the paper out of the water, and hold it in a slanting position to drain. The plant should then be pressed between two boards with blotting paper between them, and a piece of *washed* muslin or cambric interposed between the plant and the blotting paper which should be removed daily and dried, and then replaced, until the specimens are sufficiently dry.

These may then be placed in a scrap book by gumming or inserting the stem in a slit in the leaf. Some of the finer species when thus treated, from their extreme delicacy of texture present the appearance of paintings.

Several *Polypes* may be found on this coast; among them, more than one species of the sea anemone (*Actinia*) wave their green, pink-tip'd *tentacula* in the puddles left by the reflux of the tide.

For the pursuits of the ENTOMOLOGIST this district offers a varied field. The warm dry sides of the downs are favourable to the production of numerous *Scarabæi* and a great variety of the *Hymenoptera*. We are supplied by the kindness of a practical Entomologist* with the following extended list of the more attractive division of the science.

" The order Lepidoptera is well represented in the neighbourhood of Worthing as the following statistics will show :—

In the family of the Rhopalocera, or Butterflies as they are commonly termed, out of the sixty-five British species, thirty-six may be found here ; and among them we may particularly mention the beautiful Colias Edusa, and Hyale, and Vanessa Cardui, which are very partial to clover fields. Thecla Quercus and Rubi, with the pretty Nemeobius Lucina and Hipparchia Hyperanthus, occur in Goring and Clapham woods ; whilst the Downs will furnish Polyommatus Alsus and Agestis, Argynnis Aglaia Melitæa Selene and Hipparchia Semele. The lovely Polyommatus

* H. Tompkins, Esq., of Colonnade Worthing.

Argiolus may be taken flying round holly bushes, especially on the Findon Road ; and a single specimen of the rare and handsome Vanessa Antiopa was captured near Goring in 1846.

Of the thirty-five British species of Sphinges, thirteen may be said to occur here. Those most worthy of notice are the very rare Chærocampa Celerio and Deilephila Galii, both of which have been once taken in gardens in the town ; where also the curious Macroglossa Stellatarum may be frequently met with. Sphinx Ligustri and Smerinthus Ocellatus and Populi are not uncommon in the larva state every year ; and some seasons the larvæ and pupæ of Acherontia Atropos are found in some numbers. The usually scarce Sphinx Convolvuli has once or twice also occurred here in plenty.

The Bombyces have about ninety-four representatives in Britain, out of which forty-two have been obtained here, and among them we will name the pretty Lithosia Miniata, and Nemeophila Plantaginis, which with the rarer Limacodes Asellus and Testudo, and Notodonta Chaonia may be found at Goring and Clapham woods ; whilst the lanes round Worthing will furnish specimens of Arctia Villica, Liparis Salicis, Cerura Vinula, and Diloba Cæruleocephala; and a single example of the extremely scarce Deiopeia Pulchella was once beaten from a hedge in the Angmering road. Only five or six other British specimens are known of this species. A larva of the uncommon Stauropus Fagi was found also last autumn at Offington.

Out of 290 British species of Noctuæ, 114 occur in this neighbourhood ; the principal of which are Acronycta Leporina and Ligustri, Ceropacha Flavicornis and Duplaris, Triphœna Fimbria, Cosmia Diffinis, and Affinis, Polia Herbida, Thyatira Batis and Derasa ; all of these may be obtained at Goring and Clapham woods; and at the former place the uncommon Diphthera Orion, with the still rarer Triphæna Subsequa have been taken; and at the latter, the scarce Lupernia Cespitis has also occurred. Solitary examples of Cucullia Chamomillæ, and Heliothis Marginata have been captured near the town. The splendid Catocala Fraini, one of the very rarest of the British Noctuæ, was found some years ago at rest on a post near Shoreham; and the beautiful Catocala Nupta is not unfrequently to be seen at rest on walls, or flying, in the day time, in the outskirts of Worthing.

The British species of the Geometræ, number 276, of which 106 are to be met with here, and of these we may mention the lovely Geometra Papilionaria and Bajularia, with the equally beautiful Pericallia Syringaria, Angerona Prunaria and Eucosmia Undularia, and the pretty Bapta Temeraria, which occur in Goring and Clapham woods. The scarce Lobophora Sexalisaria, and the still rarer Ephyra Orbicularia, with the more common Tephrosia Laricaria, and Acidalia Sylvaria may also be taken in Goring woods. Hedges near Charman Dean will furnish specimens of Hemithea Vernaria, Phibalapteryx Vitalbaria. A single example of the rare Camptogramma Fluviaria was captured last year near Mr. Lyon's Lodge on the road to Angmering. Eupithecia Venosaria, one of the prettiest species in the Genus, occurs also near College house on the Brighton Road.

The smaller Moths, comprising the remaining families of the Pyrales, Crambites, Tortrices, Tineæ, and Pterophori, are equally well represented in this district, but want of space prevents our giving a detailed account of them."

The ORNITHOLOGY of the neighbourhood offers few peculiar features ; what such there are, it is indebted for to the proximity of the Downs. Their broad solitary scapes and secluded combs attract some species that are averse to the neighbourhood of man. Among these is the Curlew (*Œdicnemus*) which, observes Sir W. Jardine, is extremely local, being confined to this county, Hampshire, and one or two of the eastern counties. It builds no nest but lays its eggs in fallows, or beside a stone ; and the young runs immediately it leaves the shell. It flies by night, and its wailing note heard high over head, has a peculiarly eerie sound on a boisterous night, when it frequently passes over the town.

The Wheatear (*Œnanthe*) visits the Downs in immense numbers from July to September ; migrating to the continent at the latter period. It is considered a table luxury, and is captured for that purpose by shepherds, who cut a narrow passage under the sod, within which is placed a horsehair noose. The bird is said to run into this trap for shelter from storms, and even from the shadow of a passing cloud so timid is it, and is snared by the noose. A ramble over the Downs at the season of harvest will discover these traps in large numbers.

Solitary specimens of the Hoopoe (*Upupa epops*), Ring Ousel (*Turdus torquatus*), Crossbill (*Loxia curvirostra*), Dotterel (*Charadrius Morinellus*), &c., though they might swell a learned looking list, are so rarely met with, as to have little claim to be enumerated in the ornithology of the district. All the *Hirundines* abound. Little flocks often follow the equestrian on the downs in pursuit of insects turn up by the horse's hoofs.

A small bird, the Beccafico of Italy, haunts the fig

orchards at the season of ripe fruit, which has not been observed beyond this -immediate neighbourhood. It is not to be confounded with any of the native sylvan warblers to which the name of Fig-bird is given ; but is a distinct species, which, the duties of incubation over, sets out for its autumnal holiday about the beginning of September ; lives a merry six weeks at the fig-grower's expense, and then spreads its wings again for its southern home.

A very curious bird, the Goatsucker *(Caprimulgus)*, which, Gilbert White says, can be observed only two hours out of the twenty-four, viz., an hour after dawn, and an hour before dark, is common in this district, especially in the direction of Clapham. It utters a jarring note— whence it is also called the Eve-Jar—of astounding force and loudness for the size of the bird. Heard in the twilight of a summer evening, and in the stillness of a sylvan retreat, it is by no means inharmonious.

The Downs are a gathering ground for numbers of migratory species, preparatory to their passage of the channel in the autumn.

Several species of *waders* will commonly be found fishing along the edge of the water at half-tide ; they reside principally in the brooks, and along the banks of the river.

Of the ordinary British song-birds, thrushes, blackbirds, and the numerous family of the finches are plentiful all throughout the district, and even in the gardens and planted enclosures of the town ; and the nightingale "in shadiest covert hid " is often heard there, adding a charm to the soft summer night.

> Ten thousand warblers cheer the day, and one
> The livelong night.

II.—WALKS—RIDES—DRIVES.

ANGMERING : 6 *miles West.*—A village lying between the road to Arundel and that to Littlehampton. It formed a portion of the demesne of King Alfred ; was afterwards in the possession of Earl Godwin, and subsequent to the conquest, was granted to the Abbey of Feschamp, in Normandy. When alien priories were suppressed, the revenues were bestowed upon the Nunnery of Sion. While in the hands of that convent, the low embattled tower of the church, the only existing portion of the old fabric, would appear to have been built : the escutcheon of the community appearing over the entrance, with the date 1507. The remaining portion of the church, consisting of a nave and aisles, was rebuilt a few years since, in the florid English style, at the cost of W. G. K. Gratwicke, Esq., who owns the neighbouring seat - and estate of Ham. The Vicar is the REV. H. REEKS, M.A.

In the churchyard, near the entrance, stands a fine old Yew. The frequent occurrence of the yew tree in similar situations, has been surmised to be a provision to enable each yeoman to cut his bow when driven to defend the graves of his forefathers.

There are several small endowments in the parish ; the most considerable is one for the education of the poor. The school buildings, of modern erection, stand near the churchyard.

A noticeable event is recorded as happening in the family of Palmer, to whom, on the dissolution of monasteries, this manor was granted. The wife of Sir Edward Palmer, *bore three sons, born on three Sundays successively ;* and all three lived to be knighted for their valor by Henry VIII.

BRAMBER ; *7 miles N.E.*—Is a small village lying near the river Adur. It derives a picturesque character from a massive grey fragment of the castle-keep, which, rising from a mound clothed with trees, overtops the street. This mound is well worthy a visit ; the views are extensive and beautiful, and the remains of the castle walls are interesting to the antiquary. They are evidently of Saxon origin, and enclose an area of 560 feet by 280. They are bounded on the east side by a deep morass ; and on the south-west and north by a vallum and ditch, which a profuse growth of trees, underwood and wild flowers has transformed into a wilderness of sylvan beauty. The castle of Bramber was bestowed by the Norman upon one of his followers, De Braose, who had also between thirty and forty other castles and manors in this part of the country. From a descendant of De Braose it came into possession of the Howard family by marriage. In the civil wars, while held by the Parliamentarians, the fugitive, Charles II., passed under its walls on his way to Shoreham, where he embarked.

The church, seated on the south side of the mound should not be overlooked. Its style is partly Norman ; and there is a handsome east window.

Previous to the passing of the Reform Bill, Bramber returned two members, by a constituency of about *thirty!* There is an anecdote told in the life of Wilberforce, who sat for this borough in several Parliaments, which illustrates the relation of members to the 'snug' boroughs they were supposed to represent. Travelling that way once, he called to the post-boy to inquire the name of the place they were passing through. "Bramber! Bramber!" said Wilberforce, recalling the name with an effort, "why that's the place I am member for."

BROADWATER : 1 *mile N.*—Gives name to the parish
in which Worthing stands. It is supposed to have been
derived from the *broad water* which undoubtedly covered
the brooklands on the east, and flowed up to the village, at
a remote period. It consists of one long irregular street,
terminating on the west in the village Green, a place
for public sports which every 'Auburn' should possess.

The, church is the chief object of interest. Rickman
enumerates it among those which "have an admixture
of decorated portions with the Early English ; " and
Cartwright, in his valuable *Parochial Topography*, speaks
of it as "one of the most interesting specimens of
ecclesiastical architecture in the Rape of Bramber." It
consists of a nave, two aisles, two transepts and chancel,
with a low tower in the centre. All but the nave and
aisles are early English of the 12th or 13th century,—
these of later date. The arch under the tower next
the nave has a peculiarity which puzzles archaiologists—
the pointed form, with Norman ornaments. The arch
next the chancel is of the richest style of early Norman.
The chancel, of which the length is remarkable, has within
these few years been restored, and enriched with considerable additions. The ceiling is groined in a very elegant
manner. The east window is a triplet of the early
English ; the lights being divided by clustered columns
detached from the wall. The compartments are filled with
painted glass, being a joint memorial to the late REV.
P. WOOD, 53 years rector ; and the REV. W. DAVISON,
who for 40 years of that term had been his coadjutor and
friend, the Chaplain of Worthing.

Beneath the window is an elegant canopied altar-piece
executed in Caen stone from examples taken from Westminster and St. Alban's Abbeys, of a highly enriched

character and finished workmanship.   From the sides of
the reredos up to the altar-rail runs an arcade of similar
character, recessed for sedilia, and filled in with encaustic
tiling.   The whole of this was the munificent contribution
of Mrs. Thwaites of Charman Dean.   The floor within
the rails is laid with encaustic tiles.   On the inside of
the oak screen which parts the chancel from the body,
are the ancient stalls for the priests—with side seats for
choristers.   On the south side is a stone bench, with a
Norman arch recessed in the wall; said to be an unique
feature.

Here are several tabular monuments, ancient and modern ; one of the latter to eleven fishermen who perished
in attempting to succour a ship in distress, will not escape
notice.   A fine altar-tomb to Thomas, Lord de la Warre,
who died at Offington in 1526, affords an interesting
example of the blended Gothic and Italian styles.   It was
originally painted and gilt.   In the south transept is
another tomb of similar character, but smaller, of the
successor of the above Lord, who also died at Offington
in 1554.   Some ancient brasses will be found in the nave
and chancel.

Anciently there were six chantries or side chapels
connected with the two transepts, but becoming ruinous,
they were removed in 1826.   The arches which formed
the entrances to them are still visible on the outside of the
east walls.   There is record of oblations made at the altar
of St. Symphorian, which probably stood in one of these
chapels.   Symphorian was martyred A.D. 270, according
to the "Golden Legend."   The same authority relates
that "while he was yet a youth, he refused to worship the
statue of Venus on a feast day in presence of the Prefect
at Autun in Gaul.   He was accordingly beaten and sent

Broadwater Church.

to prison. Being afterwards led out and promised great rewards if he would take part in the heathen sacrifices, he said, ' Our God both knows how to reward merit, and to punish sin ; let me willingly give up to him my life, which is due to him as of right.' The judge became angry, and ordered Symphorian to be killed. While being led out to execution, his mother cried out to him from the wall, ' My son, my son, remember eternal life : look up and remember him who reigneth in heaven. Your life is not destroyed, but changed.' Many miracles were ascribed to his blood and his tomb." August 22nd was his feast. It is not known to whom the other chantries were dedicated.

The church possesses an organ, and six bells of good tone. The Rector is the REV. E. K. ELLIOTT, M.A., who resides at the Parsonage, opposite the west entrance.

The Churchyard is surrounded by trees, whose living presence lends a pensive beauty to the habitations of the dead.

A curious incident is recorded of an owner of the manor of *Bradewatre* in the 13th century—John de Camoys, who, according to parliament rolls, " of his own free will gave and demised his wife Margaret to Sir William Painell, Knight ; " and the lady passed over to the Knight's possession like any other chattel.

Within this parish, and about a mile west of the church is *Offington*, a mansion of the old manor house character, standing in a small but well-wooded park. It is the property and residence of T. Gaisford, Esq. From the end of the 14th to the middle of the 16th centuries it was held and occupied by successive generations of the De la Warre family. It was then of more considerable extent than now. In an inventory of the latter date, mention is made of sixty-five bedrooms; there was also a chapel connected with the house. The sylvan beauty of the grounds is the envy of all who obtain a glance of it in passing; especially when it is remembered that the public *did* once possess a right of way through the centre, which the apathy of a past generation suffered to be cut off. Recent alterations have done much to improve the capabilities of the spot.

Charman Dean, is a tasteful modern residence on the hill-side, commanding a very lovely landscape, the seat of of Mrs. Thwaites, a liberal patron to the local charities.

CHANCTONBURY : *7 miles N.*—On the extreme northern ridge of the Downs, 820 feet in altitude, and falling with a steep descent to the weald. The View obtained from this spot is not excelled anywhere in this country. It extends over the broad expanse of the Weald; terminating, at a distance of twenty miles, in the Surrey hills. The sea and lateral views are equally extensive and varied. Its superior height, by bringing a long range of the undulating downs under one view, gives a better idea of the peculiarities of their formation than could otherwise be obtained. We recommend as most desirable companions to this spot, a good glass and a map—the Ordnance Survey, *Sussex, sheet No IX.* is the best, and may be had for 2s. For carriages there is little choice of route : the high road must be followed as far as Findon. On foot or horseback the way may be agreeably varied, striking the downs at the back of Broadwater. There is something strangely exhilarating in a brisk walk or canter over those unenclosed pastures, where the flocks—unequalled South Down !—crop the short sweet herbage; and where the few scattered hedgerows are

—hardly hedgerows, little lines
Of sportive wood run wild—
Wordsworth.

in protest against the usurping claims of man over Nature's broad freehold. A refreshing sea breeze plays there on the hottest day ; silence and solitude brood there, and forms of beauty which never descend upon the plain. Let the genius of Copley Fielding be called in evidence, who caught the inspiration of many of his exquisite water-colour sketches among these hills. He resided for the last eight or ten years of his life at Worthing.

Chanctonbury is an old encampment, and in the days of javelins and cross-bows must have been an almost impregnable position. A plantation of half-a-mile circuit crowns it, vulgarly called "old Goring's hunting cap," from its having been planted by the late C. Goring, Esq., of Wiston, the mansion lying below, on the right. This handsome seat, which stands in a fine park well stocked with deer, has an old Elizabethan hall with groined timber roof, part of the original mansion built by the Shirleys. Two brothers of this family were great travellers ; one, Sir Robert, was sent Envoy from the Persian court to England by the renowned Schah Abbas.

CISSBURY : 4 *miles N.*—Another ancient earthwork, or fortified position, much more extensive and complete than the preceding, from which it is distant 3 miles. It includes an area of 60 acres, and has a high vallum and deep ditch. Its name connects it with *Cissa*, king of Sussex, A.D. 514—584, who was the founder of Chiches-ter. It is assumed to have constituted a refuge for the people on the incursions of the West Saxons, who under their king Ceawlin, finally conquered Cissa at the last named date.

'Tis pleasant, while plucking the wild thyme on this peaceful spot, or watching the gambols of the rabbits that have free warren here, to travel back to the time when all

the flat country round was covered by one dense forest—
for such, antiquarians agree, was the condition of this
county in Saxon days. Fancy readily sketches the outlines
of a possible, nay probable, drama enacted on this stage.
The flight of terror at rumours of a coming foe—the
confused encampment—the anxious outlook—the muster-
ing of all capable of bearing arms as the enemy's
approach is perceived—the flight of arrows and spears at
a distance—the short-sword work in the close grapple—
and then the issue, leaving them free to return to their
sylvan homes, or forcing them to bow the neck to a new
yoke. In this country, and at that period, such events
did pass ; and probability favours the supposition that
such important works as this would be their scene.

The village and vale of Findon which lie just under the
hill, form a pretty cabinet picture. The seat and grounds,
called Cissbury, belong to Hugh Penfold Wyatt, Esq.

CLAPHAM : *5 miles N.W.*—A pretty straggling village,
of which the main part lies off the highway, amid the
woods that border the Arundel road. Indeed, the traveller
who ventures to explore it by any less accommodating
conveyance than his own legs, will find himself in the
predicament many a hero has done before — he will
have to retrace his steps. The church stops the way at
the end of the street, and further progress is possible to
those only who can clamber five-barr'd gates, and who carry
a pocket compass as a guide in the wilderness. Besides
its purely rustic features, it deserves a visit for the neat
cottage homes, built upon improved modern principles
by the Duke of Norfolk, who is the chief owner of
property in the parish.

Clapham Common is a piece of table land between the
village and the Arundel road, covered with heath and

stunted birch. The views it commands in the direction of Arundel are highly pleasing.

DURRINGTON: *2 miles N.W.*—The field path from West Tarring to Castle Goring runs through this village, passing close by the ruins of an old Chapel, which mantling ivy clothes with a venerable grace. Little is known of its history, beyond the fact that a moiety of its tithes was bestowed upon the priory of Sele ; and on the suppression of that establishment, handed over to Magdalen College, Oxford—a diversion of funds which may have had something to do with the fabric's falling into disuse and ruin.

FERRING : *4 miles W.*—A small village lying between Highdown hill and the sea. The church is of early date, but of no great interest. It contains some marble tablets to the families of Westbrooke, Richardson, and Henty. The REV. H. DIXON, M.A., is Vicar. The manorial estate is held by Edwin Henty, Esq.

Connected with this place is an incident in the life of Richard de Wyche, Bishop of Chichester, A.D. 1244—1253, which, as it is the privilege of good men to hallow every spot their memory is associated with, may well claim mention here. Richard, who was of humble origin, rose entirely by his learning and blameless life to be elected Bishop of Chichester, in despite of Henry II., who had appointed an incompetent creature of his own. The struggle between the King and the Church was then at its height. Upon the confirmation by the Pope of Richard's appointment, the masterful monarch not only took possession of his revenues, but forbad anyone to lend him money. The pastor of many thousand souls was penniless. In this extremity there was found in his diocess one poor priest who was willing to brave the

c

king's wrath, and succour his bishop. "Not' far from Chichester," says his biographer, "in a nook formed by a bend of the low shore of Sussex was the little village of Ferring, of which Simon was the priest. This was the only spot in his diocess where the prelate could find rest. All men feared the king except Simon, and God rewarded the good man's courage, for his barns never failed, and he had always wherewithal to support his illustrious guest. It was in pure faith that Simon had received him as his Bishop, and, above all, a Bishop suffering for the Church; but when he saw him more closely, and witnessed his gentle bearing and unwearied patience, while all the world was against him, he learned to reverence him as a man of God. He loved to watch him as he walked in the little garden of the parsonage, wrapped in meditation, or else stooping down to watch the unfolding of the flowers. Richard turned gardener in the summer, and it was amazing to see him intent on all the details of budding and grafting, as though a king's wrath was not hot upon him, and he was again a country lad, as he had been in his boyhood, living an out-door life among bees and flowers, and listening to the song of the birds in Feckenham forest."

Very pleasant it is to call such an anecdote to mind, in passing the modest parsonage where this brave priest lived, and a humble-minded bishop worked and meditated.

FINDON : 4 *miles N. W.*—One of the most picturesque villages in this neighbourhood. Its situation, in a narrow vale, gives it a charmingly sequestered look; to which the scattered disposition of the buildings further contributes. The church, which can boast little architectural display, acquires a charm from the seclusion of its site— the downs rising close and high around it. It will scarcely be seen by the casual visitor as he passes through the village, unless upon special search. The approach is by what appears a private road running past the lodge belonging to *Findon Place*. This mansion stands in close vicinity to the church, on the site of the old manor house. Its owner is W. W. Richardson, Esq. Another large mansion in the parish is *Muntham*, the property of the Dowager Marchioness of Bath, who makes it her chief residence. The demesne is extensive and comprises some very beautiful down scenery. Good views of this are obtained by a drive turning off from the Arundel road at Patching Pond, and coming into Findon at North End. We specially recommend this route to all who are compelled to make their acquaintance with the downs by vehicular instrumentality. Muntham was owned and inhabited at the beginning of this century by an ingenious gentleman of the name of Frankland, a descendant in the female line from Oliver Cromwell. He had been a traveller, and had a singular turn for mechanics. All the chief rooms were filled by him with machines, electrical apparatus, &c., at a cost of more than £20,000. At Mr. Frankland's death in 1805, this singular collection was dispersed.

The Vicar of Findon is the REV. GEORGE BOOTH, M.A.

A considerable racing establishment exists on the hill at the back of the village, which has sent forth 'favorites' to most of the chief resorts of the turf.

GORING : 3 *miles* *W.*—Possesses a neat modern church, rebuilt a few years since at the sole cost of D. Lyon, Esq. of Goring Hall. It contains a few ancient monuments and brasses. The interior is very comfortably fitted. The REV. T. CALHOUN is Vicar.

At the northern extremity of the parish, on the Arundel

road, is *Castle Goring*, an odd admixture of Italian and
Gothic architecture, built by the grandfather of the poet
Shelley.   The woodland scenery surrounding it is of great
beauty.   Rear-Admiral Sir G. B. Pechell, Bart., is the
present owner.

Goring Hall, a low brick building, not far from the
church, is the seat of D. Lyon, Esq.

HEENE : ½ *mile W.*—A hamlet, containing a few
lodging houses of small size.   It formerly possessed a
Chapel, of which some fragments are yet standing in a
meadow before the farm house.

HIGHDOWN HILL : 4 *miles W.*—An outlying member
of the chain of downs, much resorted to for its accessi-
bility ; and for its local notoriety as the burial place of an
eccentric miller, whose mill stood on the summit, at the
close of the last century.   The tomb he caused to be
erected in his lifetime, is covered with pious texts and
moralizing couplets of the good miller's own invention.
This modern recluse passed many hours daily during the
last years of his life in a summer house which stood near
the tomb.   Reading the scriptures and meditation occupied
his time.   His coffin, which ran upon wheels, was placed
under his bed ; and in many points, his habits were a
revival of the anchorite life of the middle ages.   A
neat cottage stands on the site of his former dwelling,
and is still inhabited by his descendants ; and in the
pretty arbours surrounding the lawn, visitors may be
served with wholesome country refreshments.   Should
fastidiousness require a precedent, a most illustrious one
offers itself in the late QUEEN DOWAGER, who alighted
and partook of a cup of new milk ; a beverage which can
nowhere be procured of purer or richer quality than here.

The views from this hill, though of course far less

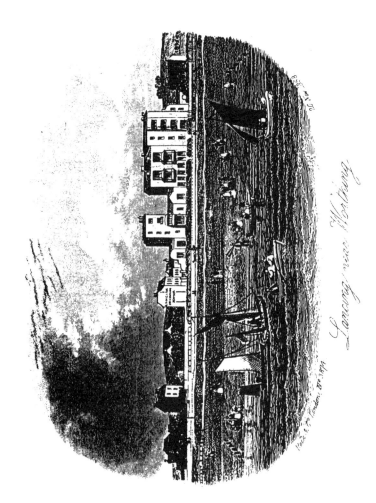

Lancing, near Worthing.

extensive than from the higher downs, are very pleasing
and varied. The close proximity of the woods gives it a
charm peculiarly its own in the profuse song of birds,
especially towards the close of day. A small earthwork
of the same character as those of Cissbury and Chanctonbury may be traced on the brow of the hill.

LANCING: 2 *miles E.*—The village consists of a
Terrace by the sea, and a few houses at its back ; and
the church surrounded by another group of cottages a
mile north, close to the downs. In the former portion
are a few houses and ornamental cottages which are let to
visitors in the season. A medical writer, Dr. King,
claims for this spot a peculiar softness of climate, which
he prefers over that of Torquay, Madeira and Malta.
The church, at *Upper Lancing,* has few peculiarities of
style to call attention to—it is part Norman, part Early
English, but possesses no very striking feature of either.
It has a few mural monuments. The REV. FISHER
WATSON, M.A., is Vicar.

The road between Upper and Lower Lancing, and the
entire neighbourhood of the latter is pleasantly rural.
The seat of Col. Carr-Lloyd stands about a quarter of a
mile distant from the church. In this parish on the side
of the downs, and at some distance from the village stands
SS. Mary and Nicolas College, an educational establishment connected with the High Church party.

On the downs north of the village, a Roman pavement
was discovered some years ago.

PATCHING : 6 *miles N.W.*—A village at the base of
the downs, lying off the Arundel road. The cottages are
of neat and comfortable appearance, this parish having
had, like its close neighbour, Clapham, a landlord alive to
the duty of improving the dwellings of the poor. The

Church, which is almost of unmixed Early English, has yet little to attract notice, beyond its situation, which is on a slope of the downs.

The Cottage is a pretty ornamental residence belonging to Sir John Kirkland, *Kt.*

Seventy years ago an experienced truffle hunter, after a four years' search in this country for the best ground on which to follow his avocation, fixed on Patching ; pretty good evidence that that precious tuber was abundant there at that date. None have been found, perhaps not sought after, of late years.

SALVINGTON : *2 miles N. W.*—A hamlet to West Tarring, notable only as the birthplace of the learned *Selden.* The cottage, though now so mean in appearance, was of consequence enough to have a distinct name in Selden's time—that of *Lacies,* as he himself mentions. It is constructed of the old-fashioned framed woodwork ; the date, 1601, yet remains on a stone over the door. On the inside of the lintel is a latin inscription, which tradition says was the work of Selden when ten years of age. Perhaps it was in reference to the humble roof and obscure situation of the spot that gave this great scholar birth, that quaint old Fuller exclaims "his learning did not live in a lane."

SOMPTING : *2 miles N.E.*—A village pleasantly situated at the base, and rising in some parts on the south slope, of the downs. The church possesses a square tower with the peculiarity of each side terminating in a gable, whence springs a shingled spire. It is mentioned by *Rickman* as among the twenty churches, which alone of all now existing, that zealous antiquary could fix as of a date prior to the year 1,000. His notice of it concludes —"it is a very curious church, and deserves to be studied with great attention." As far as antiquarian interest is concerned, this applies now only to the tower, the main body of the church having been re-built a few years since. Its situation on the acclivity of the downs, and the surrounding elms with their colony of rooks invest it with an air of seclusion that attracts many visitors. The churchyard has long been a favorite place of sepulchre for strangers dying at Worthing. REV. T. P. HUTTON is the Vicar.

Near the church is a picturesque *chateau*-like mansion of modern erection, belonging to John Crofts, Esq., called *The Abbotts.* The old mansion, on the site of which this was reared, was the residence of Queen Caroline.

Steep Down at the back of the village is a bold developement of the chalk formation, and offers a good ground for horsemanship.

STEYNING : 10, *miles N.*—Is built on an old Roman via, called by the Saxons *Stane-street,* hence its name. Its sole attraction is the church, the nave of which, of very early Norman, is magnificently enriched with ornament. The variety and beauty of the mouldings are very great, and their state of preservation excellent. The other portions of the church are of later date. Ethelwulf, the father of Alfred, and St. Cuthman, are said to have been buried here. The present Vicar is the REV. T. I. MEDLAND, M.A.

WASHINGTON : 7 *miles N.* — Is pleasantly placed among the downs ; yet close to the high road. The church is small ; Early English prevailing in the architecture. It contains a few mural monuments. The churchyard, which has some ancient yews, commands a beautiful prospect over the weald. The memorials of the ' rude forefathers of the hamlet ' are very primitive ; and altogether the place has an 'old-world' aspect which is refreshing in these days of improvement.   The REV. T. N. BLAGDEN, B.D. is Vicar.

Not far from the village is *Rowdell* the seat of Major Sandham ; and *Highden*, the residence of Sir Charles Goring, *Bart.*, is situate in a small valley on the south.

WEST TARRING : 1½ *miles N.W.*—This ancient town, which the march of improvement has completely distanced, and pert new neighbours look down upon, much as adolescence is wont to regard senility, retains in its decadence some of the claims of age to veneration.   The manor belonged to the see of Canterbury, and there is reason to believe that it was the occasional residence of the Archbishops—and notably of the Church's champion, martyr and saint, Thomas à Becket.*   An old building which tradition assigns as his palace, but which is presumed rather to have been a conventual house of the date of Edward IV., is worth inspection.   The great hall, and what is believed to have been the chapel, are the principal remains.   The Parish School is kept there ; but the stranger will meet with courteous attention if he desires to view the building.   Some old wood-work houses, with gables towards the street, of the same era as the building just spoken of, are examples of a quaint style fast crumbling out of existence.

The church is a noble building, spacious and lofty. The nave, of the date of the 13th century ; the tower and chancel, a century and a half later.   Since its rescue a few years back from the accumulated results of neglect, and the not less barbarous zeal of botchers, the noble

---

* For much curious information about this locality see " Parochial Fragments relating to the Parish of West Tarring, &c., by the *Rev. J. W. Warter, B.D., Vicar ;* 1853 "—to which we acknowledge our obligation for several facts mentioned here.

proportions of the interior have been brought out in their original effect. The altar has the unusual feature of being elevated three steps. The east window is a handsome one of five lights, in what is called the perpendicular style. The west window in the tower has been restored in Caen stone as a mortuary window to the poet Southey, whose eldest daughter is wife to the present incumbent, REV. J. W. WARTER, B.D. A tall shingle spire crowns the tower. The interior may be viewed on applying to the sexton who lives near.

The churchyard has no monuments of any pretension; nor even many of those inscriptions by "th' unletter'd muse" which chronicle the virtues of the "loving wife" or "friend sincere." One there is of somewhat quainter device and more nervous structure than the general run, which therefore deserves mention—

> "Here lieth the Bodie of John Parson : the only Sonne of William Parson of Salvington : who was buried the fowerth Day of March, 1633.
>> "Youthe was his age:
>> Virginitie his state :
>> Learning his love :
>> Consumption his fate."

Connected with the Venerable Memory which seems fittingly shrined in this quaint, mediæval town, is the tradition that the Fig, for whose growth it has acquired a celebrity, was introduced by à Becket on his return from Italy. The thought takes nothing from the zest of a walk through the low green alleys, or a repast off the fruit in its season. The *Fig Gardens*, are much resorted to by visitors, to eat the fruit in the full freshness of its aroma and flavour.

ARUNDEL CASTLE, PARK, &c.

By Rail and Omnibus 10 *miles ;* high *road* 10 *miles.*

The beauty of the scenery in the immediate neighbourhood of Arundel can scarcely be surpassed, or described.
Hill and dale, wood and water, mingle in lovely variety ;
and over all the grey, ivy-clad Castle dominates with a
grand feudal air. The Arun winds through the meadows
at the foot of the hill on which town. and castle rise,
and under the Hanger that forms one side of the park,
until it apparently loses itself among the downs. Historic
interest as well as scenic beauty invests the spot. William
Rufus occupied the castle in 1079 ; Henry I. besieged
his elder brother Robert there in 1102 ; the Empress
Maud took refuge within its walls from the persecution of
Stephen, in 1139 ; and, to pass over intermediate incidents, in the great civil wars Sir William Waller the
Parliamentarian leader sat down before it, and after a
siege of seventeen days took possession, plundered and
dismantled it. Many royal visits have been paid it in
more friendly guise, from Edward I. down to our present
beloved Queen. The keep, the barbacan tower, and a few
other portions are all that remain of the stronghold that
figured in those old historic scenes. The remainder was
restored and rebuilt about sixty years since. The ancient
portion only is shown to strangers on Mondays and
Fridays. Some celebrated specimens of the large white
American owl will be seen there. These venerable grand-
fathers of all the Owls are dignified by the possession of

proper names. There goes a story that, upon the occasion
of a celebrated Chancellor of George III., who had been
honoured with the sponsorship of one of them, dining with
His Grace of Norfolk, the Duke's Fowler rushed breath-
less into the room with the announcement "Lord Thurloe's
laid an egg!"

In the habitable portion of the castle which is not shown,
there are a few apartments worthy notice; especially the
Barons' hall, with its fine open roof of Spanish chesnut on
the model of Crosby Hall, and thirteen painted windows of
historical subjects. The library contains some carvings
by *Grinling Gibbons*; and some old tapestry lines the
walls of a suite that used to be set apart for the Prince
Regent, who was a frequent visitor here. There are no
paintings of interest beyond a few portraits of the Dukes
of Norfolk, some of them enamels by *Bone*.

The Park presents a charming alternation of hill and
vale, thick covert and open lawn. By the side of the
lake, which mirrors many exquisite bits of sylvan character in its pellucid depths, with effects of light and shade
most tempting to the artist, there is a fine growth of
Beech. The path by its margin conducts to an ornamental
and well-appointed Dairy—which the public are permitted
to inspect on the days before mentioned for seeing the
castle. Its site was once that of the baronial mill, which
stood, up to the last generation, a picturesque reminiscence
of times when the seigneur claimed an exclusive right to
grind the vassal's corn as well as his bones.

Arundel Church is an extensive and beautiful structure,
satisfying both the artist and the antiquary: indeed, few
parochial churches so well combine the exigences of these
varied tastes. It is lengthened on the east to the extent
of 80 feet by a Collegiate Chapel, which communicates

with the nave by an elegant pointed arch. This chapel formed part of an adjoining ' College of the Holy Trinity of Arundel,' of which remains may be observed in the churchyard. It contains a number of fine monuments to members of the Fitz Alan family, Earls of Arundel ; but upon them, as also upon the fine features of the building itself, grim devastation has left its mark—the mad zeal of the iconoclasts of the parliamentarian forces. Many members of the house of Howard rest in the vaults below.

But our brothers of the Angle are waiting all this time, rods in hand, to hear of the shady banks and clear reaches of the stream, compared with which all these antiquated figments are as nought in their eyes. Buckling on their tackle, then, let them start for the hostelry of the " Black Rabbit," a mile from the town—and if they be not the veriest gobble-worms they will not grudge the length of the way—where, under the poplars, they may whip for grey mullet and trout ; or follow the stream in its further windings with profit and pleasure. Having thus started our gentle craftsman on his way, we may dismiss him with the benizon of honest Izaak—' that if he be an honest angler, the east wind may never blow when he goes a-fishing.'

The high road to Arundel runs through some very pretty woodland scenery ; and the preference of that route is recommended to those to whom time is not an object.

————o————

CHICHESTER CATHEDRAL, AND GOODWOOD.

Chichester 18 *miles by rail ; Goodwood* 4 *miles beyond, by road.*

This ancient capital of the *kingdom* of Sussex invites a visit, not for any lively display of the stirring incidents of the present, which seldom flourish where the minster's shadow falls, but for those palpable evidences of "the pomps of old religion" which carry the not unwilling mind back into the past. The long-drawn aisle and fretted vault are favourable to the birth of fancies delicate and refined, all sensuous though they be.

The Cathedral is by no means entitled to rank among the finest specimens of that class of building. Not there are the richest fancies of Gothic art displayed ; nor its most imposing grandeur achieved. But its pretensions are respectable, and taste will not turn ungratified from an inspection of many of its features. The tower, and lofty spire, which is greatly similar to that at Salisbury, are its finest external features ; the former is 133, and the latter 138 feet in height. The interior consists of a nave, double aisles, transepts, choir and Lady Chapel (now transformed into the Chapter library). Among the monuments is a very beautiful one in statuary marble, against a pillar in the north aisle, to the poet Collins, whose troubled day dawned and closed amid the darkest clouds in this city. A very lovely figure in white marble by the younger Flaxman—"THY will be done "—adorns the south aisle. Many ancient tombs and tablets to the Bishops are scattered over the nave and transepts ; among them the shrine of St. Richard—good Richard de Wyche —faces the window in the south transept. There also are two panel paintings by a Flemish artist (1519) of subjects connected with the history of the church of Chichester. Also a series of portraits of the Bishops up to 1543, and of the Kings of England up to George I. Up in the tower is a room in which the boots, thumbikins, and other gentle persuasives to a right view of theological matters were wont to be applied. Some of the instruments yet remain. The cloisters on the south side, enclosing an open space of sepulchre called "The Paradise" were the frequent resort of the unhappy poet of The Passions. There himself presented the woful spectacle he paints in the lines—

> With woful measures wan Despair
> And sullen sounds his grief beguiled;
> A solemn, strange and mingled air;
> 'Twas sad by fits, by starts 'twas wild.

Next to the Cathedral, the elegant market Cross, *temp.* Henry VII., demands notice. It is a beautiful specimen of a kind of structure fast disappearing from the land before the ravages of time, and the rage for 'improvement.' Its form is an octagon, with an open arcade, and buttresses with finials at the angles.·

GOODWOOD, the seat of His Grace the Duke of Richmond, situate on a declivity of the downs, about 4 miles north-east of Chichester, is worthy a visit for its collection of paintings and articles of virtu; as also for the fine views obtained in its neighbourhood. The latter comprise no small portion of the Isle of Wight; and the flat shores of West Sussex and East Hampshire. In the vicinity is an earthwork, and numerous tumuli.

Among the paintings at Goodwood are many of great excellence; several by Vandyke, some Guidos, Vander Meulens, Titians, Canalettis, Rembrandts, Salvator Rosas, Ostades, Teniers, &c.; besides many modern English Artists of the first merit.

The house may be seen any day between the hours of 12 and 4, on applying at the front entrance.

———o———

DEVIL'S DYKE.
By road 14 *miles.*

A name borne by a remarkable cleft between two almost perpendicular hills. The stranger may well be puzzled

to conceive why the father of mischief should be honoured
by the dedication of a very interesting spot on these
downs, which, in their pastoral simplicity, might be presumed to be a *terra incognita* even to that indefatigable
traveller.   And so they are, almost—at least one glance
sufficed him, if the tale is to be believed.   It is *not* to be
found in the "Legenda Aurea"; though whether that
fact militates most against the authority of the tale, or
the completeness of that truthful history, may be left an
open question.

The people of the Weald, runs the story, were uncom-
monly pious, and built churches so thick as not to leave
a village or hamlet the devil could call his own.   So he
hit upon a neat little plan to let the sea in upon them and
swamp them together.   But it happened, an old woman
in a cottage hard by hearing an extraordinary scratching,
hobbled out with her rushlight to discover the cause.
Conscience that makes cowards of us all, magnified this
farthing dip into the rising sun; whereupon the surrep-
titious navvy fearing to face the eye of day, flung down
his tools and fled, leaving that little gap in the hills as
the fruit of his night's work.

The Dyke, or rather the hill above it, offers some of the
boldest down scenery ; and the whole aspect of the neighbourhood is wilder and sterner than the general character
of these hills.   It is much frequented by *improvised* gip-
sies, who recklessly venture to 'camp out' for a long
summer day !   One of these baggages has been known
to exhibit greater skill in palmistry than a whole camp
of the darker sisterhood !

The road lies through Shoreham, Beeding, and Edburton.   The first named of these, *Old* Shoreham, has a curious
church, the mother church of the county.   Its character

is early Norman. Beeding was the ancient Sele, where was a convent of Benedictine monks ; but no portion of the building now remains. Edburton church lies a little out of the way, and is scarce worth turning aside for— its most noticeable feature being an ancient leaden font.

———o———

PETWORTH HOUSE.
By road 20 miles.

Twenty miles distant and a hilly road, tedious to the traveller and trying to horseflesh—and yet, Petworth House well repays a visit. The treasures of art amassed there, principally by the late Earl of Egremont, rank it among the richest private collections in this country ; and the liberal spirit in which the public are admitted every day, irrespective of the presence of the family, whose privacy is often sacrificed, is yet rarer than the treasures it adorns.

The town of Petworth may be likened to an assemblage of decently reputable stable yards met in a quadrille ; but with an utter disregard to figure, all *setting* simultaneously to different points of the compass. The visitor has therefore only to thread the intricacies of the set as quickly as possible, and get to the mansion.

"Lord Egremont's house," says Cobbett, in his Rural Rides, "is close to the town, and with its outbuildings, garden-walls, and other erections, is perhaps nearly as big as the town, though the town is not a small one. The park is very fine, and consists of a parcel of those hills and dells which nature formed here when she was in one of her most sportive moods. I have never seen the earth flung about in such a wild way as round about Hindhead and Blackdown ; and this park forms a part of this ground."

But the excursionist for the day will do well to avoid a divided attention. There is enough of sight-seeing within to fatigue the strongest eyes; and of a kind of which it is worth bringing away distinct impressions. One glance at the long Italian façade, and another at the pond and general outlines of the park, with their webbed and antlered occupants, and the visitor should turn to the serious business of his visit.

No introduction is needed beyond that of a respectful request at the proper portal for permission to see the house; and a civil domestic at once constitutes herself your "guide, philosopher and friend" for an art-ramble of indefinite duration. The works of art here do not merely fill a gallery, but also a succession of noble apartments— themselves worth taking a pilgrimage to view. Above all others should be noticed one called the " carved room," which probably has no match for its carved work in the world. The hand of the famous *Grinling Gibbons* has here wrought out such profuse and exuberant fancies as would never enter the conception of those who have not seen them. The exquisiteness of the execution equals the poetry of the design. Festoons of flowers, fruits, shells, birds, foliage in every variety and play of line, with vases graceful as Grecian artists ever moulded, are suspended from the walls and ceilings in endless combinations. It is in this room, if memory serves us, that the priceless, life-size Harry VIII. of Holbein, dazzles with a matchless lustre of jewellery—a regal presence rather than a painted canvass. High up on the stairs, in the corridors, as well as through the grand suite of apartments, wherever there is hanging room, art asserts its reign. The collection of paintings comprises many by Claude, Cuyp, Rubens, and others of the old masters; and an extensive series of Vandykes. English art is represented by Lely (including the 'celebrated Court Beauties) Reynolds, Gainsborough, Romsey, Fuseli, Leslie, Wilson, Wilkie, Northcote, Callcott, and Turner. In no one collection, save his own, are there so many of the latter painter's works to be seen as here; and they illustrate all the varieties of style of that most unequal artist. The rooms contain also a large number of antique statues, busts and tazze; as well as many works of English sculptors, as Carew, Nollekens, Chantrey and Flaxman—of the latter especially, the sublime group of ' Satan and the archangel Michael,' and the graceful ' Pastoral Apollo.'

The Petworth collection is little known, from the inaccessibility of the place; but it may be hoped that the iron horse will ere long have found a track into the neighbourhood, so that the liberality of the owner, Lord LECONFIELD, may be more widely known and generally availed of.

About midway of the distance from Worthing, the road skirts PARHAM PARK, where is an old mansion, now belonging to the Curzon family, but previously to a Sir Cecil Bisshopp, whose half-mad pranks were the gossip of the country-side half a century ago. The mansion is of the Elizabethan era, and contains a handsome stone hall, picture gallery, painted glass windows, and other features peculiar to that date.

———o———

SWISS GARDENS, SHOREHAM.

By rail 4 miles, road 5 miles.

Hey, for a frolic! a rouse to get rid of the rust! one turn on life's merry-go-round! If your joints are not too stiff, or your prejudices too strait-laced for joining in the fun, go to the Swiss Gardens on a gala day. The company may not be select; but it is of a character that many who take exception at here, would not scruple to mix with on a Parisian Boulevard. Indeed the scene has many features in common. The open-air concert and restaurant; the whirligigs, see-saws, puppet-shows and *jeux* of various sorts; the rush and flutter of fine raiment —all, except the *gaieté de cœur*, which, not being in the people can't come out. But it behoves to make the best of a bad business, and they who can't laugh must grin.

The amusements of the SWISS GARDENS may truly be styled legion. Boating, batting, bowls and quoits; music, singing, dancing and dramatic performances; panoramas, cosmoramas, dioramas and dissolving views. Avenues, arbours and lawns for the sentimental; for the curious there is 'a prophet kept on the premises'; for the agile there are spacious saloons where they may dance, like Sanderson's bear, to the genteelest of tunes.

One word more. The caution may not be needed; but it is no harm to bear it in mind—It's good to be merry and WISE!

APPENDIX.

A.—*page 8.*

A TABLE shewing the COMPARATIVE ANNUAL MORTALITY of the TOWN OF WORTHING, and that of certain other places, taken from the latest Reports of the Registar-General.

In all ENGLAND and WALES there was in the year *one death* to .... } 40 persons.

The METROPOLIS 37

SUSSEX 45

WORTHING DISTRICT, including the Town of Littlehampton & intervening Villages } 47

WORTHING TOWN 52

The year to which the above refers—1858—was one of great *general* mortality; and the results given are *comparative* and not *positive*—being calculated on the population returns of 1851.

The following Extract from the Registrar-General's Quarterly Report—January, February and March, 1859—further supports the above favourable result as regards Worthing :—

"In Worthing where Sanitary measures have been carried out, 83 deaths occurred; in Brighton, 459: the respective populations of the two districts having been 18,746 and 65,569 in 1851. Assuming that the population increased at nearly the same rates, the mortality out of equal populations was about as 4 in Worthing to 7 in Brighton. All the facts tend to shew that Sanitary improvement is a question of life and death to the population of every town."

B.—*page 10.*

List of the principal Streets in the Town of Worthing.

Alfred Place,

Ambrose Place,

Ann Street,

Market,

Augusta Place,

Bath Buildings,

Bedford House,

Bedford Row,

Billiard Rooms,

Wesleyan Chapel,

Belle Vue,

Christ Church,

Humphrys' Alms Houses,

Belle Vue Cottages,

List of the principal Streets continued.

Brunswick Cottage,
Caledonian Place,
Camden Terrace,
Casina,
Chapel Road,
  Chapel of Ease,
  Chapel House,
  Collerton Cottage,
  Davison School,
  Dispensary,
  Girls' National School,
  Stamer Lodge,
  Tudor Cottage,
  Worthing House,
Chapel Street,
Clarendon House,
Colonnade.
East Street,
  Gas Works,
Egremont Place,
Greville Terrace,
High Street,
  Manor House,
  Warwick Hall, *School,*
  Warwick House,
  Worthing Cottage,
John Street,
Lancing Road,
  Beach House,
  College House,
  Eden Cottage,
  Eden Villa,
  Navarino,
Lansdown House,
Liverpool Terrace.
Marine Parade,
Market Street,
  Market,
Marine Terrace,
Marlborough Terrace,
  Royal Baths,
Montague Cottage,

Montague Place,
Montague Street,
  Eldon Cottage,
  Independent Chapel,
  Montague Hall,
  North Villa,
  Western Cottages,
Montpellier,
New Street,
North Street,
  Adelaide Cottage,
  Box Cottage,
  Railway Hotel,
  Wortley House, *School,*
Paragon,
Park Crescent,
  Swiss Cottages,
Park Lane,
  Fairfield,
  Gothic Lodge,
  Heslington House
  North Lodge,
  Park Villa,
  Westerfield House,
Portland Lodge,
Portland Place,
Prospect Row,
  Lawn Place,
Richmond Place,
  Boys' National School,
  Richmond Cottage,
Smith's Brickyard,
  Ivy Cottage,
  South Villa,
South Place,
South Street,
  London and County Bank,
  Marine Hotel,
  Railway & Omnibus Office.
  Sea House Hotel,
  Town Hall,
Springfield House,

List of the principal streets continued.

Steyne,
   Assembly Rooms,
   Steyne Hotel,
   Summer Lodge,
   Union Place,
   Richmond Villa,
   Union Cottage,
   Warwick Buildings,
   Warwick Lodge.

Warwick Place,
   Warwick Street,
   Bank,
   Stanford's Cottage,
West Buildings,
West Terrace,
Westbrooke Villas,
   Christ Church Parsonage.
York Terrace.

C.—*page* 18.
Town Well.

Mr. T. REDWOOD, Professor of Chemistry to the Pharmaceutical Society, London, gives the following attestation to the Analysis of the water from this well, made by Mr. E. C. Stanford :—

"The carbonate of lime which it contains, and which is held in solution with free carbonic acid, renders it agreeable to the palate when used as a beverage; while that constituent can be readily removed by boiling, and a very soft water thus produced, which is well suited for washing, brewing, and other domestic uses. Thus the hardness, which, before boiling, is 14.3 is reduced to 4 by boiling, in consequence of the carbonate of lime being precipitated, as the carbonic acid is driven off. It is very *free from organic matter*, and from color; and it is well aerated."

PROFESSOR BRANDE, also, 'in the *Pharmaceutical Journal,* gives the result of a comparison of this water with water from other well-known sources, on the two points of hardness, and solid ingredients.

With respect to the degree of hardness, the professor's deductions are as follow :—

Thames Water, at Medenham .... 17 deg.
Thames Water, Chelsea Company ⎫
Thames Water, Southwark and ⎬ 15½—16
   Vauxhall Company .... ⎭
Lee Water, East London Company 17 —17¼
WORTHING WELL, 365-ft. deep .... 14 —3-10th.

With regard to the solid matters contained in it, the comparison is equally favourable :—

Trafalgar Square, London .... 68 grains per gallon.
Coombe's Brewery............ 56   ,,
Royal Mint 37   ,,
WORTHING WELL .... 20½   ,,

D.—*page* 20.

List of Local Officers, &c.

HIGH CONSTABLE OF THE TOWN.

A. Sharpe, Esq. M. D., 14, Steyne.

RESIDENT MAGISTRATES.

Bridger, W. L. Esq. Chapel House.
Hargood, Rear-Admiral, 1, Liverpool Terrace.
Pilcher, Jeremiah, Esq. 1, York Terrace.
Whitter, W. Esq. Heslington House.
Whitter, W. W. Esq. Heslington House.

Magistrates' Clerk.—Mr. W. F. Tribe, Office, Chapel Road.
Sergeant of Police.—Mr. Stevens, Police Station.

LOCAL BOARD OF HEALTH.

Chairman.—W. Harris, Esq. 4, Marine Terrace.
Clerk.—Mr. W. H. Dennett, 5, Bedford Row.
Surveyor & Inspector of Nuisances. } Mr. S. J. Smith, Office, Town Hall.
Collector of Rates—Mr. W. Harris, Office, Town Hall.
Cryer.—H. Richardson, 4, Montague Place.

PAROCHIAL OFFICERS.

Guardian.—Mr. Braby, Holly Cottage.
Overseers. } Mr. W. Newland, Broadwater,
Mr. G. B. Bennett, 38, Warwick Street.
Collector of Rates and Assistant Overseer. } Mr. W. Verrall, High Street.

REGISTRARS.

District Registrar.—R. Edmunds, Esq. 8, Bedford Row.
Acting ditto for Birth and Deaths. } Mr. Patching, 14, High Street.
Ditto for Marriages.—Mr. Hide, 2, Colonnade.

THE CHURCH, &c.

Broadwater Parish Church.

Rector.—Rev. E. K. Elliott, Rectory.
Churchwardens. } Mr. G. Heather, Chapel Street.
Mr. G. Ede, Chapel Road.
Organist.—Mrs. Parker, 24, Warwick Street.
Sexton.—Mr. John Price, Broadwater.

List of Local Officers continued.

Chapel of Ease.

Perpetual Curate.—Rev. W. Read, Church Cottage.

Chapelwardens. } Mr. S. T. Bennett, Steyne Hotel.
              Mr. Munday, 18, Warwick Street.

Organist.—Mr. A. H. Messiter, 19, Warwick Street.

Clerk.—Mr. James Blaker, Chapel Street.

Christ Church.

Incumbent.—Rev. P. B. Power, Parsonage.

Churchwardens. } Col. Keene, Westerfield House.
              Mr. R. Leader, Richmond Place.

Organist.—Mrs. Ovey, 10, Bedford Row.

Verger.—Mr. T. Harmer, Royal Baths.

Independent Chapel.

Minister.—Rev. W. Bean, Westbrook Villas.

Presbyter.—Mr. Walters, Montague Street.

———

E.—*page* 27

Time of High Water off Worthing. Having ascertained the age of the Moon, the following table will indicate the *proximate* time of high water.

Moon's Age.	days.	New 1	2	3	4	5	6	7	8	9	10	11	12	13	14
		or 15	16	17	18	19	20	21	22	23	24	25	26	27	28	29
High Water.	m.	15	3	51	39	27	15	3	51	39	27	15	3	51	39	27
	h.	11	12	12	1	2	3	4	4	5	6	7	8	8	9	10

The intermediate tides are found by adding 12*h.* 24*m.* to the times in the lower column.

A

DESCRIPTION

OF THE

MILLER'S TOMB,

ON

HIGHDOWN HILL,

SUSSEX.

THIRD EDITION.

WORTHING:

PUBLISHED AND SOLD BY HENRY PATCHING,

STATIONER, WARWICK STREET;

1859.

Wilkins & Patching, Printers, Worthing.

THE MILLER'S TOMB.

————o————

Visitors to the many pleasant places of summer
resort on the Sussex Coast, in their enquires after the
various points of local interest, seldom fail to hear
of the Miller's Tomb ; and comparatively few leave
these shores without first making a pilgrimage to that
celebrated spot. The visit forms an incident in the sea-
side sojourn, and stores the mind with imagery which
does not readily fade away. The youthful and buoyant
carry away with them lively recollections of pleasant
picnic parties—the open-air meal and green sward dance :
the sedate and contemplative find pleasure in dwelling
upon the features of the rich and varied scenery ; and to
all it furnishes an agreeable subject for after description
to friends at home.

The Miller's Tomb stands on Highdown Hill, an
outlying member of the range of South Downs, equi-
distant between Brighton and Chichester, about two miles
from the sea, and within three quarters of a mile of the
line of the South Coast Railway. It is thus easy of access
from all places on the coast, from Hastings to Portsmouth.
If the traveller alights at the little road-side Station of

Goring, an easy walk of half-an-hour will take him to the summit of the Hill. For such as are domiciled nearer, as at Worthing, pleasant lanes and green fields invite another mode of approach.

Legs are an older invention than wheels, and in their use reward with a more exquisite pleasure the heart that is stout enough to trust itself to their conveyance. As in the city a thousand traits of character, so in the country unnumbered sources of interest by the way-side, escape the notice of him who is content to be whirled along at the pace, and on the precise route of another's will, instead of following the unfettered guidance of his own. If strength and distance concur, therefore, let not indolence rob the jaunt of more than half its charms.

The nearest route the pedestrian from Worthing can take is something short of four miles. Leaving the town by Park Crescent, he should proceed in a north-westerly direction through the fields, from which a view of the downs and the opening of the vale of Findon will be gained. Through the little old-fashioned town of Tarring, with its grey traditions of Thomas à Becket and the luscious Italian fruit he planted there, to evoke archaiological or gustatory fancies, as one or other of these tendencies predominate in the rambler's composition. Skirting the Church-yard, with a passing glance at the venerable fabric in its centre, the path leads into a large field beyond. From this point the direction of the route is sufficiently indicated by the hill itself, which now comes distinctly in view. On the north is seen the hamlet of Salvington, under one of

whose thatched roofs was born the learned author of
" A Treatise on Titles of Honour," whom Milton charac-
terises as " chief of learned men reputed in this land."
Yet further to the west is Castle Goring, built by the
grandfather of the poet Shelley, now the property of Sir
G. B. Pechell, Bart. The high road will be regained at
Northbrook Lodge ; whence a long lane, with hedges,
overhanging trees and a running brook, conducts to the
base of the hill.

Two ways of ascent offer—from the south and from
the east. The latter may be preferred as being the
easier, and as it discloses the prospects on either hand in
more pleasing succession. Turning north, then, from the
point at which the roads intersect, we proceed as though
to penetrate the woods, but stop short, and turn in by
some cottages through a rustic gate ; and so, with some
pauses to take breath, and many more to admire the
beautiful views that open upon us, proceed to climb the hill.

About half way towards the summit stands the object
which gives notoriety to the spot. It is a simple altar-tomb,
surrounded by iron railings, and over-shadowed by a few
stunted trees. Probably the first impression is that of
disappointment ; but this is soon succeeded by a feeling
that the humble, time-stained record under the eye is
more in harmony with the situation and the sentiment it
embodies than a more pretentious monument would have
been. " Decay's effacing fingers " have passed over the
inscription ; but by close inspection the following can be
trace on the several parts of the tomb :

On the south side—

In Memory
of John Olliver Miller,
who departed this life
the 22nd of April. 1793,
Aged 84 Years.

On the top slab—

For the reception of the body of John Olliver, when deceased to the will of God; granted by William Westbrooke Richardson, Esq. 1766.

As in Adam all die, even so in Christ shall all be made alive. I. Cor. XV, 22.

The law was given by Moses: but grace and truth came by Jesus Christ. John I. 17.

God so loved the world that he gave his only begotten Son, that whosoever believeth in him should not perish, but have everlasting life. John III. 16.

Wherefore I perceive that there is nothing better than that a man should rejoice in his own works, for that is his portion; for who shall bring him to see what shall be after him. Eccles. III. 22.

Knowing that shortly I must put off this my tabernacle; even as our Lord Jesus Christ hath shewed me. 2 Peter, I. 14.

On the west end are rudely sculptured figures of *Time* pursuing *Death,* who is poising a dart as though in act to strike; and the following descriptive lines underneath:—

Death, why so fast?—pray stop thy hand,
And let my glass run out its sand!
As neither Death nor Time will stay,
Let us improve the present day.
Why start you at the skeleton?
'Tis your own picture that you shun;
Alive it did resemble thee,
And thou when dead like it shall be.
But though Death must have its will,
Yet old Time prolongs the date
Till the measure we shall fill
That's allotted us by Fate;
Then, Time no longer staying Death,
Both agree to take our breath.

Encircling the allegorical figures is the following—

The fear of the Lord is the beginning of wisdom; but to keep his commandments is holiness to the Lord.

On the eastern end are these apologetic lines :—

Why should my fancy any one offend
Whose good or ill does not on it depend?
'Tis at my own expense, except the land,
A generous grant, on which my tomb doth stand.
This is the only spot that I have chose
Wherein to take my lasting long repose;
Here in the dust my body lieth down,
You'll say it is not consecrated ground!
I grant the same, but where shall we e'er find
The spot that e'er can purify the mind;
Or to the body any lustre give?—
This more depends on what a life we live;
For when the trumpet shall begin to sound
'Twill not avail e'en where the body's found.

One passage of the foregoing inscription will hardly fail to excite the curiosity of the stranger—namely, that on the top of the tomb which intimates that it was reared by its present occupant, for himself, nearly thirty years before his decease. The strangeness of this fancy is well calculated to raise a doubt in the mind—was he madman or enthusiast, or merely swayed by inordinate vanity, who affected such singularity in death. This natural enquiry renders a few words on the manner of his life neither devoid of interest, nor out of place in this account.

Miller Olliver, as he was known to all the country-side, used a mill which, till overthrown in a boisterous gale some thirty years ago, stood on the crown of the hill, half-a-mile to the west of the tomb. A cottage on the north slope of the hill, on the site of which the present one stands, was his dwelling. While yet in the prime of life he executed the singular purpose of building his own tomb ; and at the same time had his coffin made, which was thenceforth kept under his bed. The passage from Ecclesiastes inscribed on the top of his work, before quoted, may possibly supply a key to these ghastly fancies. But that other and better motives mingled with the not unusual yearning of human weakness "to see what shall be after him" may be gathered from the tenour of his latter years. During many of these he passed some hours daily in a wooden house he had erected at the head of the tomb, where a rustic seat since stood. There, in the study of the Scriptures, and in the contemplation of his destined resting place and the perpetual homily it preached, the old man's evening of life waned calmly away. The selection of such a spot shews that he was not insensible to the more soothing inspirations of the situation ; and we may feel assured that the landscape around had for him a voice as audible as that of the grave at his feet, and probably cheered and lighted his long passage towards it. In choosing his place of sepulture, the honest Miller only gave way to a weakness in which wiser and greater men have shared—a desire that the bones may rest on the spot wherein the living spirit rejoices. "Let my ashes repose on the banks of the Seine," was the aspiration of the dying captive of St. Helena.

> Mine be the breezy hill that skirts the down,
> Where a green, daisied turf is all I crave,
> With here and there a violet bestrown—
> And many an evening sun shine sweetly on my grave.
>
> *Beattie's Minstrel.*

The sentiment has had a thousand utterances, and been in some moment of tenderness the passing, if unspoken, aspiration of many hearts.

The funeral itself partook of the unusual character of the preparations for it. The coffin, which was made to run upon wheels, was drawn round the foot of the hill, followed by a large concourse of people from the villages around ; and the service for the dead was read by a young girl who had been reader to the Miller during the last few years of his failing sight.

It would appear that the old man was the author of the lines on the tomb, as well as of others that once decorated the Summer-house. Strong common-sense and piety characterized these effusions ; and they were sufficiently like poetry to be a country marvel in the old man's day, and long after. Among the fragments that have been preserved, the following was written over the rustic building :—

> Stranger enjoy this sweet enchanting scene,
> The pleasing landscape and the velvet green :
> Yet though the eye delighted rove
> Think on better scenes above.

and in the interior of the house—

> My Friend ?
> Let us secure an interest in the other world,
> Let this be as it list toss'd and hurl'd.
> He's great and rich enough who wills to die,
> And can with joy expect Eternity.
> Friend ? this is the best counsel I can tell,
> Think on't and practise, and so farewell !

Should the visitor's curiosity crave further information, there is an ancient female, sibylline of aspect,

Hannah White by name, who stands daily on the hill with her basket of sweets, and may be consulted as an oracle of country-side gossip.

* * * * * * * * * * * * *

Highdown Hill is of the upper chalk formation; and the cuttings or pits shew the horizontal layers of flints peculiar to that deposit. These are the remains of zoophytes, which attracted the silica, and sunk to the bottom of each separate deposit of cretaceous matter while the latter was in a state of suspension. Fossils of the higher organisms are comparatively rare.

The London clay which rises to a considerable elevation on the north side of Highdown Hill, shews that a great upheaving must have occurred at this spot since the period of that deposit.

The flora of the locality is varied and interesting. In the spring and earlier months of summer, the neighbouring woods, besides a profusion of Primroses, wild Hyacinths and Violets, both *V. odorata* and *V. canina*, exhibit Meadow Lychnis, Germander Speedwell, Forget-me-not, both the large *(Myosotis palustris)* and the smaller variety *(M. arvensis)*, or Field Scorpion Grass. The spotted Orchis is abundant in June, as is also the Crane's Bill or wild Geranium. Later in the season the Scarlet Pimpernel, or Shepherd's Weather Glass, with its rarer congener, the blue flowered Pimpernel, *(anagallis cerulea)* disputes the ground with the beautiful Crows-foot trefoil. The Honeysuckle, Sheep Rose, and wild Clematis will be found clustering on the copse-wood and hedges. About the same season, the open down, especially towards the crown of the hill, will be found speckled with Harebells—

> These little bells of faint and tender blue,
>   Which gracefully
> Bent their small heads in every breeze which strayed
> From lawny sunshine to the woodland's shade—

and the sward will be fragrant with wild thyme.

Any description of this noted spot must be held defective that fails to call attention to what indeed constitutes its prime attraction—the charming views it offers. From the isolated position of Highdown, its summit affords an unbroken panorama of the country around. On the South, from the bold cliffs of Beachy Head to the Isle of Wight, a broad expanse of sea stretches forth ; its varied line of coast dotted with towns and villages. Westward, the eye wanders over a range of country intersected by the tortuous windings of the river Arun, till it is arrested by the spire of Chichester Cathedral standing out in the horizon. The turrets of Arundel Castle, backed by the fine woods of its hill-park, bound the view on the north-west. Thence, on the north, the line of downs carries the eye on to the Devil's Dyke, and the hills at the back of Brighton. Extensive woods, stretching almost to the observer's feet, clothe portions of the range ; embosomed in which, near at hand, appear the pretty churches and villages of Patching and Clapham.

Nearly on a line with the latter, but on the furthest ridge of the range of hills, rises Chanctonbury, crowned with a ring of trees, the highest point of the Sussex Downs.

On it was established a beacon at the time when this coast was all bustle and commotion from the anticipated invasion of Buonaparte. Somewhat to the east and south of this may be remarked Cissbury, a Roman earthwork; as was also Chanctonbury, and the spot on which we have taken our stand, the summit of Highdown, which gives unmistakeable evidence of artificial formation, and still bears the name of Cæsar's Hill.

Prospects diversified as those obtained from this spot cannot fail to please, under whatever aspect they are viewed. Early morning and high noon has each its peculiar charm. But for an hour thoroughly accordant with the genius of the spot, commend us to the subdued splendour of evening in summer, or early autumn. At that time, from an arbour in the cottage garden, seated at the sober repast of country dainties which the Miller's descendants provide for visitors, to watch the early shadow steal down the hill-side, throwing the distant cliffs into brighter relief by contrast, and settling down upon the dense foliage in various shades of brown, excites and charms the fancy. The whispering of the leaves, which the passage of the light evening breeze makes audible in the hush of the country, sooths the ear; and as the notes that made the woods vocal gradually cease as day closes, the jarring note of the Fern-owl from the branches of some tree near at hand, reminds the listener of his proximity to the most secluded haunts of sylvan life. Altogether it is a situation of rare enjoyment to minds open to the charms of rural objects.